D1265068

THE TIME OF POPULAR SOVEREIGNTY

PAULINA OCHOA ESPEJO

THE TIME OF POPULAR SOVEREIGNTY

Process and the Democratic State

The Pennsylvania State University Press
University Park, Pennsylvania

All foreign-language translations are by the
author unless otherwise indicated.

Library of Congress Cataloging-in-Publication Data

Ochoa Espejo, Paulina, 1974–
    The time of popular sovereignty : process and the
    democratic state / Paulina Ochoa Espejo.
        p.   cm.
Includes bibliographical references and index.
Summary: "Examines the concept of the people and the
problems it raises for liberal democratic theory,
constitutional theory, and critical theory. Argues that
the people should be conceived not as simply a
collection of individuals, but as an ongoing process
unfolding in time"—Provided by publisher.
ISBN 978-0-271-03796-7 (cloth : alk. paper)
1. Constituent power.
2. Sovereignty.
3. Democracy.
I. Title.

JC330.O28   2011
320.1'5—dc22
2010044098

TO *Tom*

CONTENTS

ACKNOWLEDGMENTS

Over the years I have received institutional support for my research from El Consejo Nacional de Ciencia y Tecnología (CONACYT), the Institute of International Education, Johns Hopkins University, and the Erasmus Institute at the University of Notre Dame. I am particularly grateful to Yale University's Department of Political Science for granting me a junior sabbatical leave, and to the División de Estudios Políticos of the Centro de Investigación y Docencia Económicas (CIDE) for hosting me during the 2009–10 academic year. The book was published with the assistance of the Frederick W. Hilles Publication Fund of Yale University.

I thank those who helped me finish this project. My first intellectual debt is to my teachers at Johns Hopkins: Jane Bennett, Jennifer Culbert, Dick Flathman, Mimi Keck, Hent de Vries, and especially Bill Connolly, who helped me understand the relevance of the problem at hand and encouraged me to deal with it creatively. I also thank those fellow students and friends who commented on specific parts of the manuscript: Riccardo Pelizzo, Matt Scherer, Mina Suk, and particularly Lars Tønder. They, together with all the other members of the political theory community at Hopkins, have been a constant source of intellectual stimulation over the years.

At Notre Dame I had much help and encouragement from the 2005–6 fellows at the Erasmus Institute, and particularly from the institute's director, Robert Sullivan, and from the Department of Political Science, Fred Dallmayr, Catherine Zuckert, Michael Zuckert, Vittorio Hoesle, and especially Ruth Abbey. At Yale, I thank my colleagues Bruce Ackerman, Seyla Benhabib, Bryan Garsten, Stathis Kalyvas, Karuna Mantena, Andrew March, Ian Shapiro, Steven Smith, Sue Stokes, and Libby Wood. I also thank the students in a graduate seminar on "The People" for their reflections and critical comments on some of the ideas that I develop here, and Tom Donahue for giving me permission to use parts of our cowritten paper "What Is a People?"

I am particularly grateful to those colleagues who have given me advice on specific chapters, and those who have commented on parts of the book I presented at conferences and workshops: Arash Abizadeh, José Antonio Aguilar Rivera, David Álvarez García, Anders Berg-Sørensen, Barbara Cruikshank, Lisa Disch, Lisa Ellis, Kennan Ferguson, Chris Meckstroth, Sofia Näsström, Kevin Olson, Andrea Pozas-Loyo, Rogers Smith, Lasse Thomassen, Andrew Volmert, and Alan Wood. I owe special thanks to those who read the whole manuscript: Jason Frank, Claudio López-Guerra, and particularly Angelica Bernal, who helped me improve the prose; as well as to my editor, Sandy Thatcher, and his team at Penn State University Press. I also thank those anonymous reviewers who pointed out weaknesses in the manuscript. I have tried to respond to their concerns, and I am sure the book is better for it.

I owe most to those without whose constant help and love I could not think clearly, let alone write a book: Andrea Fuentes Silva, Ek del Val de Gortari, Alejandra Fregoso Domínguez, Mariana Cordera Rascón, Adriana Parcero Malagón, Dulce Espinosa de la Mora, Sabina Alazraki Fantoni, Kate Donahue, Bill Donahue, Sofía di Lodovico, Claudia Ochoa Espejo, and Ofelia Espejo González. Most of all, I want to thank Tom Donahue, who has helped me, and this manuscript, much more than I could say in these pages.

Introduction:
The Time of the People

Imagine a black-and-white photograph. Its coarse grain tells you that it is an enlargement of another picture. The photo depicts a man wearing a broad-brim hat. He gazes beyond the frame, raises his clenched fist, and opens his mouth: he may be shouting or singing. Now imagine a second photograph. This one zooms out from the first. The man remains the focus, but the image now reveals a larger area around him, with a crowd thronging the picture's frame. You can see men and women carrying banners; many of the people raise clenched fists and seem to chant. Zoom out again. A third photograph depicts buildings framing the open space where thousands gather. The assembly fills a big city square, and you lose sight of the man in the hat. He blends with all others in support of their common cause.

This series of photographs illustrates a widely held conception of the people.[1] It depicts the people as an aggregate: individuals compose a people, and individual political wills compose a people in the political sense. This conception underlies many arguments for democratic legitimacy. In these arguments, all individual wills in the community become a popular will when they agree, and only the resulting unified will is said to legitimize rule democratically.

Democrats everywhere cherish this traditional conception of the people. But it is as problematic as it is attractive. If you return to the photograph

---

1. I use "the people" as a singular noun ("The people is . . . ") when it refers to a single political community. This is the traditional conception and most commonly used form in political philosophy. I use the plural noun ("The people are . . . ") to refer to an undefined group of unassociated individuals.

of the city square, you will see that the people, thus conceived, is not there. Look again at the third photograph. The aggregate it captures excludes many individuals. For instance, children, the mentally ill, and foreigners cannot contribute their political will. The photograph also shows many individuals who chose not to join the rally: some stand aside, and others peek at the crowd from the balconies surrounding the square. With more pixels, you would see that many do not chant or raise their fists. But not even the highest resolution could show you those who did not go to the rally or those who changed their minds and no longer believe in the cause.

The traditional conception of the people is problematic because it holds that only a unified popular will legitimizes the foundation of a state. Hence it has to show that a given people is or was unified in order to prove that a state is legitimate. Yet the conception cannot point to any instance of this unification because the populace changes constantly. Every time you try to frame an actual populace according to the traditional conception of a unified people, the populace has already changed. How can you legitimize a democratic foundation if you cannot show that the people are or have ever been unified?

Observe the people in the square again. Return to the photograph of the man in the hat. Now imagine you could add the dimension of time by pressing a Play button. Almost immediately after you press it, the man exits the frame, but as he leaves, other men and women enter the picture. Some chant, some keep silent, others push their peers, while the crowd as a whole pulls others along. Occasionally you can distinguish their faces, but they quickly leave your field of view, and often you can only get a quick glimpse of their shirts, their backpacks, or their hair. You struggle to focus your attention because the image changes rapidly. Nevertheless, if you zoom out until you can see the whole square at once, something will catch your eye. Suddenly you discern patterns of sound, of movement, and of stillness: patterns like the ululation of the chants, or the tendency of groups to form in some parts of the open square and not in others. Over time the constant alteration acquires a peculiar character. Some events occur regularly, and the movement in the city square may become something recognizable over a longer period. This "something recognizable" is not the unified people that the traditional conception seeks to capture. In fact, it is not even a unified thing, just as hurricanes, heat waves, and football matches are not unified things. Yet this something is just as real as a hurricane. When you consider time and change, you realize that a people does not originate when individuals merge into a bigger thing. Instead, a people arises when many actions and movements combine into novel patterns of change. For a people is always in the making or unmaking.

This book is about the people changing in time. I will argue that we should conceive of the people as a process rather than as an aggregation of individuals. Doing so, I argue, dissolves the problem of legitimizing rule democratically as the composition of the people changes. The people conceived as a process can be a source of democratic legitimacy that moors state institutions but is compatible with surprise and innovation. But before I discuss the people as process, let us step back and review the source of the problem I address: the thesis of popular sovereignty.

Popular Sovereignty

Popular sovereignty is the contention that the unified will of the people is the supreme authority in a state. Many political thinkers dislike this contention, and it is not difficult to see why. The idea that all individuals in a whole state could unify their wills is odd at best and dangerous at worst. Many a tyrant has abused this idea and committed atrocities in the name of the people. So it is not surprising that many political thinkers reject the thesis on the grounds that supreme authority is a dangerous idea, or that the unification of popular will is improbable, and maybe even impossible.[2] Yet this odd and dangerous thesis prevails in the history of political thought. In fact, politicians and political thinkers have used it incessantly for at least two hundred years. So why has this implausible and risky idea survived in politics and political thinking for such a long time?

You could argue that the thesis of popular sovereignty stays in circulation because of its rhetorical force. By evoking images of a unified people, the idea often persuades individuals to support a particular cause, leader, or government. Detractors of the thesis commonly argue that the will of the people cannot be unified, and that no honest politician could use the concept with a straight face. In this view, crafty leaders manipulate naïve publics to believe that the leader's aim is the general will. But even if this were true, neither the innocence nor the ignorance of the public can

---

2. This view is common among those who equate popular sovereignty with popular will as an aggregation of votes. If you seek a common will through voting mechanisms, these may produce results that do not reflect the will of the majority, let alone the will of all. Social choice theorists have produced elaborate arguments on the basis of "Condorcet's paradox." See, for example, Riker, *Liberalism Against Populism*, 238–41. The original formulation can be found in Arrow, *Social Choice and Individual Values*.

explain why the idea of popular sovereignty recurs in politics and, a fortiori, why it recurs in political philosophy. Invoking the people's will may
bring cheers at a rally, but this alone cannot sustain the idea of a unified
will in philosophical arguments. Rhetorical power does not explain why
the thesis appeals to philosophers and the public alike. Why, then, is the
thesis so prevalent? Why does it have such influence?

The answer lies in a promise implicit in the thesis's traditional formulations: that of a good and just state. Those who employ popular sovereignty
tacitly argue as follows: A state is good and just only when it guarantees
individual freedom and equality, as well as social coordination. And this
guarantee can be made good only when all individuals govern together or
unanimously consent to rule—that is, when they all agree. They all agree
when they recognize a true principle, obvious to reason, the recognition of
which harmonizes all individual wills. The thesis of popular sovereignty
presupposes this harmony and thus implicitly asserts that there exists a
principle that harmonizes all wills through reason. It then promises that,
provided we find this principle, we can have a state that is good and just.
I believe this promise explains the resilience of the concept and the force
of the image of "the people."

The promise also explains why popular sovereignty is so problematic.
For centuries politicians and writers have waved the flag of a unified and
reasonable popular will in the rhetorical battle of liberty against tyranny.
William Hazlitt's prose is a model of this spirit and discourse:

> [Common interest and abstract reason] taken together, as the test of
> the practical measures or general principles of Government, must
> be right, cannot be wrong. It is an absurdity to suppose that there
> can be any better criterion of national grievances, or the proper reme-
> dies for them, than the aggregate amount of the actual, dear-bought
> experience, the honest feelings, and heart-felt wishes of a whole peo-
> ple, informed and directed by the greatest power of understanding
> in the community, unbiased by any sinister motive. Any standard of
> public good or ill must, in proportion as it deviates from this, be
> vitiated in principle, and fatal in its effects.[3]

In Hazlitt's text, the aggregated experiences, feelings, and wishes of the
people directed by the "greatest power of understanding in the community" are what I call the "coincidence of popular will and reason": the

3. Hazlitt, "What Is the People?" 12.

harmonization of all individual wills through a principle of reason. This harmonization unifies a people, and it may legitimize the state. This notion is powerful because it can legitimize rule, as well as political change in the guise of popular revolutionary movements.

In sum, this traditional conception views the people as the supreme authority in the community when popular will coincides with reason. But if you hold that only an *actual* coincidence of popular will and reason can legitimize rule, popular sovereignty remains an odd idea. Consensus rarely obtains among small groups, and it is unfeasible among large populations. As Locke wrote, unanimous mutual "consent is next to impossible ever to be had."[4] If we ask ourselves where does popular sovereignty get its strength, we find that the answer is not from actual unification, but rather from the *promise* of it. That is, popular sovereignty depends on the hypothetical coincidence of popular will and reason. Even Hazlitt, who seems to hold that the actual people can have a unified will, says that the people is unquestionably right only if the will of the people is led by "the greatest power of understanding in the community." This condition implies that the people may not actually be unified, but if popular will coincided with reason it *could* unify.

This hypothetical view of popular sovereignty explains why the thesis prevails. Even when rulers commit abuses in the name of the people, a supporter of popular sovereignty could always argue that the abuse was not due to the idea but rather to its application. The people "cannot be wrong," the supporter could argue: what passed as popular will was simply an abuse or a failed attempt at achieving an ideal of unification. The real people could still legitimize the state some other time.

A hypothetical unification of the people can legitimize rule because democratic rule does not require actual consensus: it is enough that state decisions are those that the people *would* make if they were unified. But how can we know what the unified people would decide? According to the thesis of collective autonomy and hypothetical unification, you can know what the unified people would decide if you can discover a principle that every free and rational individual would agree with, under the appropriate conditions. All the people would necessarily agree to this principle because it guarantees both autonomy and social coordination. Since it would be universally agreed to, it is a principle for the hypothetical unification of the people.

Such a principle can ground the legitimacy of a democratic state without an actual consensus. Even without unanimity, some members of the

---

4. Locke, *Two Treatises of Government*, 332.

community could deduce, from the principles of freedom and autonomy, norms and procedures for constituting a democracy. So hypothetical unification can ground the constitution of a legitimate representative democracy. If you argue for a hypothetical version of popular sovereignty, you assume there is actual disagreement because the appropriate conditions do not obtain. Such conditions might be access to education and other requisites for moral development, or the provision of complete information and time to deliberate. You also assume that there is no good reason to disagree with the principle if the appropriate conditions did obtain. The possibility of agreement is good enough to legitimize a constitutional democratic order. Of course, at this point the whole argument turns on how to determine the principle that grounds a constitutional democracy. This may explain why theories of democracy that emphasize principles, like John Rawls's contractualist theory of justice, are not concerned with the unification of the people. Instead, they concentrate on determining whether the principle that grants the possibility of agreement is morally adequate.[5]

But determining the basic principle that justifies democracy cannot itself legitimize a democratic state. Knowing that the people ought to agree does not establish that individuals would *will* to do so, and if they do not actively will their government's existence, their state cannot be legitimate. Even hypothetical versions of popular sovereignty implicitly go beyond the basic principle and guarantee the actual coincidence of will and reason at some point in the past or future. They may, on the one hand, displace the promise of unification to the past, as a reference to the original agreement that founded a democratic state. Constitutionalists, for instance, often use images of the past to legitimize the state. On the other hand, hypothetical theories displace the promise to the future as an ideal to be realized. An example comes from those theories that hold that a reasoned discussion, or deliberation, could produce agreement on principles of political morality. In short, theories of popular sovereignty sometimes posit popular unity in the future, and sometimes in the past, but they never demonstrate unification in the present, though they insist it must be there.

But how can you legitimize the state if the people is not unified at any given time? The question of unification and its displacement in time uncovers a grave problem with profound consequences for the theory of democracy and political theory in general. I will call this problem the "indeterminacy of popular unification."

5. Rawls, *Theory of Justice.*

The Indeterminacy of Popular Unification

The problem is this: how do you legitimize rule democratically as the people's composition changes? The problem arises from a condition for democratic legitimacy implicit in the thesis of popular sovereignty. This condition says that a state is legitimate only if those who are ruled consider that rule appropriate. But given that in a democratic state those who are ruled think rule is appropriate only when the body of the people accepts rule, the legitimacy of a democratic state depends on the people's agreement on the reasons that justify rule. That is, in order to prove that a democratic state is legitimate, you must show that the people are or were unified in their agreement. Yet it is impossible to show this. Individuals never come together at one moment; the people changes continuously. While a hypothetical version of popular sovereignty presupposes that the people could unify in the future, the problem of popular indeterminacy shows that the people will *never* unify. Indeterminacy, therefore, challenges the legitimacy of the democratic state and poses a difficult problem for democratic theory.

Popular indeterminacy has been an important concern in political theory in recent years. But new research into the edges of the political community, the composition of the demos, and the popular legitimization of the state treats the problem only tangentially, since it often takes the unified people as a given. Thus it tends to ignore the question underlying the problem: What is a people? What is its nature? For example, much of the recent research dealing with the people in political philosophy and constitutional theory assumes that there already exists a people, and then turns to examining what this people can do. These scholars ask: Can the people make collective decisions and rule itself?[6] Can the people agree on a justification for its government?[7] Can the people bind itself?[8] Can there be democracy beyond a given people?[9] But they usually do not ask whether their implicit assumptions about the nature of the people are correct or coherent.

The indeterminacy of popular unification also poses a problem for political theory dealing with the boundaries of the people. Unless we have unification, we cannot tell whether there is a people, and thus we cannot

6. Elster and Hylland, *Foundations of Social Choice Theory;* Mueller, *Public Choice III.*

7. D'Agostino and Gaus, *Public Reason.*

8. Holmes, *Passions and Constraint,* chap. 5.

9. Benhabib, *Another Cosmopolitanism;* Bohman, *Democracy Across Borders;* Held, *Democracy and the Global Order.*

determine who ought to be included in the demos. Yet most contemporary theorists who examine the political problems produced by massive immigration, extension of civil rights, and changes in national borders concentrate on the franchise. They have ignored the problem of who or what is the people underlying the electorate. These scholars also assume that there is a democratic people *already*, and then ask what are the appropriate rules for extending the franchise or constituting an electorate,[10] or when secession or partition is justified.[11]

The problem of popular unification is also relevant for constitutional scholars, but they see it from a different perspective. These scholars care about popular indeterminacy insofar as it produces a tension between constitutionalism and democracy. That is, they interpret the lack of popular unification as a rift between the liberal principles embedded in constitutions and the democratic practices that channel the concerns of actual mobilized populations.[12] The indeterminacy of popular unification thus poses a problem for constitutional theory because unless we establish that a people has unified at a given time, we cannot understand how it is possible that free and equal individuals under democratic rule could be obligated to obey laws they did not create or approve.[13] Unsurprisingly, however, constitutional scholars discuss this tension from within the democratic constitution; they do not focus on the people, without which the constitution would not even be possible.

The problem of indeterminacy is also important, though tangential, for recent scholarship dealing with popular legitimization or populism. This body of work asks how political regimes use the concept of the people to legitimize existing institutions, or how revolutionary groups rely on the concept of the people to justify radical change.[14] This work has a similar approach to studies of the people from a historical perspective. Generally, both approaches assume that popular indeterminacy is unavoidable.

10. Benhabib, "Borders, Boundaries, and Citizenship"; Dahl, *Democracy and Its Critics;* Goodin, "Enfranchising All Affected Interests"; López-Guerra, "Should Expatriates Vote?"; Whelan, "Democratic Theory and the Boundary Problem."

11. Beran, "Border Disputes and the Right of National Self-Determination"; Buchanan, *Secession;* Buchanan, "Making and Unmaking of Boundaries"; Dahbour, "Borders, Consent, and Democracy."

12. Benhabib, "Deliberative Rationality and Models of Democratic Legitimacy"; Habermas, *Between Facts and Norms;* Habermas, "Constitutional Democracy"; Honig, "Dead Rights, Live Futures"; Michelman, "Constitutional Authorship"; Michelman, *Brennan and Democracy.*

13. Elster, *Ulysses Unbound;* Holmes, *Passions and Constraint,* chap. 5.

14. Canovan, *Populism;* Laclau, *On Populist Reason;* Panizza, *Populism and the Mirror of Democracy.*

Hence they study how the concept of the people in nationalist narratives and political philosophy helps hegemonic groups legitimize rule throughout history, even though unification (and thus democratic legitimacy) is always an elusive target.[15] For this reason, they study how the people functions as an ideological stopgap. They do not try to understand the nature of the people, or whether the problem of indeterminacy can be overcome. In short, they are concerned with the sociological aspects of the problem of popular indeterminacy, not its normative aspects.

Finally, those scholars who deal critically with the theory of popular sovereignty also care about popular indeterminacy. They acknowledge that unless you show that the people unify at some point in time, it is hard to explain how the people could be sovereign. Like the scholars in the previous group, these critics of sovereignty often stress that the populace does not correspond to an ideal unified people. They frequently assume that the people is necessarily indeterminate, and on this basis they describe the inconsistencies, paradoxes, and perplexities that underpin the theory of popular sovereignty.[16] So even though these scholars deal with the nature of the people in reference to the problem of indeterminacy, they are not directly concerned with overcoming the problems that indeterminacy poses to democratic theory. Instead, they offer a critique of the justification of democracy that relies on popular sovereignty.

In sum, all these discussions circle the concept of the people and the logical difficulties with the thesis of popular sovereignty. But none of them deals directly with the problem of indeterminacy of popular unification, or the underlying question of what is the people's nature. Yet if you are interested in the normative aspects of the thesis of popular sovereignty, you cannot afford to ignore the problem. Unless you tackle it head-on, democratic theory is left exposed to charges of self-contradiction, and democratic politics in danger of losing any normative foothold.

A Dilemma in Democratic Theory

The indeterminacy of popular unification undermines the foundations of democratic theory. As I will argue in chapter 3, popular indeterminacy

15. Canovan, *The People*; Morgan, *Inventing the People*; Palti, *La invención de una legitimidad*; Rosanvallon, *La démocratie inachevée*; Rosanvallon, *Le peuple introuvable*; Smith, *Stories of Peoplehood*; Yack, "Popular Sovereignty and Nationalism."

16. Agamben, *Homo Sacer*; Honig, "Between Decision and Deliberation"; Honig, "Declarations of Independence"; Honig, *Emergency Politics*; Keenan, *Democracy in Question*; Näsström, "Legitimacy of the People"; Rancière, *Dis-agreement*.

makes the traditional concept of the people collapse under the weight of logical problems, and with it, the legitimacy of democracy collapses as well. Moreover, without the concept of the people, even the principles of freedom and equality lose their traction within those arguments that seek to justify democratic rule. Further, these difficulties are not just abstract conceptual problems. Chapter 2 shows with historical examples that these theoretical difficulties can make it impossible for actual states to achieve political stability.

Many of the theorists mentioned above acknowledge the indeterminacy of popular unification. The two major strategies they have chosen for dealing with it, however, seem equally unsavory. In fact, these options lead to a dilemma: either you sustain democratic legitimacy while embracing the paradoxes of democratic theory, or you reject these paradoxes and give up on finding a democratic foundation for the political order.

The first horn of the dilemma—sustaining democratic legitimacy while tolerating paradox—may seem a sensible approach, for it presents a compromise that may be the best available policy. Such an approach appears both sensitive to the complexity of political life and flexible in the face of the irrationalities of practical politics. And it may also divert violence and avoid pain, as Paul Ricoeur has argued.[17] But the position is ultimately unsatisfying because sustaining a paradox is a form of intellectual capitulation. It is also politically fragile because by acknowledging that democracy cannot achieve its aim, the position leaves democracy exposed to attacks. It is easy to argue, against this position, that any government that claims to be democratic is in fact using the name of the people to establish the hegemony of a group. If an open people produces a hegemony like any other group, the critics would argue, there is no good reason for preferring an indeterminate people to other versions of the people (such as an ethnic nation or a chosen people), since these appear to provide a more stable ground on which to build a state.

The second horn of the dilemma accepts the existence of the paradox, rejects logical inconsistency, and thus gives up on the people as a ground of legitimacy. Many radical critics on the Right and on the Left believe that the people is a chimera, and they deal with it as one would an imaginary animal. Some, including philosophical anarchists and critics of liberal democratic politics, dismiss the people as a dangerous fabrication that masks the realities of power. They urge us to do away with it, but they do

17. Ricoeur, "Political Paradox."

not offer much in its stead.[18] Others see the people as a form of idolatry. According to this traditional conservative view, the unachievable people usurps the state's legitimate religious foundation.[19]

In conclusion, the condition of indeterminacy in popular unification is costly because it produces two unpalatable reactions. The first rejects democratic legitimacy. The second tries to close the gap between the scattered individuals and the ideal people through such nondemocratic procedures as religious authority, nationalism, or political enmity. But there is an additional cost for political theorists. The indeterminacy of popular unification leads to stalemate in discussions about the legitimacy of the democratic state. Hence this indeterminacy challenges not only the legitimacy of the state, but also the imagination of political theorists. In sum, tackling indeterminacy is important, for at stake are the legitimacy of the liberal democratic state and our capacity to think creatively about the kind of political order we should strive for.

The People as Process

Dilemmas can be misleading, as there are often more than two possible solutions. As Julio Cortázar wrote, there is an infinite wind rose between yes and no.[20] The problem of how to legitimize the state democratically despite popular indeterminacy can be solved, provided one looks beyond the dilemma's two horns. But to find a genuine solution we must uncover the problem's roots, and we must also be willing to make profound changes at those roots.

The root of the indeterminacy problem is the demand made by theories of popular sovereignty that the people be a fixed and stable thing that seeks to conform to the ideal version of itself, such that its internal changes do not alter the essential nature of the state it founds. Most theories of popular sovereignty require that the state have a unified will. This requirement depends on beliefs and metaphysical commitments that are seldom questioned, despite not often being justified in moral or political terms. In fact, most of the beliefs that ground arguments for the state's legitimacy are not the most adequate or desirable for this purpose. For example, according to one set of beliefs, the will of the people is always what it ought to be: it is

18. Agamben, "What Is a People?"; Hardt and Negri, *Multitude;* Wolff, *In Defense of Anarchism.*

19. Schmitt, *Political Theology.*

20. Cortázar, *Historias de cronopios y de famas,* 43.

good, permanent, and enduring, without a shadow of change, like the will of God.[21] Yet if you question these beliefs further, you find that, unlike the will of God, there is no good reason why the will of the people must have these characteristics. Take another example. According to a second set of beliefs, the ideals that constitute the hypothetical versions of the people are unchanging and thus formulated as principles sub specie aeternitatis.[22] Yet upon further inspection we find that these unchanging ideals are incompatible with dynamic social processes and the indeterminacy of nature.

If these beliefs and metaphysical commitments generate the indeterminacy problem, you might ask, why not drop them? Political theory implicitly gives two reasons why this is hard to do. First, the demand for one will in the state is embedded in contractarian arguments, which are those most commonly used to legitimize the modern state. This unitary-will tradition is implicit in many arguments, practices, and institutions and therefore is difficult to abandon.

Second, the most common arguments in political philosophy depend on widely available beliefs and metaphysical arguments. In the West, the most prevalent arguments are those of a philosophy of being, which requires fixed identities over time, instead of a philosophy of becoming or process. This latter kind of philosophy does exist, but unfortunately those political theorists interested in legitimizing the state democratically have by and large ignored it.[23]

This book seeks to make such philosophy available to democratic theorists. I will argue that a philosophy of becoming is better suited to studying the people than is the widespread philosophy of being. I am helped in this because a philosophical commitment to time and change has been systematized in the philosophy of process.[24] This philosophical outlook is committed to describing the world in dynamic terms. On this philosophical approach, process—rather than things or substance—is metaphysically ultimate. Here I rely on those aspects of process philosophy that have direct implications for the problem of indeterminacy.

21. Riley, *General Will Before Rousseau*.

22. Rawls, *Theory of Justice*, 514.

23. Those contemporary political theorists who are interested in process or becoming, such as William Connolly, are generally not interested in legitimizing the state. See, for example, Connolly, *Pluralism*.

24. The terms "philosophy of process" and "process philosophy" are often associated with Alfred North Whitehead and his followers, but his work is part of a long tradition whose main exponents include thinkers as diverse as Gottfried Leibniz, G. W. F. Hegel, Friedrich Nietzsche, C. S. Peirce, William James, Henri Bergson, Gilles Deleuze, and Nicholas Rescher.

I take this processualist approach in order to get a new grip on the indeterminacy problem. You may object that a metaphysic is not something one can decide to change, as one would a jacket. This is true and especially important in political theory, where the metaphysical commitments of theories are tied to conceptions held by institutions and the public at large.[25] Additionally, concerted political action and perceptions of legitimacy depend on the public's entrenched ideas about identity and stability. This means that a solution to the problem that takes this new approach must at the same time consider historical habits and generalized expectations. That is to say, it must allow us to retain the general will, not as a set goal but as a tendency defined by the expectations of many individuals. What I am looking for, then, is the source of an open-ended tendency, one that is as stable as the self-perception of a people but flexible enough to allow for adjustments to novel and surprising events.

What, then, is a source of democratic legitimization that can avoid the problem of the indeterminacy of popular unification? The thesis of this book is that if we conceive of the people as a process, a series of events, rather than a collection of individuals, then we can solve the problem of legitimizing rule democratically as the people's composition changes.

The people as process is a source of democratic legitimacy that moors state institutions but is compatible with change, surprise, and innovation. It can both sustain democratic institutions and accommodate people's indeterminacy because it does not seek a predetermined goal. Rather, it fosters creative freedom as it recognizes historical tendencies and the current need to search for relatively stable state institutions. As I will show, a people as process is an unfolding series of events coordinated by the practices of constituting, governing, and changing institutions. On the one hand, the people requires a set of practices and institutions, some of which are obligatory and constrain individual action. On the other hand, it also includes a fleeting community of hopes, expectations, memories, and fraternal feelings, periodically subject to drastic and unexpected changes. These two sets, as I will show, are related in a process of becoming. As I will argue, a theory of democratic legitimization that appreciates these distinct changing sets can deal with the logical problems that beset other conceptions of the people. Moreover, it can be a ground for democratic legitimization, since it is flexible enough to admit change, yet realist

---

25. These conceptions are tied to a particular way of understanding ourselves and our society, what Charles Taylor has called a "social imaginary." See Taylor, *Modern Social Imaginaries*.

enough to recognize the staying power of institutions and the dangers involved in both change and stability.

Outline of the Book

Chapter 1 begins with a question that has perplexed democrats for more than two hundred years: how can you tell the people from a mob? "The Mob and the People in Mexico" presents a historical example of the problem of indeterminacy of popular unification, illustrating why the idea of the democratic people as an aggregation of individuals cannot legitimize a new state.

Chapter 2, "A Problem in Liberal Democratic Theory," presents the indeterminacy problem in more detail, this time from the perspective of contemporary political thought. In this chapter I argue that the problem afflicts all contemporary liberal democratic theories, and I go on to consider objections against this view that might be made by majoritarian democrats (Robert Dahl), egalitarian democrats (Thomas Christiano), social choice liberals (William Riker), and liberal contractarians (John Rawls). I conclude that liberal democratic theories cannot legitimize the state because they require a popular unification that they can never prove would be possible.

The indeterminacy problem first appears as an epistemological difficulty. At first glance, it seems that the problem is not the actual lack of unification, but rather that we cannot know that it ever happens. Yet if the problem were only epistemological, then hypothetical conceptions of the people could solve it. But I argue that they cannot. Thus, in chapter 3, "Mechanical and Teleological Conceptions of the People," I argue that the indeterminacy problem also plagues hypothetical versions of democratic theory, which helps explain why a processual conception of the people is a better solution.

Chapter 4, "Dynamic Constitutionalism and Historical Time," examines one of the most promising current solutions to the indeterminacy problem: Jürgen Habermas's theory of co-originality. This theory makes the concept of the sovereign people a function of a flexible constitution open to self-creative change over time. That is, it conceives of the people partially as a process. In this chapter I argue that while it is compelling, Habermas's solution is only partial. For instead of dealing with the indeterminacy problem in the present, he displaces it in historical time.

Chapter 5 examines other constitutional theories that espouse the idea of a changing people. In "The People Between Change and Stability," I argue that constitutional scholars who conceive of the people as a dynamic process (e.g., Frank Michelman, Sheldon Wolin, and Bruce Ackerman) offer a promising solution, but they also fall prey to the indeterminacy problem because they frame the process of constitutional change within a difficult tension between rigid stability and unruly change.

In chapter 6, "Creative Freedom and the People as Process," I develop a theory of the people as process that draws on the process ontologies of Henri Bergson, Alfred North Whitehead, and Nicholas Rescher. With their help, I define the people as an unfolding series of events coordinated by the practices of constituting, governing, and changing a set of institutions. Within this process, I call "creative freedom" the aim that coordinates the becoming of such a people. The chapter also explains how to distinguish a people from other types of process, and how to distinguish a specific people from other peoples.

Finally, chapter 7, "A Democratic People as Process," explains why this conception of the people can better deal with the indeterminacy problem than can other conceptions. In this chapter I show that a democratic people as process can avoid the logical problems that are insoluble for those theories that conceive of the people as a collection of individuals. I further argue that a justificatory democratic theory that rests on process philosophy can coherently claim that a democratic people creates itself and rules itself. In sum, the theory of the people as process offers a democratic justification of the state that is compatible with popular indeterminacy.

1

The Mob and the People in Mexico:
A Historical Example of the Indeterminacy of Popular Unification

How can you tell the people from a mob? For more than two hundred years, this question has gone hand in hand with democratic politics. Ever since Rousseau's *On the Social Contract*, we have known that to establish the legitimacy of a democratic state you must first "distinguish a regular, legitimate act [of the people] from a seditious tumult, and the will of an entire people from the clamors of a faction."[1] How to tell the people from the mob is an unanswered question in political theory, often dismissed as a concrete historical difficulty rather than a serious philosophical problem. But making this determination is a specific instance of the wider question of what is the nature of the people, a philosophical problem that democratic theory cannot afford to ignore. In this chapter I use a historical example to illustrate that the problem has philosophical import as well as actual political relevance.

I draw my example from nineteenth-century Mexico. I move away from the familiar examples of the United States and France to underline that this is a theoretical problem, one that arises in all countries that have tried to justify government using liberal democratic arguments. Moreover, presenting an example that is rare in the political theory literature reminds the reader that the establishment of relatively successful democratic regimes in western Europe and the United States is also a concrete historical experience. For this reason, the generalizations drawn from the American and European experiences should not be taken as neutral points of departure applicable to all cases. This is particularly true concerning the concept

1. Rousseau, *On the Social Contract*, 106.

of the people, which Anglo-American democratic theory has traditionally considered a stable background assumption. So I turn to early nineteenth-century Mexico to illustrate the problem of the indeterminacy of popular unification and to emphasize why it is relevant for any abstract theory of democratic legitimacy.

The Vicious Circle That Grounds the State

Mexico became an independent country in 1821. Since 1824, most Mexican governments have tried to justify their rule using democratic arguments, but they have generally failed to obtain a solid generalized agreement on their legitimacy. To date, a surprisingly large number of Mexicans continue to doubt the legitimacy of their ruling institutions.[2] Why would they do this even when they have good evidence that these institutions follow democratic principles?[3] I will argue that one of the main causes of this legitimacy deficit is an internal problem in democratic theory.

The problem is that when you try to determine the source of legitimacy in a new state, you get caught in a vicious circle. Where did the legitimacy of the newly created Mexican republic come from? To this question, you might reply that in Mexico, as in any other democratic state, legitimacy comes from the collective decision of citizens, who are the free and equal parties of a social contract. In sum, legitimacy comes from the people. The people's collective decision, you may say, authorizes the creation of representative governmental institutions. Yet in Mexico it was not clear that such consent could legitimately ground the Mexican republic because, from the beginning, logical difficulties with a democratic legitimization of rule were apparent. For one, before independence there was no people. That is, there was no single, unified population with rights to ground a state.[4] In the Spanish colony of New Spain, most individuals were neither

2. Klesner, "2006 Mexican Election and Its Aftermath."

3. Eisenstadt and Poiré, "Explaining the Credibility Gap in Mexico's 2006 Presidential Election." See also Cleary and Stokes, *Democracy and the Culture of Skepticism*.

4. This theoretical problem became obvious after the independence of the new Spanish American republics, but it first appeared during the historical crisis that preceded independence: the abdications of Bayonne, following Napoleon Bonaparte's pressure, and the constitutional convention in Cádiz. The Spanish people who founded the new legitimacy of the empire was not easy to find. See Chust, "Legitimidad, representación, y soberanía," 232. In Mexican historiography there is much debate on the effects and consequences of the "first liberalism" introduced after the 1808–12 period through the Cádiz Constitution. Yet, independent of the outcome of the first liberalism, the introduction of citizenship could not have settled the limits of the Mexican people without appeal to a preexistent nation. See Annino, "Pueblos, liberalismo, y nación en México," and Ochoa Espejo, "Paradoxes of the People in Spanish American Political Thought."

free nor equal participants in political life. They were not modern citizens, but rather neighbors who participated in the political life of their villages.[5] When some of these subjects mobilized politically outside those institutions, they constituted a mob as opposed to a people. For this reason, they could not be the origin of democratic institutions. Moreover, before independence, the political jurisdictions that would later become the territory known as Mexico did not have clearly distinguishable edges. These jurisdictions overlapped and did not clearly encompass or define the population of a single people.[6] Therefore, appealing to the people to legitimize the state produced a vicious circle because democratic citizenship presupposed democratic institutions, and democratic institutions presupposed citizenship. How could individuals have voiced their intention to create democratic institutions if their ability to express their political intent depended on the existence of those very institutions?

This vicious circle is often considered a purely theoretical problem because generally a people already exists at the inception of democracy. But this was a real problem for Spanish American political elites at the time of independence. The issue first emerged as they debated whether to establish an empire, a constitutional monarchy, or a liberal democratic republic. Vicente Rocafuerte, an ideologue of independence, reporting the opinion of the republican faction in the first independent congress of 1822, provides us with an eloquent statement that best captures the problem: "To ask that the ground of the republic be the virtue or enlightenment that is fruit of this very republic creates a vicious circle, it wishes the effect to be the foundation of the cause that should produce it. The sensible patriot should content himself with finding in the constituted people disposition to sow, and to allow the seed of virtue to bear fruit: that should suffice to erect a republic that will soon be worthy of admiration."[7] Rocafuerte talks about "virtuous republics," a term better suited to a classic city than a modern state; nonetheless, what he depicted was a modern (representative) liberal democracy.[8]

5. There is an important difference between the ideas of "ciudadano" and "vecino," which defined the terms of political participation in the republic and the prior monarchy. See Aljovín de Losada, "Ciudadano y vecino en Iberoamérica." For the Mexican case, see Breña, "Mexico." See also Herzog, "Communities Becoming a Nation."

6. This can be explained through the conceptual disputes regarding the ideas of "el pueblo" and "los pueblos." See Annino, "Soberanías en lucha," 162–65; Guerra, *Modernidad e independencias*, 354; and Roldán Vera, "'Pueblo' y 'pueblos' en México," 3–5.

7. Rocafuerte describes the main arguments for the republican position given in Congress before the establishment of Iturbide's empire in 1822. See Rocafuerte, *Bosquejo ligerísimo*, 164–65.

8. In fact, the republic he had in mind looked very much like the system just inaugurated in the United States. See Aguilar Rivera, "Dos conceptos de república," and Rocafuerte, *Ideas necesarias*.

In Rocafuerte's time it was widely held that citizenship required virtue—in his words, the "virtue or enlightenment" that grounds the republic. Rocafuerte's words reflect the demand shared by all modern liberal
democracies for a personal disposition to seek individual freedom and to
recognize the freedom of others. This personal virtue is said to be important because it enables mutual consent, which in turn guarantees individual freedom and collective autonomy. In this way, virtue allows citizens to
legitimize the state.

Rocafuerte conceded to the critics of republicanism that most existing
Mexicans lacked this disposition. He knew that republicans would not find
virtuous individuals on the ground, so he proposed that democratic institutions be legitimated hypothetically using a representative model.[9] According to this model, the people's representatives could constitute a legitimate
government on behalf of those who were not yet enlightened. Although
seemingly a solution, this approach ultimately reintroduced the vicious
circle. Here Rocafuerte called for institutions to represent free and equal
individuals within a democratic state, but unless real individuals actually
demanded such institutions, the democratic state would not be instituted.
To constitute a state, Rocafuerte required free citizens to create institutions
and democratic institutions to create free citizens: one term presupposed
the other.

Rocafuerte and his fellow republicans throughout the new countries in
Latin America recognized that only universal male citizenship together
with real popular support would provide the required social legitimacy for
the philosophical justification to have any traction.[10] But prevailing social
conditions did not favor their project. Many of those who held political
power were royalists and would appeal to traditional forms of legitimacy
to found the state. The bulk of society was not composed of individuals
who regarded themselves as free and equal to others, but rather of individuals who belonged to various hierarchical corporations: families, Indian
towns, convents, guilds, the church, and the army. Most would-be citizens
did not know, understand, or care about the machinations of the big city's
political coteries. From this small glimpse into Rocafuerte's world, you can
see why he was so concerned to foster a disposition toward self-government among those who would legitimize the state with their consent. He

9. On the idea of representation as the distinguishing mark of modern democracy, see
Manin, *Principles of Representative Government*, 79–93.

10. In all of Spanish America (with the exception of Venezuela), the franchise was
extended to the entire adult male population soon after independence was achieved. See
Colomer, "Taming the Tiger," and Sábato, "On Political Citizenship in Nineteenth-Century
Latin America."

needed individuals to have such a disposition so that, once aware of their rights, they would actively consent to and ratify the principles that independence and the constitution had upheld on their behalf. But Rocafuerte could not wait for the consent and participation of those individuals in the creation of institutions, lest he get caught in the vicious circle. The question thus became how to plant the seed of democratic virtue when there is no ground where it can take root. As we have seen, the champions of representative democracy searched for a democratic people, a ground to legitimize the republic, but they were trapped in a vicious circle between the civic virtue that establishes democratic institutions and the democratic institutions that create civic virtue.

Constitutional Paternalism

By the 1820s, most countries in Spanish America had gained independence from Spain, yet they began their independent life with heavy debts, internal discord, and theoretical problems of grave political concern. For one thing, the principle of popular sovereignty that justified their independence did not guarantee the legitimacy of their governments.

In Mexico, the lack of legitimacy manifested itself in constant civil strife during the first decades of independence. The political instability became even more complex after Texas seceded in 1836 and was annexed by the United States nine years later. The political uncertainty reached unexpected intensity during the American invasion of 1846–47. As it was then felt, the very survival of the country hung on a thin thread, and the death of the Mexican people was a real possibility.[11] After the war, conservative elites turned to monarchism as a last resort against political fragmentation. They began to argue in the press that the real problems of the republic did not come from bad application of the principle of popular sovereignty, but rather from the principle itself.

For these thinkers, the theoretical difficulties in the notion of sovereignty became a favorite target.[12] For example, the vicious circle in the foundation of the state did not go unnoticed. Writers in *El Universal* asked,

> Are the faculties and entitlements that are contained in constitutions and granted to citizens real rights because the constitutions granted

11. Palti, "Introducción," 19.

12. The essays against popular sovereignty can be found in *El Universal* for the month of December 1848. See Palti, *Política del disenso*, 148–89.

them, or did they exist before the constitutions so declared it? If the first is true, then citizens did not have any right to elect those representatives who drafted the constitutions, and for that reason, the constitution is nothing but a sheet of paper written by the representatives of men without rights, who, for that very reason, could not do anything legally, and thus [the constitution] has no substance, and all of this has been a farce. If the second option is true, how, when, and wherefrom did they acquire those rights?[13]

But these writers did not only find fault in the legal founding of the state. They also doubted the very idea of the people as its ground. In their view, the wielder of popular sovereignty was not a solid entity. Popular sovereignty cannot "constitute a people in a stable, firm, or lasting manner because the social edifice rests on a shaky base, and this ground floor cannot be propped with fulcrums. For, were these solid, they would bring the floor down; and, were they weak, they would not be sufficient to keep the base in place."[14] The people could not exist without legitimate institutions. Even the liberals agreed with this grim view of the people. According to the writers of El Siglo XIX, "The elements of disintegration . . . are so numerous that at first glance one may doubt if our republic is really a society or only a simple collection of men without the bonds, the rights, or the duties that constitute a society."[15]

With these political and theoretical antecedents, Mexican liberal governments faced a dilemma in the second half of the nineteenth century. The triumphant liberal rulers had to choose between a strong state that would attack corporate privilege and build up the civic culture that would legitimize the state, and a limited state that would focus on guaranteeing individual liberty.[16] Liberal governments chose the first horn of this dilemma, and the original liberal democratic project soon gave way to "liberal" dictatorships.[17] Thus a problem within the philosophical justification of institutions became a political problem that manifested itself in the design of the

13. Ibid., 179.

14. Ibid.

15. El Siglo XIX, June 1, 1848, quoted in Hale, "The War with the United States and the Crisis in Mexican Thought," 155 (Hale's translation).

16. Hale, quoted in Escalante Gonzalbo, "La imposibilidad del liberalismo en México," 14.

17. The liberal constitution of 1857 supported the government-by-decree of Benito Juárez and the thirty-year rule of Porfirio Díaz. According to Brian Loveman, "The liberal victory of 1857 bequeathed permanent language and authority for constitutional regimes of exception that buttressed the dictatorship from 1884 to 1910." Moreover, this is not a phenomenon particular to Mexico: "In the name of popular sovereignty and in 'defense of the constitutional order,' governments in Europe and the Americas sought to legitimate barbaric repres-

institutions,[18] resulting in a type of government I will call "constitutional paternalism."

Constitutional paternalism arises when governments interfere with individuals against their will, using the legal sanction of the constitution and the state, and the justification that individuals will be better off despite coercion.[19] The early Mexican state established constitutional paternalism in the name of liberal democracy. Yet, given that the legitimacy of liberal democracy depends on consent or reasonable agreement, these governments soon fell into a contradiction. They sought to follow democratic principles, but paradoxically, in doing so, they betrayed those very principles.[20] Nineteenth-century Mexican jurists gave a nickname to those lawmakers and politicians who zealously adhered to democratic principles and, in their zeal, were tempted by constitutional paternalism: "Jacobins."[21]

Like French Jacobins, Mexican liberal democrats fell into the temptation to impose a liberal social order "from above," through the constitution and the state.[22] In the second half of the nineteenth century, liberals captured the government after decades of civil war against conservative forces. Once in power, they imposed their idea of citizenship in order to transform an ancien régime society into a democratic polity. They used legal means to destroy the corporate privilege of the church and the military, and to break up guilds and the communal or otherwise antiliberal institutions in Indian communities. Like French Jacobins, Mexican liberals often let violence go unchecked if it helped realize their hopes. They blurred the distinction between the people and violent mobs, and they justified such violence with a discourse of republican patriotism, claiming that these actions would generate an enlightened community in the future. Once

sion of adversaries, to justify the unjustifiable, and to legalize slavery, slaughter, and mayhem." Loveman, *Constitution of Tyranny*, 3.

18. Ibid.; Negretto and Aguilar Rivera, "Rethinking the Legacy of the Liberal State in Latin America."

19. Dworkin, "Paternalism," 65.

20. A good example of a theoretical defense of "liberal dictatorship" can be found in Laureano Vallenilla Lanz's defense of Paez's dictatorship in Venezuela. See Vallenilla Lanz, *Cesarismo democrático*.

21. Hale, *Transformation of Liberalism*, chap. 2; Rabasa, *La constitución y la dictadura*, 63, 85.

22. As Luis Castro Leiva and Anthony Pagden write, "The politics of freedom was intended to secure a *res publica* in order to create a civil society, which would be capable of delivering public happiness for all its members. It was the state that was seen as the only instrument capable of generating civility within a polity which, until independence, had been wholly devoid of any autonomous political culture." "Civil Society and the Fate of the Modern Republics in Latin America," 182.

created, this community of virtuous individuals would unify under principles of reason and thus would subsequently legitimize the state.[23]

Mexican constitutional paternalism thus depended on hope. As a result, it sought to create institutions that would socialize individuals into the new system of government in the present but also legitimize the state in the future. But this hope cannot solve the lack of legitimacy. Paternalism, like Rocafuerte's solution to the vicious circle, presupposed that the people were already constituted as a people. Yet, as noted earlier, we can ground a democratic order on the hope that virtuous institutions generate virtue among individuals only if the republican institutions have a steady ground. This steady ground is a well-defined group of individuals who recognize one another's freedom and equality—which is precisely what was missing after Mexican independence.

Constitutional paternalism thus bet heavily on the future, but that was not even its biggest problem. Perhaps the main difficulty for this democratic project was how to justify the original violence involved in the creation of the state and its institutions. Such violence emerged because it was not "the people" but rather a political and economic elite who forcibly created a modern state from above, a situation that was difficult to justify. And while original violence might reluctantly be justified in retrospect, perhaps because it would be compensated for by the social changes and other advantages made possible by the creation of a modern state, there nevertheless remained an original taint. How could the state justify that the original representatives of the people claimed to represent something that did not yet exist? The people was the genuine source of legitimacy in the state, but it never coincided with the actual institutions. Throughout the nineteenth century, Mexican liberalism carried this stigma in the ever-present risk of insurrection.

By the last decades of the nineteenth century, republican Mexico had all but given up on the hope that consent would legitimize the state. The republic had suffered decades of social and political unrest: it barely survived the 1847 war against the United States and the consequent loss of half its territory, and in the 1860s it nearly lost the civil war against a

---

23. This republican patriotism became common in the discourse of the ideologues of triumphant liberalism after the Guerra de Reforma (1857–60). According to Carlos Monsiváis, "Which were the qualities of the Mexicans who would forge the nation? . . . patriotism, good principles, loyalty, hard work, love without conditions or regard for the self, duty toward their fellowmen, honesty, lack of self-regard, bravery against injustice." "Prólogo a *El Zarco*," 18. According to D. A. Brading, who also looks into the texts of Ramírez and Altamirano, "Liberal Patriotism was the Mexican version of classical republicanism." *Mito y profecía en la historia de México*, 146.

French-backed Second Mexican Empire. After all these tribulations, legitimizing the liberal republic required more than visions of the future. Liberals thus propped up their discourse with nationalistic images of the past. These images grounded the republic in a myth of origins and virtuous laboring classes, embodied symbolically in the Catholic Virgin of Guadalupe and her Indian features.

A popular nationalism rife with religious imagery thus came to replace the civic liberalism of the first republicans as the government sought to build a state.[24] After the war against the United States, the governing elites resorted to romantic nationalism and religion to build popular political unity. The sanctuary of a Mexican Virgin seemed the "only place of reunion for all Mexicans, the only chain which unites their sentiments . . . the only principle of force and unity which makes it appear as a nation through whose action we can even now regenerate ourselves."[25] After the subsequent civil wars, even the liberals turned to the Virgin of Guadalupe. Fifty years after independence, Mexicans were still bitterly divided on all political issues, and the official ideology turned to religious nationalism as a last resort. But in the end, liberal democratic theory failed to legitimize the state: the unified people never materialized outside political discourses, and even these discourses had to resort to nationalistic images of the past to justify rule.

La bola: The People and the Mob

The failure to consolidate a liberal democratic government in nineteenth-century Mexico has been explained in two ways by historians and political scientists.[26] The first blames this failure on the lack of civic engagement of most of the population.[27] The second explanation blames it on mistakes in the original design of the democratic institutions.[28] The first explanation

24. For clear literary examples of the way national and religious images propped up the political discourse of the people, see Illades, "La representación del pueblo en el segundo romanticismo mexicano," 20, 23, 27.

25. Miranda, "Sermón pangeneryco de Santa María de Guadalupe," quoted by Brading, *Mexican Phoenix,* 244.

26. An exception to this position can be found in the work of Carlos Forment, who argues that despite small failures there *was* democracy. See *Democracy in Latin America.*

27. Among political scientists, this position is best represented by Morse, "Heritage of Latin America," and Véliz, *Centralist Tradition of Latin America.* In recent historiography, it is best represented by Escalante Gonzalbo, *Ciudadanos imaginarios,* and François-Xavier Guerra, *México.*

28. Aguilar Rivera, *En pos de la quimera;* Loveman, *Constitution of Tyranny.*

implies that a legitimate democratic order comes "from below." The second inverts the dependence, positing that the order comes "from above." This disagreement, however, is only apparent. As we have seen, both explanations converge in Rocafuerte's vicious circle. In either instance, establishing legitimate democratic institutions requires a democratic people, a well-defined group of citizens socialized into democratic culture. At the same time, in both cases, legitimate institutions are also necessary to produce citizens. In either of these explanations, the legitimate liberal democratic state both causes and results from popular consent to just institutions. Both explanations are therefore stuck in the practical and theoretical problem of how to "jump-start" a liberal democratic state.

In nineteenth-century Mexico, legitimacy did not arrive from above or from below.[29] Such was the shared sentiment of a generation grown tired of petty leaders invoking the power of "the people." This generation is perhaps best represented by Emilio Rabasa, a novelist and constitutional scholar, who captured its sentiment of discontent when he wrote in his novel *La bola*, "The Revolution develops around reason, it rouses nations and requires citizens. *La bola* [the mob] does not demand principles and never has them, it is born and it dies in a short material and moral space, and requires ignorant folk. In a word: the Revolution is the daughter of world progress and the ineluctable law of mankind; *la bola* is the daughter of ignorance, the unavoidable punishment of backward folk."[30]

Like Rabasa, most Mexicans who wrote about politics did not believe that nascent democratic institutions had turned the mob into a people. For almost a century, Mexico had suffered countless uprisings and rebellions, which according to Rabasa were the mob's handiwork. *La bola* attracted the rabble, not the people. Moreover, if constitutional law was indeed the people's collective will and the expression of its rationality, it made no sense that the people could act outside the limits of the established law. Those taking up arms sought legitimacy beyond the law and therefore did not deserve to be called the people, and their uprisings did not deserve the name "revolution." But while the mob was not the unified people that elite ideology envisioned, these uprisings did expose the early Mexican government's lack of legitimacy.

29. According to Eric Van Young, during and after independence popular and elite insurgency aspired to quite different goals. Rather than liberal democracy or independence from Spain, popular rebellions were characterized by cultural resistance against forces of change. This pattern continues until the time of the revolution. Van Young, *The Other Rebellion*, 496–504.

30. Rabasa, *"La bola" y "La gran ciencia,"* 167–68.

But the view of those bearing the arms clashed with those who called them a mob, for those who revolt believe in the legitimacy of their cause. This clash of views was evident in retrospect, especially after the popular insurrection that later became known as the Mexican Revolution. While this insurrection brought the liberal dictatorship to an end in the early twentieth century, it also raised the question: was this a "real" revolution or just another *bola*? According to the liberals then in power, the popular uprising that accompanied the political movement was another instance of the mob. But the resistance against paternalist coercion seemed to justify rebellion, even according to some of the liberals in power. Such civil strife, in a country that was nominally a liberal democracy, lent itself to two mutually exclusive interpretations. On the one hand, it was argued that the law and the institutions were after all legitimate, and therefore that the uprising reflected only bad leadership and lack of civic awareness among the ignorant masses. On the other hand, it was argued that the mobilized population expressed the people's will, and that the people's opposition to existing institutions gave further proof that the government and its institutions had been illegitimate all along.

These contrasting positions illustrate a political problem that arises when liberal democratic theory seeks to legitimize the state. The first position holds that the mobilized masses lack the reason required to ground a legitimate state. The second position holds that the government is illegitimate without the masses because without popular support, not even just law can legitimize rule. The first position requires that all individuals be unified in the awareness of their rights within the existing institutions, while the second requires the consent of the unified people. The problem with both positions was that they require the coincidence of will and reason in a unified people to legitimize the state, when neither can actually show that the people were unified at a given time. And without unification, all that remains is a mob.

It is true that the will of the unified people was missing in nineteenth-century Mexico, just as much as it is missing today. Yet this was not solely the fault of Mexico's weak civil culture, or a product of the fragile Mexican state and economy. The example of Mexico's tribulations resonates with the deficit of democratic legitimacy suffered by many democracies, new and old. A unified will would have been just as hard to find in the United States in 1789, in France in 1793, or in Iraq in 2007. Could it be, then, that this deficit arises within democratic theory itself, and not solely from the features of the populations to which the theory is applied? That is, could we be facing a problem of design rather than a problem of application?

2

A Problem in Liberal Democratic Theory: The Indeterminacy of Popular Unification

We saw that the people was nowhere to be found in nineteenth-century Mexico. This is no anomaly. Democrats and democratic theorists have not been able to find the unified people anywhere. It is perhaps for this reason that they have relied on a mixture of democratic and liberal arguments when seeking to justify the democratic state. Liberal democratic theory offers arguments to justify political principles and institutions, yet rather than appealing to the people to legitimize the state, it appeals to individual consent. According to liberal democratic theory, if everyone could consent to and thus agree on a set of principles that justify the state, any state satisfying those principles would be legitimate. This theory thus presupposes that there is a group of individuals the totality of whom we could call "everyone." It presupposes the existence of a well-defined political community whose members could agree on a principle legitimizing the state. In short, the theory assumes that there could be a unified democratic people, even if in actuality we cannot find one.

Individual consent and generalized agreement seem like compelling criteria for legitimizing the state because today almost everybody thinks that a people could unify if reasonable individuals recognized one another's equal worth and right to freedom. But can such unification ever occur? Could there be well-defined communities where all members recognized one another as free and equal? Unless both liberal democrats and their critics ask this question directly, they are not entitled to their assumptions about the state's legitimacy. In this chapter, I argue that contemporary liberal democratic theory is threatened by the indeterminacy of popular unification. The problem is that to justify rule, the theory requires that the people unify (actually or hypothetically), but it cannot show that the people do or could unify at any given time. As a result, the theory cannot justify the state.

That consent and reasonable agreement cannot themselves legitimize the state becomes clearer if you consider that the indeterminacy problem in liberal democratic theory is closely connected to the idea of popular sovereignty. You can see this connection in the following argument. To legitimize the state, liberal democratic theory envisions what would happen if individuals agreed to establish a legitimate liberal democratic order. The theory assumes that when all individuals come together in their consent, they can agree both on the rules of the political game and that these rules will legitimately bind them in the future. But this in turn implies two further assumptions: first, that all the members of a well-defined group could unify their political wills, even if only hypothetically; and second, that the institutional arrangements arising from their consensual agreement are the group's supreme authority. Since we usually call such a politically unified group "a people," and their supreme authority "sovereign," we can say that most liberal democratic theories assume a moment of popular sovereignty. In what follows, I will argue that given this assumption of popular sovereignty, these theories stumble over the indeterminacy problem. Consequently, whenever they try to show that the people can unify, they either fall into a philosophical regress or get trapped in a vicious circle.

The argument advanced in this chapter consists of two parts. First, I claim that most available liberal democratic theories embrace popular sovereignty. For this reason, I argue, they face the problem of the indeterminacy of popular unification. Second, I answer objections to this claim. For instance, many liberal and democratic theorists would object that this problem damages their justifications of the state. In reply, I argue that currently dominant theories—such as majoritarian democratic theory, egalitarian democratic theory, social choice liberalism, and the liberal versions of contractualism (including Rawlsian political liberalism and some theories of deliberative democracy)—must still come to terms with this problem.

Popular Sovereignty and the Indeterminacy of Popular Unification

In the previous chapter, I showed how an incipient state can fail to establish legitimate democratic rule. Scholars who study similar cases have

often claimed that new countries often fail to consolidate liberal democratic regimes because they lack material resources or modern organization.[1] Their underlying assumption is that poverty and other material
obstacles prevent individuals from developing democratic institutions. But
few of these scholars ask whether the failure to establish democracy might
originate in the very design of the democratic project, rather than in the
obstacles to its application. That is to say, they do not ask whether the
problems may reside within the normative theory of the proposed institutions. Yet the history of countries such as Mexico shows that democratic
theory failed to legitimize rule, at least partly because the unified democratic people could be neither found nor represented in institutions. Could
it be, then, that this failure illustrates the problem in democratic theory I
have called the indeterminacy of popular unification?

The indeterminacy problem arises in the justification of rule for the
following reasons. First, to establish the terms in which a legitimate liberal
democratic order can exist, most liberal democratic theories rely on the
theory of popular sovereignty. Second, the theory of popular sovereignty
requires popular unification, yet it cannot show that the people is unified
at any given time. In what follows, I will illustrate each of these claims. Of
these, the first is perhaps more contentious than the second: it may well
be doubted that liberal democratic theories postulate popular sovereignty
at all. Therefore, let me begin by making the case for this proposition.

Generalized Consent in Liberal Democratic Theory

Most theories of liberal democracy require popular sovereignty when they
offer arguments to legitimize the state.[2] This last claim is not controversial
among democratic theorists,[3] but it will make many liberals cringe. The

---

1. The details of the relation between democracy and development have been one of the
main concerns of the empirical studies of democracy since the middle of the last century. As
Seymour Martin Lipset wrote, "Perhaps the most widespread generalization linking political
systems to other aspects of society has been that democracy is related to the state of economic
development." "Some Social Requisites of Democracy," 75. It has also been an important
concern for rational choice theorists. According to Mancur Olson, for example, "The conditions necessary for a lasting democracy are the same necessary for the security of property
and contract rights that generates economic growth." "Dictatorship, Democracy, and Development," 567.

2. By "liberal democratic theory" I mean normative political theory that focuses on
autonomy when it seeks to legitimize the state, in the tradition of Rousseau and Kant, but I
also mean the tradition that concentrates on equal rights and opportunities. By "liberal,"
then, I mean liberal egalitarianism, which "is concerned with equality as a political value that
is concerned with the regulation of legitimate coercion." Kelly, *Liberalism*, 13.

3. Popular sovereignty is a central assumption in some of the most prominent contemporary democratic theory. See, for example, Christiano, *Rule of the Many*, 3, 70.

people? Is that the ultimate source of authority in liberal theory? Against this objection I argue that, indeed, according to liberal democratic theory, the people is sovereign. Rule is legitimate only when the ultimate source of political authority in the state is the actual or hypothetical consent of all individuals to those principles and institutions that make rule acceptable.

Consent thus undergirds this last claim.[4] And the claim that all liberal democratic theorists require actual or hypothetical generalized consent holds even for libertarians who have claimed, like Robert Nozick, that the invisible-hand process by which the state could legitimately emerge "looks nothing like unanimous joint agreement."[5] For him, the legitimacy of rule need not come from joint agreement—that is, from an actual social compact. Generalized consent may come from "voluntary actions of separately acting individuals . . . even though no one had the pattern in mind or was trying to achieve it."[6] But the resulting state rests on generalized consent and is equivalent to such agreement. A "state of nature" theory, as he calls his thought experiment, explains and legitimizes the state hypothetically. It tells us how a state could emerge without violating anybody's rights, but this requires each individual's consent. If libertarian theories adopt this view, we could say that, a fortiori, other liberal democratic theories that are less concerned with consent and individual liberty are likely to concede that state legitimacy depends on (hypothetical) generalized agreement. They also assume that only generalized consent, or unification, can fully justify rule and legitimize state institutions. They thus presuppose that the unifying of the people is possible, whether generalized consent comes from joint agreement or from egoistic individual actions.

In contrast to consent theories such as Nozick's, other liberal theories accord even more importance to generalized agreement. Liberal contractarian theories, for instance, hold that rule is legitimate only when reasonable individuals would consent to it. And individuals would consent to rule only when rule depends on institutions designed according to reasonable principles on which everybody ought to agree, such as those that justice requires. Thus they assume that if legitimacy is possible, then generalized agreement, or popular unification, is also possible.

4. For a general view of consent theory, see Beran, *Consent Theory of Political Obligation*.

5. Nozick, *Anarchy, State, and Utopia*, 132.

6. Ibid. This position is also consistent with political economic thinking, specifically with social choice theory. According to Mueller, "The state can be defined as a kind of involuntary membership club that exists to economize on transactions costs when resolving the many market failures the community faces." *Public Choice III*, 40. The state is presumably justified if it economizes on transaction costs.

Popular unification through consent is also important, albeit less obvious, in many other liberal theories. For example, it is important in theories that hold that you cannot eliminate disagreement from a liberal polity because even when there is disagreement, any liberal democratic state presupposes a prior agreement on basic institutional arrangements. In *Law and Disagreement,* one example of such an approach, Waldron makes central to his theory of constitutionalism the fact of disagreement. Yet he also assumes that authority is illegitimate if it cannot be justified to each person it claims to bind. This means that although individuals may disagree on every specific question they debate in a liberal state, they still share a common ground established by hypothetical agreement. This generalized agreement on good reasons for having a government justifies the exercise of rule and the production of law. Hence, even in theories centered on disagreement, the state's legitimacy hinges on the possibility of generalized consent or unification on basic procedural rules.[7]

Liberal theorists may disagree on the details of how generalized agreement legitimizes the state, and especially on whether legitimization must be actual or hypothetical. Yet all contemporary liberal theories legitimize the state by relying on the possibility of generalized consent to basic principles that allow for life in common.[8] They implicitly claim that generalized consent may obtain because there are reasonable principles on which everybody ought to agree. These principles are the normative ground for democracy. For most liberal theories, such principles state that all persons are free and equal, so that a state is legitimate when it respects the equal worth of persons and protects the rights that derive from that proposition. Given that *ought* implies *can,* this form of justification presupposes the possibility of consensus because it asserts that all individuals ought to agree on these principles. Liberal democrats, then, assume that in a legitimate state there is a framework of understandings or practices based on the primacy of an equal personal right to freedom. They also assume that the source of political authority is the actual or hypothetical generalized

---

7. Waldron, *Law and Disagreement,* 229. See also Estlund, "Jeremy Waldron on Law and Disagreement."

8. Joseph Raz and other scholars sharing his view would argue that government is not legitimate due to the consent of the governed, but rather due to the good reasons that underpin the consent of individuals to authority. See Raz, *Morality of Freedom,* 89. But this objection does not refute the point that I try to make here. My point is that the authority of government depends on the *possibility* of consensus—and this consensus would also obtain where all individuals accept that they have good reasons to accept authority, as happens when we accept that by obeying authority we are more likely to comply with reasons that apply to us than we would otherwise be. See Raz, *Morality of Freedom,* 38–69.

consent all individuals give to the institutions that uphold individual rights.

Why does this form of justification entail that liberal theories postulate "popular sovereignty"? Most liberal democratic theories, I contend, postulate such sovereignty when they justify the state on the basis of generalized consent. All theories that seek to legitimize the state in this manner assume that there could be a consensual agreement, and that this unification, *when available,* is the ultimate source of authority in the democratic state.[9] Given that sovereignty is an attribute of those having the supreme authority in a state, we can say that most liberal democratic theories assume that the unified consent of individuals is sovereign.[10]

Most liberal thinkers would agree with these claims, but they might still be uncomfortable with the idea that the hypothetical consent of individuals amounts to popular sovereignty. Why assign sovereignty to "the people," they might ask, rather than to the individuals who consent to rule? To support this claim, I first have to show that the unified consent of individuals that grounds a liberal democratic state is equivalent to a unified people.

Liberalism and Popular Sovereignty

So far I have argued that liberal democratic theories assume the possibility of popular sovereignty. That is, they admit that while generalized agreement may not actually be available, it is still a real possibility that, if it existed, would be the ultimate source of authority for all individuals. We can say then that for liberal democrats, generalized consent is sovereign. But is "generalized consent" equivalent to "the people"? Perhaps generalized consent does not come to mind when you think of popular sovereignty, so you might ask: What precisely do I mean by "popular sovereignty"? How does the concept I use differ from other uses?

Popular sovereignty is the claim that the people's unified will is the supreme authority in the state. The theory of popular sovereignty can justify the state because it guarantees individual freedom and social coordination simultaneously. According to the theory's traditional versions,

9. Note that this agreement need not be substantial. All that is required to satisfy the condition for popular sovereignty is that all agree to accept the authority of decisions produced through a particular procedure. Even if all disagree on substantial matters, they can agree on the procedure that generates collective decisions. These decisions are binding for all, and for this reason generalized agreement constitutes the sovereign.

10. On the history and conventional uses of the concept of sovereignty, see Benn, "Uses of Sovereignty"; Hinsley, *Sovereignty;* and Philpott, "Sovereignty."

common recognition of a reasonable principle justifying rule on the basis of freedom and equality can harmonize all individual wills into a unified will, which in turn legitimizes a state. This agreement, whether tacit or explicit, guarantees that every individual obeys only herself, and thus preserves freedom (or autonomy) and legitimizes rule. Democratic institutions can thus represent a people if such agreement, or generalized consent, is possible. Hence, for those who believe in popular sovereignty, a democratic people, or "the people," is the collection of all those individuals who agree or would agree to organize ruling institutions according to principles of freedom and equality. When a democratic people exists, it is the ultimate source of authority for itself. Given that liberal theories seeking to legitimize the state assume that there is, or could be, a unified people based on common recognition of a principle on which they ought to agree, they therefore espouse a version of popular sovereignty.

I want to distinguish this conception of popular sovereignty from others because the term can be used to express views that I do not hold. For example, many mistakenly use the term to express the view that the majority of the electorate (whether right or wrong) has unlimited and irrevocable authority over the minority. This use is mistaken because popular sovereignty entails legitimacy, and the arbitrary rule of the majority, which this usage suggests, does not. While it may be true that the sheer force of numbers can compel compliance with rule, it certainly cannot legitimize the force that powers such compliance. The majority may be sovereign as a matter of fact, but few believe that this alone justifies its supreme power.

The idea that the will of the majority is sovereign is often said by intellectual historians to be a misappropriation of Rousseau's conception of the "general will." Their work shows how the theological conception of God's sovereign will became the will of the people: an all-powerful will that is necessarily right.[11] It also shows how, over time, "the majority" became equivalent to "the sovereign people." This happened after political philosophers introduced the idea of representation into their discussions and politicians began to use both sets of ideas in political debates.[12] But the history and political theology of the sovereign will need not concern us here. While it may be true that politicians have used the concept of popular sovereignty as an appeal to a divine power capable of summoning a unified

11. Riley, *General Will Before Rousseau;* Schmitt, *Political Theology.*

12. An excellent genealogy of democracy that traces these developments can be found in the work of Pierre Rosanvallon for the case of France. See Rosanvallon's *La démocratie inachevée, Le peuple introuvable,* and *Le sacre du citoyen.*

people, such appeals are neither sufficient nor necessary to justify the state through liberal democratic arguments.[13]

Perhaps in reaction to the view of the sovereign people as divine, many critics have come to caricaturize the concept of popular sovereignty. They portray it as the idea that the majority of citizens in a state are right to do as they please, and are also right to impose their opinions on those who disagree. I believe that this caricature distorts the concept to the point of contradiction. According to this view, the popular sovereign (understood as the majority) could overturn the principles of freedom and equality, and thus a democratic majority could legitimately use democracy itself to overturn democracy.[14] This does not make sense, and no genuine theory of popular sovereignty espouses this view.

Yet the caricature, like all caricatures, does capture some important truths. Ideologues and politicians have used the term "popular sovereignty" to support the view that an oppressive majority could stand for "the people." For example, in the antebellum United States, many used the term to justify extending slavery to the territories acquired during the Mexican War. Stephen Douglas frequently appealed to the notion in his famous debates with Abraham Lincoln.[15] Douglas argued that if the settlers rather than the federal government decided the issue, "popular sovereignty" could justify introducing slavery to the new territories of the United States. He used "popular sovereignty" rhetorically to defend an unjustifiable conception of the people in which slaves did not count as citizens or equal persons.

This use of the term is evidently inconsistent with any contemporary normative view of liberal democracy centered on equal individual worth and a right to freedom. In fact, the belief in everyone's equal freedom is one of the central marks distinguishing modern democracy from oligarchy or despotism.[16] Douglas also made the term incompatible with any liberalism. Given that for liberal thinkers the authority of legitimate rulers is never unsupervised and irrevocable—even if they have the authority to make law, judge, and enforce compliance with law—Douglas's use corrupts the term, which is otherwise compatible with liberal democratic theory.

---

13. See Ochoa Espejo's "Does Political Theology Entail Decisionism?" and "On Political Theology and the Possibility of Superseding It."

14. Jaffa, *Crisis of the House Divided*.

15. Angle, *Complete Lincoln-Douglas Debates of 1858*.

16. The American South may have been democratic, but it was "undemocratic in relation to its black population." Dahl, *Democracy and Its Critics*, 121.

According to the above definition, contemporary liberal democratic thought presupposes popular sovereignty when it justifies the state. But this definition carries with it a problem because the theory of popular sovereignty assumes yet cannot show that the people are unified. To support this claim, however, I must first determine what liberal democratic theory conceives a people to be.

The People in Liberal Democratic Theory

In the previous section, I claimed that liberal theory implies that a people is the collection of all those individuals who agree, or would agree, to organize ruling institutions according to principles of freedom and equality. But is this what most liberal democratic theories mean by "the people"? How does this conception differ from others?

In everyday language, the term "people" often refers to a person's kin. In this sense, "your people" are your extended family and those who share with you a common origin and history. This meaning figures in the expressions "this land belongs to my people" or "those are the songs of my people."[17] The usage in these expressions differs, however, from a second sense of the term, found in Exodus 8:1, when God instructs Moses to tell Pharaoh, "Let my people go!" In this sense, "the people" is a group of individuals who share cultural and historical ties. These two types of grouping are communities that may share biological ties, but they are mostly bound by shared beliefs or culture.[18] Hence these senses of the people are cultural, while the sense of the term "people" I discuss here is primarily political. So it is important to underline that by "a people" I do not mean a nation. The nation may resemble political conceptions of the people, and it obviously has political relevance, but it remains distinct from the most relevant people conception in modern political philosophy. While the first two senses of "people" (a kin group and a nation) relate to the Greek term *ethnos*, the sense we are dealing with, which has a tradition going back to the time of Rousseau, relates to the term *demos*.[19]

The demos refers to all the citizens of a city-state. Much political theory imagines the history of the term "the people" to begin in ancient Greece

17. Here I do not discuss a definition of a people based on language (I equate it with a nation), but this specific criterion was very influential in the nineteenth century. Jacob Grimm claimed that "a people is the essence of all those who speak the same language." Quoted by Habermas, "What Is a People?" 18.

18. See Anderson, *Imagined Communities*, and Miller, *On Nationality*, chap. 2.

19. For current discussions on this distinction, see Balibar, *We the People of Europe?* and Benhabib, *Another Cosmopolitanism*.

and to continue its way through Rome to modern times. The claim that the term has a classical origin is not implausible. "The people" may indeed go back to the Greek *demos* and the Roman *populus,* and it could have made its way into modern political theory by way of Enlightenment classicism, such as that of the American Founding Fathers.[20] Indeed, the definition of the people that I have propounded as central to modern democratic theory closely resembles Cicero's. In *On the Commonwealth,* Scipio, the famed Roman general and main protagonist of Cicero's text, proclaims, "The commonwealth, then, is the people's affair [*res publica*], and the people is not any group of men associated in any manner, but is the coming together of a considerable number of men who are united by a common agreement about law and rights and by their desire to participate in mutual advantages."[21]

Understanding the people as demos or populus, however, requires a further distinction. Just like today, in classical Roman political thought populus chiefly meant the whole of the political community as well as "the masses."[22] The second classical sense conceives "the people" as those who do not rule directly, and by association it became shorthand for "the poor." This sense of the term has a long political history of pitting the poor against the rich, and often ascribing righteousness and political virtue to the former.[23] Yet this second sense is not the one that theorists use in democratic theory. Although appealing to the people may help to legitimize the state sociologically, the appeal itself is not a definitive justification of the state. For this reason, "the masses" or "the many" do not map onto "the people" in the sense I gave in the previous section. While you cannot completely sever the modern democratic sense of the term "the people" from other associated meanings, you can say that the democratic sense has little to do with social justice and the distribution of wealth.

In contemporary democratic theory the people is generally conceived of as a collection of individuals. Among political theorists, the commonsense view is that the people is the "mass of the adult population in a polity."[24] But democratic theorists often restrict membership in this collection

20. Canovan, *The People,* 10–39.

21. Cicero, *On the Commonwealth,* 129.

22. Lintott, *Constitution of the Roman Republic.*

23. Politicians and political ideologues have often used this connotation to fan the fires of revolutionary movements and peasant rebellions; political scientists have used the blanket term "populism" to describe this political discourse. For a mapping of this concept in the literature, see Canovan, *Populism.*

24. Geuss, *History and Illusion in Politics,* 113.

according to competence. For example, Thomas Christiano defines the subject of popular sovereignty as "all minimally competent adults coming together as one body."[25] Both James Fishkin and Henry Richardson also offer a collection-of-individuals account. In this view, the democratic people is the citizenry: the sum total of all those in the polity who have full citizenship rights, including the right to vote and the right to publicly discuss political matters.[26] There are also more elaborate views of the nature of the political collective, or what Philip Pettit calls "political ontology." For example, Pettit's own account (a view he also attributes to Rawls) is a conception of the people under representative government. According to Pettit, such a people is correctly seen as "a civicity." By this, Pettit means a group of individuals who "have certain purposes in common, and have a representative agency in place to advance those purposes."[27] But even this elaborate view shares in common with the more traditional conceptions the idea that the people is a collection of individuals brought together for the purpose of organizing ruling institutions.[28] More specifically, they all assume that a democratic people is a collection of individuals who would agree to principles that uphold freedom and equality.

This conception of the people has traditionally been tied to the notion of a territory, a place, or a "there."[29] Because the possibility of agreement calls for individuals who are already "there," so to speak, it requires a group already existing in a particular place. As Bernard Yack says, what distinguishes this conception is that "it presents an image of community over space. It portrays all individuals within given boundaries of a state as members of a community from which the state derives its legitimate

25. Christiano, *Rule of the Many*, 3.
26. Fishkin, *Voice of the People*, 97–143; Richardson, *Democratic Autonomy*, 65–72.
27. Pettit, "Rawls's Political Ontology," 166.
28. Two recent conceptions of the people that contrast with more traditional views are those of Rogers Smith and Ernesto Laclau. According to Smith, a people "is a potential adversary of other forms of human association, *because* its proponents are generally understood to assert that its obligations legitimately trump many of the demands made on its members in the name of other associations." *Stories of Peoplehood*, 20. Laclau also holds that the people is constructed in contrast to a different group because the people does not have a stable referent—it is constructed as an "empty signifier." *On Populist Reason*, 67–72. I do not consider these views here because they are not offered as the basis for a public justification of the democratic state. That is, they are part of explanatory theories showing how the concept of the people is used in modern political life, rather than how it is used as the ground for a normative democratic theory.
29. It may not be a pure coincidence that in Spanish the term "for the people" is also the term for "town." On the development of the historical idea of "pueblo" and "pueblos" in Latin America, see Annino, "Soberanías en lucha."

authority. . . . The concept of the people allows us to imagine the community that we share at any particular moment in dealing with the state's coercive authority."[30]

Hence the modern political use of the term "the people" goes hand in hand with liberal democratic thought. This conception of the people thus differs both from the national or ethnic sense described above and from the idea of the masses. A people, in its modern democratic sense, is not a nation (itself often associated with the German *Volk*).[31] Further, it is neither the mob nor the deprived masses that nineteenth-century thinkers so feared. Nor yet is it the majority. In its modern democratic sense, the people emerges from the belief that all the individuals in a given territory are free and equal, and that they may rule themselves when they create institutions by uncoerced association.

With these elements in hand, we can now give the complete definition: in the modern liberal democratic view, the people is the collection of individuals in a given territory who agree, or would agree, to organize ruling institutions according to principles of freedom and equality. Given this, a unified people actually agrees and wills that this democratic government come into being. Moreover, the individuals who form a people are the parties to the social contract, the complete count of members in the political set. Further, any theory that legitimizes government based on consent and autonomy must, as I have argued, assume that there is an actual or hypothetical general agreement. That is, any such theory takes for granted the possibility of a unified people. This conception of the people accompanies most justifications of the state in liberal democratic theories; it is distinctly modern, and something that democratic theory usually takes as given.

Democratic Theory's Three Intractable Logical Problems

The possibility of a unified people is such a deep assumption in democratic theory that democratic theorists hardly notice it and seldom discuss it. But who composes the people? Democratic theories often assume that the people is "already there," and hence that its criteria of membership is not a matter of discussion. Robert Dahl believed that this common assumption among democratic theorists is one of the core components of the "shadow theory of democracy," a set of "half-hidden premises and

---

30. Yack, "Popular Sovereignty and Nationalism," 521.
31. For a discussion of the term *Volk*, see Habermas, "What Is a People?" 6, 17.

unexplored assumptions that forever dogs the footsteps of explicit, public theories of democracy."[32] But even Dahl failed to dig much deeper into the assumption's roots.

I believe we must pay more attention to the question of who composes the people, because without such attention we leave obscure a problem in normative democratic theory: the indeterminacy of popular unification. In short, the issue is that to legitimize the state you would have to show that the people are unified or could unify in their agreement on democratic principles. In order to do this, however, you first have to determine whom the people comprises. In its current configuration, however, democratic theory cannot answer this latter question. The conception of the people on which democratic theory relies is subject to three intractable logical problems: the problem of constituting the demos, the vicious circle of self-constitution, and the problem of the people in time. Let us consider each issue in turn.

When you ask who composes the people, contemporary political theory gives different answers. These depend on diverging criteria, which are often grounded on territory, history, or individual political competence. But which is the right criterion of exclusion? Determining how we ought to allocate political rights within a constituted polity is known in the literature as the problem of constituting the demos.[33] Let us see why the standard conception of the people cannot give a coherent answer to this question.

In the previous section, I claimed that most democratic theories assume that those who ought to be part of the demos are all adults in a given country. But it does not take much to see that this answer will not solve the problem of constituting the demos. For one thing, the actual borders of a country tend to be arbitrary. They do not fit well with liberal democracy's commitment to the idea that government guarantees collective autonomy through individual freedom and equality. To lessen the arbitrariness of this first response, democratic theory often takes history and geography into consideration. These features highlight ethnic ties and territorial friendships, and thus they are not random criteria. In this view, citizens owe special regard to one another because they are also "siblings" and "neighbors" of sorts.

But ethnic ties and territorial friendship have their own problems as criteria for exclusion. Blood and soil may provide criteria for determining

32. Dahl, *Democracy and Its Critics*, 3.
33. Ibid., 21–23, 30.

who belongs to a nation, but they do not justify the limits of the people understood as a collection of free and equal citizens. For example, if you argue that geographical limits define a people, you will find it hard to classify those living in borderline geographic areas. Are those living in South Tyrol part of the people of Austria or Italy? Moreover, problems of this kind arise even when you encounter settled and stable geographic borders. Consider an island like Great Britain. Water determines the limits of Britain's population, yet in Britain the accident of history, rather than the accident of geography, defines the people. The Welsh and Scots could attest to this.

Could history better determine the limits of the people? At first sight, history does seem to solve these problems. But a closer look shows that relying on history rather than on geography does not make our situation any easier. Making the people an accident of history conflates it with the nation. As I argued in the previous section, a democratic people must come together by choice rather than chance, and therefore it cannot map onto a nation. Considering a people an accident of history and geography is problematic, because while those contingent borders may accurately describe a people, they do not help us achieve our goal: justifying rule. A good justificatory principle would require that this group be a democratic people that comes together by reason and will. That is, history and geography do not tell you which individuals in a given territory could willingly agree on a principle that guarantees everyone's freedom and equality. Those who could willingly agree must be free and equal individuals who can choose to rule themselves according to democratic principles, and only they can legitimize the state on the basis of agreement or consent.

Neither territory nor history, then, can define a democratic people.[34] Instead, individual will and explicitly relevant moral criteria must define it. But a "shadow democratic theorist" might object that finding a territorially or historically based people is still possible. Couldn't you find an island with a steady population, universal citizenship, a homogenous democratic culture, and no immigration? If we argue that these conditions have never obtained, the committed shadow theorist could reply that we may yet find such characteristics in an island we have yet to discover: our own utopia.

Yet even in utopia the people are never "already there," and they cannot be taken for granted. On our imaginary liberal democratic island, full citizens would exclude children and the mentally ill from participation in

---

34. Arrhenius, "Boundary Problem in Democratic Theory"; Whelan, "Democratic Theory and the Boundary Problem."

politics because citizenship requires consent. Someone would have to define mental health and adult age, thus narrowing citizenship to those who are considered fit to agree on a principle of political freedom and equality. And that criterion for delimiting the people—that rule of exclusion—could not come about by geographical or historical accident.

To legitimize rule democratically, you need a morally relevant rule of exclusion that determines the people's boundaries. But what constitutes such a rule? Few have ever dealt with the problem of constituting the demos, and those who do consider it usually run into trouble. Dahl, for instance, bravely advances the following rule of exclusion: "The demos must include all adult members of an association except transients and persons proved to be mentally defective."[35] This rule pleases democratic theorists because it respects democratic criteria: it does not define the people on ethnic grounds, it establishes that all those who are subjects of rule should also make the decisions that govern them, and thus it ensures freedom and equality and the state's legitimacy. Yet this rule, too, has a problem. It hides a premise that introduces a territorial condition through the backdoor. The "subjects to the decision" are those whom the decision's makers can compel to obey. This means that subjects must be within the territory for the association to enforce its decisions. Thus subjects to the binding decisions of the association must be in a specific area: they are those who "are already there." Hence this rule depends on existing geographic borders.[36] It makes the people an accident of geography yet again, and thus undermines the normative principle underlying Dahl's exclusion rule.

The principle underlying the exclusion rule is the "all affected interests" principle, which holds that all those whose interests are affected by a decision should be participants in making the decision. The principle initially appears to be the best candidate for determining the limits of the demos, since it leaves intact the democratic requirement to preserve individual freedom and equality. So, for example, populations living on either side of

35. Dahl, *Democracy and Its Critics*, 129.

36. Alternatively, you could argue that the modern state can actually compel compliance beyond territorial borders. A bomber airplane, a missile, or commercial sanctions can effectively coerce (and thus make subjects of decisions) those outside territorial boundaries. In this case, Dahl's rule would include those outside the territory of a given state, but then *everybody* would be potentially subject to the decisions of *any* given state. Democracy would have no bounds and the rule would not be an *exclusion* rule anymore. The criteria would determine the worldwide reach of democratic politics, but it could not help us constitute a state or fix boundaries. See the discussion of Goodin's solution below.

a river that is also an international border should have a say in those democratic decisions that determine the quality of the river's water.[37] The rule
works, but only when territorial boundaries and democratic institutions
on both sides of the river already exist, and individuals living on either
side could agree on an analysis and interpretation of the meaning of "having one's interests affected by a decision." But in the cases that concern
this book, where the decision in question would establish the very ground
and legitimacy of the democratic state, the rule is not useful. Given that
the decision we need to make will determine which individuals will have
rights of political participation, those who get to participate in the decision
would have to determine whether their own interests are affected by this
very decision. As a result, the rule generates a vicious circle.[38]

So what is an adequate criterion for constituting the people? If we
demand that the criterion be selected democratically, we fall into paradoxes.[39] You cannot determine, by means of a vote, who will belong to the
demos that is to vote on that very question. But if choosing the criterion
for exclusion is not itself to be done democratically, then we face another
problem. If we justify an exclusion criterion by appeal to nondemocratic
principles (such as abstract principles of justice), then we fall into what I
have called "constitutional paternalism." This is a condition in which that
appeal will be made by the group already in power, who will then treat the
rest unequally, since those others could not participate in the very definition of the principles. So the problem of constituting the demos turns out
to be closely related to the vicious circle that haunted Vicente Rocafuerte.
Unless the people is already there, there is no way to jump-start a democratic people legitimately. This is the paradox of self-constitution that goes
hand in hand with democratic theory.[40]

37. Arrhenius, "Boundary Problem in Democratic Theory."
38. Goodin, "Enfranchising All Affected Interests," 40–68.
39. Dahl holds that "we cannot solve the problem of the proper scope and domain of
democratic units from within democratic theory . . . [for] the criteria of the democratic process presuppose the rightfulness of the unit itself." *Democracy and Its Critics*, 207.
40. Hannah Arendt talks about "two vicious circles, the one apparently inherent in
human law-making, and the other inherent in the *petitio principii* which attends every new
beginning, that is, politically speaking, in the very task of foundation." *On Revolution*, 161.
The second circle is equivalent to what William Connolly described as the "paradox of political founding." Going back to Rousseau, Connolly explains this conundrum by saying that
"for a general will to be brought into being, effect (social spirit) would have to become the
cause, and the cause (good laws) would have to become effect. The problem is how to establish either condition without the previous attainment of the other upon which it depends."
Ethos of Pluralization, 138–39. On this problem, see also Keenan, *Democracy in Question*.

This vicious circle is another version of the problem of how to legitimize a democratic state democratically. Indeed, this problem of how to create democratic institutions has been a source of concern since Rousseau's time.[41] All democratically determined rules of exclusion fall into this vicious circle. As a result, the democratic people is always indeterminate because every attempt to find the ground of unification produces an infinite regress. As on our utopian island, the people may unify, but every attempt to show that they unified produces a vicious circle, since the people must determine the criterion for belonging to the very same people we are trying to define. If, on the other hand, you try to show that the people unify by the very act of their common agreement, you must also show that the people have themselves produced the terms of their agreement, and this sends you into a philosophical regress.[42] As Robert Goodin writes, the vicious circle and the infinite regress underlie a silence at the heart of democratic theory: "It is simply incoherent to constitute the electorate through a vote among voters who would be entitled to vote only by virtue of the outcome of that very vote."[43] That is like saying that one could bring oneself out of a mire by pulling at one's hair, like the Baron von Munchausen.

In recent years, however, there have been attempts by Goodin and others to solve the parallel problems of constituting the demos and the vicious circle of self-constitution by extending the demos to its natural limits. If the principle of affected interests is a good normative ground for establishing rights of democratic participation, so this line of thought goes, then we should extend the demos to all those who could possibly be affected by a democratic decision. But upon analysis, we can see that the principle of all possibly affected interests is not really a criterion of exclusion; rather, it is an escape' from exclusion rules. Given that every time we make a democratic decision it can possibly affect all other interests in the world, the principle will ultimately yield a people encompassing all humanity.[44]

---

41. Rousseau wrote, "In order for an emerging people to appreciate the healthy maxims of politics, and follow the fundamental rules of statecraft, the effect would have to become the cause; the social spirit, which should be the result of the institution, would have to preside over the founding of the institution itself; and men would have to be prior to laws what they ought to become by means of laws." *On the Social Contract*, 69. For a discussion of this problem, see Benhabib, "Deliberative Rationality and Models of Democratic Legitimacy," and Honig, "Between Decision and Deliberation."

42. Derrida, "Declarations of Independence," 10.

43. Goodin, "Enfranchising All Affected Interests," 43.

44. Ibid., 63.

Is this, then, the best available solution to the problem of constituting the demos?

Of course, this cosmopolitan solution is not to everybody's liking.[45] But independent of the further difficulties a cosmopolitan solution may cause, I hold that it does not really solve the problem. Even if you were willing to accept this demanding criterion for democratic legitimacy, it fails in its purpose because it cannot conclusively determine the limits of the cosmopolitan demos. Even the community of all humankind would require a rule of exclusion in order to constitute the ground of democratic legitimacy. Just as on the utopian island mentioned above, there would have to be an additional criterion for determining which humans are fit to be citizens. Such a criterion could perhaps be the same as that for being a human, but this last criterion is not natural, settled, or stable. As the ethical debates surrounding the beginning and end of life illustrate, the criteria for being a human are not obvious. In politics, therefore, some person or group would have to make a decision regarding who counts as a person, and hence as a citizen. This, of course, would be a political decision that affects most people, which means that if the principle of all affected interests were being applied, the regress would arise anew.

Some may object that I have set the bar too high. Traditionally, democrats everywhere begin with the assumption that peoples already exist, such that we can simply assume the rightfulness of the political unit. But is this assumption sufficient to bypass the problem of indeterminacy of popular unification? My claim here is that even with well-defined democratic boundaries, there remains a third difficulty with democratic theory's demonstration that the people unify, and thus with the theory's attempt to legitimize the state. This is the problem of the people in time. Imagine that in our utopian worldwide community the following conditions apply: an obvious natural mark distinguishes children from adults, mental illness does not exist, everyone understands the arguments that sustain democratic government, and everyone accepts democratic principles. In this ideal context, everyone can see the boundaries of this cosmopolitan political community.

Even if these boundaries were settled, we would not be able to show that the people unify at any given time. Thus democratic theory would not be able to legitimize the state because the boundaries of the people would be settled in space but not in time. We cannot establish temporal boundaries for two reasons. First, the individuals whose interests are possibly

45. See, for example, Miller, "Democracy's Domain."

affected by a present political decision extend beyond the present generation.[46] This means we cannot make decisions that they have an obligation
to consider legitimate, lest we fall into the problem of constitutional paternalism. The rift between generations thus generates a tension between
constitutionalism and democracy. This tension becomes obvious as soon
as you accept that the people changes. Individuals change constantly: we
change our minds, our wants, our emotions, and our interests, depending
on our geographical and temporal situation. Individuals do not just have
conflicts with one another; they often have conflicts with themselves. Yet
every time that you try to frame an actual populace according to their political agreement, it is as though you had picked a photographic still out of a
moving picture; the still misleads because the picture goes on. The people
likewise change continuously. Even if the people seem unified at a given
time, as when they vote unanimously or give thumbs-up in a rally, you
would not be able to show that they have in fact unified; by the time you
declare that all individuals have consented, some individual's will may
have already changed.

Second, even if we do not rely on individual consent to build institutions, but rather use only normative principles that everybody ought to
accept, we still have the problem that societies change and the criteria they
consider normatively adequate change with them. These changes in the
perception and interpretation of the normative criteria underlying political
institutions also create a rift between legal institutions and democratic politics: the perceptions and beliefs of a population change while the legal
institutions remain static.

Political theory seldom takes into consideration that the people
changes. Yet it is enough to reflect on this fact to doubt that the idea that
hypothetical consent, or generalized agreement, could legitimize the state.
You cannot show that the people unify, because unification requires a temporal abstraction and the people always exist in time—that is, they change.
Consequently, you cannot show that the people are unified at any given
time.

This has to make us wonder whether individuals could give the consent
that democratic theory hypothesizes. How can you legitimize rule democratically if the people constantly changes in composition? This question

---

46. This problem was already noted and discussed by Thomas Jefferson. For a contemporary consideration of the "problem of generations" in constitutional theory, see Rubenfeld,
Freedom and Time.

underlies the problem in democratic theory that I have called the indeterminacy of popular unification. Below, I answer objections to the claim that this problem affects all liberal theories.

Does Liberal Democratic Theory Really Need Popular Unification?

To legitimize the state, liberal democratic theory requires the unification of individual wills in their consent to democratic principles and institutions. Since Rousseau's time, theorists have thought of this condition as the coincidence of popular will and reason in a unified people. This coincidence creates a unified and well-defined democratic people, it justifies rule, and it may subsequently legitimize the state. Yet, as I have argued, we cannot show that popular unification is possible.

Liberal democratic theory has traditionally taken for granted the possibility of unification. As I argued in the previous section, such unification requires generalized agreement on a principle of practical reason, such as the mutual recognition of freedom and equality that guarantees collective autonomy. Democratic theory takes the possibility of unification as the ground to justify rule, while liberal theories emphasize the principles of reason. These two types of theory generate two types of objection against the claim that the indeterminacy of popular unification is a problem for democratic theory.

The first set of objections would come from democrats. For instance, majoritarian democrats (democrats who favor majority rule) do not believe that the failure to unify the will of the people leads to illegitimacy. In their view, democratic legitimization rests on the will of the biggest group within the political community.[47] Moreover, those who hold that consensus and collective autonomy are unnecessary might raise a second democratic objection, holding that democracy can be justified on the basis of the principle of equality alone.[48]

The second set of objections would come from liberals. One of the earliest well-known challenges to unification comes from the standpoint of social choice theory.[49] Like most liberal thinkers, social choice critics of popular sovereignty conceive of popular participation as voting. According to them, the votes of citizens control and limit the power of rulers in a liberal polity, and the act of voting and electing rulers suffices to legitimize

---

47. Przeworski, "Minimalist Conception of Democracy."
48. Christiano, *Rule of the Many*, chaps. 2 and 3.
49. Riker, *Liberalism Against Populism*.

rule. For this reason, they believe that liberal polities do not require or desire the people's unification.

A second line of liberal objections arises from a position I call "liberal contractualism," whose adherents use the methods of contemporary contractualist thinking, most notably Rawls's *A Theory of Justice* and *Political Liberalism*, to offer arguments to legitimize the state. Among them the champions of deliberation stand out.[50] Like other liberals, contractualists believe that the people cannot achieve actual unity and that expecting such an outcome can be dangerous. Yet unlike social choice thinkers, contractualists acknowledge that any method of aggregation of individual preferences presupposes a popular consensus. This prior consensus allows for the creation of institutional arrangements, including legitimate electoral procedures and spaces for deliberation. But liberal contractualists would object to the claim that the indeterminacy of popular unification causes problems, on the grounds that democratic legitimacy does not require an actual consensus legitimizing the state as a whole. Liberal contractualists envision the grounds for legitimacy as a hypothetical consensus within existing institutions. On their view, in existing democratic orders the terms of political participation are already established according to general principles whose formulation is open to revision in an ongoing discussion.

Why does the indeterminacy of popular unification challenge these four views? In what follows, I will address each issue and respond to these objections.

Majoritarian Democracy

Democrats who favor majority rule could object to my description of the indeterminacy problem based on their belief that those who expect consensus hold an obsolete view. For example, Adam Przeworski suggests that we "put the consensualist view of democracy where it belongs—in the Museum of Eighteenth-century Thought—and observe that all societies are ridden with economic, cultural, or moral conflicts."[51] In this view, no consensus can come about and it is not realistic to expect that it will, yet we can still have legitimate democratic rule. Can you have legitimate democracy without popular unification, as Przeworski proposes?

Majoritarian democrats deny that the failure to unify the people's will leads to illegitimacy; rather, they hold that legitimacy ultimately depends

---

50. Gutmann and Thompson, *Democracy and Disagreement.*
51. Przeworski, "Minimalist Conception of Democracy," 46.

only on the will of the majority. On this conception, elections are sufficient to legitimize a state; that's all there is to democracy.[52] This view prevails not only among those who hold a minimal conception of democratic rule, such as Joseph Schumpeter,[53] but also among those who, like Dahl, believe that the inclusiveness of the democratic process itself adds to legitimacy by sheltering minorities' rights and the rights and interests of individuals.[54] In either case, majoritarian democrats assume that democracy does not require the actual people's unification. But I argue that this position also requires popular unification and hence runs afoul of the indeterminacy problem. According to majoritarian democrats, all those involved in the democratic process must agree on the legitimacy of electoral procedures and institutions.[55] That a minority agrees to submit to the majority's will, or that it can have expectations of getting its turn in the next election, requires some assumptions about the future stability of the democracy. Consequently, it necessitates a general agreement on the political system as a whole.

Let us examine this more closely. That the losers of an election accept its outcome is, for Przeworski, nothing short of a "miracle,"[56] and explaining this miracle is as difficult as explaining popular unification itself. As Dahl put it, "The democratic process is a gamble on the possibilities that a people, in acting autonomously, will learn to act rightly."[57] I take "acting rightly" here to mean upholding institutions that support freedom and equality. In this view, the bet on the stability of institutions amounts to a bet on the possibility of popular unification. That is, political stability obtains only if you and almost everyone else also bets on stability. Obviously, gambling only makes sense if you believe that you can win—or, in this case, that there can be generalized consent. In other words, such gambling makes sense only if the people could all agree in approving and sustaining democratic principles. Hence majoritarian democracy requires the possibility of popular unification.

A majoritarian democrat might reply that you can explain the stability of minimal democracy without recourse to gambles, magic, or miracles,

52. Ibid., 44.

53. Schumpeter, *Capitalism, Socialism, and Democracy.*

54. Dahl, *Democracy and Its Critics,* 130.

55. This does not mean that, according to majoritarian democrats, everyone must agree with every decision, but it does mean that all opposition must be "loyal." See Shapiro, *Democratic Justice,* 39.

56. Przeworski, "Minimalist Conception of Democracy," 15.

57. Dahl, *Democracy and Its Critics,* 192.

provided that you acknowledge the potential disruptive power of the majority. Paradoxically, they would argue, the threat of disruption guarantees stability. According to majoritarians, elections amount to a peaceful revolution, where the majority informs the minority that it would be willing to take up arms for its cause. This view, however, still suffers from the indeterminacy problem. The potential physical strength of majorities may guarantee the sociological stability of a democratic state, but it could never justify such an arrangement, because any democratic justification of majoritarian rule still rests on popular unification. That is, the democratic justification of the state requires that all the people, winners and losers, accept the show of force without resorting to actual force. In this way, democratic legitimacy requires a general tacit agreement that electoral institutions will mediate conflicts. Even in this example, democratic legitimacy depends on a popular unification (even if unacknowledged) on the fairness of the rules and the procedures that govern elections.

As any student of democracy knows, you do not simply bump into this tacit agreement. It requires certain social and economic conditions, and more important, it requires institutions. Yet this requirement sends us back to Rocafuerte's vicious circle, since we once again encounter the problem of the self-constitution of a democratic state. In a situation where no previous agreement on institutions exists, or where a consensus on the principles creating them is lacking, we need a democratic decision to establish institutions. But how could democracy establish them? Moreover, if to solve this problem an individual or a group in power makes a decision and imposes institutions undemocratically, how could they be legitimate?[58]

Since the eighteenth century, liberal democratic theorists have argued that only a social pact can jump-start a legitimate democratic system. This pact may be a hypothetical social contract or an actual consensual democracy. In either case, the arrangement presupposes some type of popular unification, yet no one can show that this unification could obtain. Thus even for majoritarian democrats the indeterminacy of popular unification is a real problem. But does this also create problems for egalitarian democrats, given their claims that popular sovereignty does not require consensus or consent?

58. Such formulation would amount to moral vanguardism, or liberal paternalism as I have been calling it, yet all liberal democratic theories "are rooted in the antivanguardist conceptions of the good; their proponents resist the idea that values should be imposed on people against their wishes in the name of some greater social good." Shapiro, *Democratic Justice*, 31.

Egalitarian Democracy

As alluded to above, egalitarian democrats might argue that the indeterminacy problem does not affect their theory because they hold that consensus
is neither necessary nor sufficient for justifying democratic rule.[59] According to Christiano, for example, "Substantial consensus of judgment on the
proper terms of association we live under . . . flies in the face of the common and pervasive experience we have of disagreement and conflict in
society and thus must fail as a strategy for defending democracy."[60]
Instead, egalitarian democrats resort to the principle of political equality
to mount their defense. Is it possible, then, to ground democracy on the
basis of equality without resorting to popular unification?

Christiano argues that a justification of democracy based on individual
freedom or autonomy is insufficient because it leads to two insurmountable difficulties.[61] The first is that if the justification of democracy is individual liberty through consent, there is no reason to accept mechanisms
of rule that satisfy collective autonomy. After all, individuals can simply
opt out of collective institutions and choose individual freedom. The second difficulty is that if collective rule is justified on the basis of consent,
then it is incompatible with self-rule, unless there is consensus at all
times—and as we have seen, this is not a realistic goal in modern political
life. Christiano thus acknowledges the problems that arise in every attempt
to legitimize democratic rule on the basis of consent; and for that reason
he shares my concern for finding a different ground on which to justify
democracy. Like other egalitarian democrats, however, Christiano holds
that the principle of equality is sufficient to justify democratic rule, while
I claim that this strategy drops you right back into the indeterminacy problem. Let us see why the principle of equality is also subject to this difficulty.

Christiano justifies democracy on the ground that it is intrinsically fair.
He sustains this view by appeal to the principle that "the interests of all
individuals are to be advanced equally by the society."[62] Moreover, he
argues that equal treatment must be public.[63] The best way to fulfill the
requirements of equal consideration and publicity, Christiano holds, "is to

59. Christiano, "Authority of Democracy"; Christiano, *Rule of the Many*; Singer, *Democracy and Disobedience*; Waldron, *Law and Disagreement*.
60. Christiano, *Rule of the Many*, 57.
61. Ibid., chap. 1.
62. Christiano, "Authority of Democracy," 269. See also Christiano, *Rule of the Many*,
54–70.
63. Christiano, "Authority of Democracy," 271–74.

give each person an equal say in how the society ought to be organized."[64] That is, each individual ought to have a say in determining the common legal, economic, and political institutions under which they live. Adopting this principle in political life, he claims, is sufficient to justify democracy. Moreover, the principle does a better job justifying democracy than does individual consent for at least two reasons. First, it incorporates an argument for the necessity of collective rule: given that some individual interests are tightly bound to others, it is in everybody's personal interest to have a say in decisions over the basic institutions in society. Second, interests are attributes of persons, not a product of individual judgment. This fact protects the theory from the infinite regress that arises when individual participation is a matter of consent or personal judgment. Given that interests, as attributes, are objective, one could argue about other people's interests without their consent, and thus there is no need to have an agreement on which interests are correct. For this reason, there is no regress of agreements required to justify the principle of public equality.

Now, this reasoning is attractive because it does not need a prior democratic sanction to justify democracy, and it can thus avoid the regress of democratic justification. According to this argument, there can be a public justification based on the assumption that nobody should be treated as an inferior member of the community or society. But the argument falters once we ask: Who constitutes the community? Equality presupposes equality among members of a given society, but how do we establish who, among all human beings, has a right to membership in this society? The theory does not provide us with the tools for finding a satisfactory rule of exclusion. So the egalitarian justification of democracy works, but only on the condition that a democratic society is already constituted. It is true that this justification does not rely on consensus, for as Christiano tells us, "To say that the people are sovereign is not to say that they all agree or that they have a common will." And it is also true that the theory does not require agreement on any substantial issue. But popular sovereignty does imply "that all citizens ought to come together in one group to make decisions together as a group."[65] In short, while Christiano's argument does not require consensus to justify democracy, it does assume that there already is a constituted people. But if we have reason to doubt this assumption, the theory falls into the vicious circle of self-constitution.

Given that the theory does not tell us how to find a morally relevant rule of exclusion, the egalitarian justification of democracy remains trapped in

64. Ibid., 276.
65. Christiano, *Rule of the Many*, 70.

the vicious circle of self-constitution. This is because in order to publicly treat a person as an equal, you require public rules and a common authoritative rule maker.[66] To establish authoritative rule-making institutions and public rules, however, you need to ensure that all individuals are given an equal say and are publicly treated as equals in the process of making institutions (for if you exclude some from the process, you violate the principle of equality).[67] So you need democratic institutions to treat individuals as equals, but you need equally treated individuals to establish democratic institutions. Again, one term presupposes the other. In sum, while the argument from the perspective of equality does not need consensus to legitimize the state if a democratic people already exists, it still requires generalized agreement on the terms of rule making in order to create a democratic people.

I believe that the theories of egalitarian democracy formulate a solid normative argument for justifying democratic rule. (In fact, in chapter 7 I will defend my own view of the democratic people based, in part, on the principle of equality.) But such theories cannot be sustained unless they first overcome the problem of popular unification, specifically the vicious circle of self-constitution. Can we do better if we do away with the requirement of having a people, as social choice liberals do?

Social Choice Liberalism

According to liberal critics of populism, the legitimacy of the liberal democratic order depends on the impossibility of unity. In this view, a liberal democracy provides the mechanisms for resisting any claims to popular unification. Hence it can resist the danger that one individual or group will illegitimately appropriate the state's power in the name of the people.

Social choice liberals hold that popular unification is not only undesirable but also impossible.[68] In general, social choice thinkers try to determine how to aggregate a set of individual preferences such that the aggregation satisfies a set of plausible normative criteria. In the case that concerns us, they try to determine how to aggregate individual preferences

66. Christiano, "Authority of Democracy," 282.
67. Ibid., 287.
68. Here I call "social choice liberals" only those social choice thinkers who accept the conclusion of Arrow's theorem, which Riker calls the "paradox of voting": "Arrow's theorem or the general possibility theorem [is] the proposition that, if a social choice function satisfies universal admissibility, unanimity (or monotonicity and citizen's sovereignty), independence from irrelevant alternatives, and non-dictatorship, then the social choice may not satisfy transitivity." Riker, *Liberalism Against Populism*, 293.

(individual freedom) within a general order (collective autonomy). Thus they try to determine whether you can attain individual freedom and collective autonomy simultaneously by aggregating individual wills under a set of conditions commonly found in contemporary countries. So far, they have concluded that this is not possible. According to these theorists, the aggregation of individual preferences requires electoral mechanisms, but voting cannot harmonize individual wills. I lack the space here to go through all the elements of their claim, so, for the sake of this argument, we may concede to social choice liberals that it is impossible to achieve unification by an aggregation of votes.[69]

A well-known social choice liberal argument is found in William Riker's *Liberalism Against Populism*. Riker argued that electoral results cannot represent the will of a people because the mechanisms for aggregating individual choices distort such will. According to him, in a liberal democracy any attempt to attain popular unification leads to coercion.[70] There are no fair and accurate methods of aggregating individual preferences through voting because every one of them violates some reasonable canon of fairness and accuracy.[71] In his words, "We do not know and cannot know what the people want,"[72] so it makes no sense to try to legitimize the state by appeal to the people's will. Hence we should content ourselves with a negative view of democracy. He says that "the meaning and goal of a liberal democracy is to allow an electorate to rid itself of offending rulers."[73]

At first glance, this limited view of democracy seems consistent with the conclusions reached in previous parts of this chapter. Riker's version of democracy acknowledges the indeterminacy of popular unification, yet it puts forward a modest and feasible version of democracy that may legitimize rule. Nonetheless, there are two features of Riker's view that subject it to the indeterminacy problem.

First, social choice liberalism's interpretation of democracy takes for granted that even if we cannot have conclusive electoral results, "we all" can agree on the legitimacy of voting procedures. This resembles a feature of the theories of majoritarian democrats: both presuppose a generalized agreement on electoral practices, even if these practices do not provide electoral consensus. But the indeterminacy of popular unification does even more damage to this theory than to majoritarian democracy, since

69. Mueller, *Public Choice III*, 596.
70. Riker, *Liberalism Against Populism*, 13.
71. Ibid., 115.
72. Ibid., 238.
73. Ibid., 244.

for social choice liberals more is at stake in the stability of electoral institutions. In their view, democracy should establish procedures for removing bad officers from office and nothing more. In short, then, democracy means voting.[74] According to Riker, the existence of voting procedures is a necessary and sufficient condition for a legitimate liberal democratic state. For this reason, you could not have democracy if the participants in elections did not agree on the limiting conditions of electoral procedures. But those limiting conditions are the size and shape of the electorate, and as we have seen, voting cannot help us in establishing these limiting conditions. As I argued above, to suppose that we could vote on who gets to vote generates a philosophical regress. Thus, without the democratic constitution of the people, the limiting conditions of electoral procedures are unjustified. As a result, social choice liberals also face the problem of how to constitute the demos, and so they face the indeterminacy problem.

There is a second reason why social choice liberalism falls into the indeterminacy problem. If the people do not unify, then the liberal conception of democracy cannot justify rule. Riker argues that because we cannot know the people's will, individual freedom and collective autonomy are incompatible. Were this true, the state would also be unjustifiable on liberal democratic grounds. You could not justify a liberal constitution if it were impossible to achieve generalized consent on principles that guarantee freedom and equality. It would also be impossible to justify constitutional restraint on rule, which, on Riker's view, is necessary to keep electoral mechanisms going. Democracy (even in its minimal version) requires unification, otherwise this form of rule would be nothing but a euphemism for tyranny limited by periodic voting.

For these reasons, the indeterminacy of popular unification poses a grave problem for social choice liberalism. And it is also a problem for other libertarian, or rights-based, conceptions of democracy that give no explicit moral principles aimed at legitimizing electoral institutions or constitutional restraints on government. These views, as I shall examine below, do not legitimize the state, and they cannot tell you why to choose democracy over anarchy.

Liberal Contractualism

Liberal contractualism has a deeper link to the problem of indeterminacy of popular unification than do the views of liberal democracy discussed

74. Ibid., 4–8.

above. Liberal contractualists use the standards of contemporary contractualist thinking, mainly Rawls's *A Theory of Justice* and *Political Liberalism,* to offer arguments that legitimize the state democratically by appealing to the idea of reasonable agreement among equals.[75] Like social choice liberalism, liberal contractualism acknowledges the need for institutions that allow individuals to oust bad rulers. Unlike social choice liberalism, this view also acknowledges that liberal democratic institutions must be publicly justified by a contract. This contract is logically prior to voting and amounts to a consensus among all individuals in a given group. This agreement sustains the creation of institutional arrangements, including electoral procedures, and it also justifies them, thus leaving liberal contractualism particularly vulnerable to the indeterminacy problem.

Yet liberal contractualism would reject this last claim. Contractualists would maintain that their view is protected against these obvious objections. First, the view acknowledges that mass approval alone cannot legitimize the state. Second, it does not require an actual popular unification to ground a liberal democratic political order. Liberal contractualism envisions the grounds for legitimacy as a hypothetical consensus that may justify actually existing institutions. According to contractual theories, in existing democratic orders the terms of political participation are already established by general principles, whose precise formulation is open to revision in ongoing theoretical reflection.[76]

Some versions of liberal contractualism stress the importance of this ongoing reflection or deliberation for the viability of the doctrine. For this reason, many of its adherents call themselves "deliberative democrats." Deliberative democrats argue that we cannot take for granted an agreement on moral views, and they hold that these positions are always open to challenge.[77] In fact, the liberal ground for this form of justification requires that any moral claim put forward by any group or person be open to contestation, while its democratic element resides in its postulated terms of equal participation. Why then would popular indeterminacy be a problem for this position?

These theories seek to provide the terms to justify rule in already existing political communities with particular cultural characteristics and

---

75. See also Barry, *Justice as Impartiality,* and Beitz, *Political Equality.*

76. This is what Rawls calls a "reflective equilibrium." *A Theory of Justice,* 18.

77. Gutmann and Thompson, *Democracy and Disagreement.* Despite the similarities between Rawlsian deliberative democracy and its Habermasian counterpart, I do not count Habermasian versions of deliberative democracy within this group because they deal directly with (one version) of the indeterminacy of popular unification. I deal with Habermasian theory in chapter 4.

defined borders.[78] As such, they overlook the problem of how to constitute the demos. The problem becomes obvious, for example, when you ask liberal contractualists who is the subject of rights, or when you ask deliberative democrats about who gets to participate in the deliberation, and who gets to set the agenda for discussion.

Second, these theories generate justifications of the state based on the assumption that citizens are willing to make and keep promises to other persons whom they regard as equal. That is, citizens must be reasonable,[79] or more important, they must think of one another as reasonable. According to Rawls, "Insofar as we are reasonable, we are willing to work out the framework for the public social world, a framework it is reasonable to expect to endorse and act on, provided others can be relied on to do the same."[80] The argument for why one person's disposition to cooperate encourages others to follow suit may explain the evolution of a just society. Further, a just society is the basis on which these theories seek to justify the state.[81] But the theories cannot tell us why or how the first individual would cooperate when there are no institutions guaranteeing that others can be relied on to reciprocate. A person may cooperate spontaneously if she is reasonable, but reasonableness is a disposition of persons and we may require legitimate liberal institutions to foster such disposition. Therefore, reasonableness requires institutions, and institutions require reasonableness. In sum, such a requirement brings us back to Rocafuerte's vicious circle, or to the problem of the self-constitution of the democratic state. If the political community cannot constitute itself, how can the existing boundaries and institutions that created these boundaries be legitimate?

Liberal contractualism, like most other contemporary normative liberal democratic theories, relies on some form of popular unification, and hence it cannot solve the problem of showing that the people is or could be unified at any given time. Thus, like all other normative liberal democratic theories that rely on consent, it cannot legitimize the state. All of these theories require the unification of the people to justify rule, but they cannot show that the people do unify or could unify. And when you try to show that a group is unified, you get trapped in a vicious circle or a philosophical regress. Moreover, when you seek to bypass the logical difficulty

---

78. "Deliberative democracy asks citizens and officials to justify public policy by giving reasons that can be accepted by those who are [already] bound by it." Ibid., 52.
79. Rawls, *Political Liberalism*, 48–49.
80. Ibid., 53.
81. Mueller, *Public Choice III*, 14; Rawls, *Theory of Justice*, 434–41.

by relying on an already existing group, you find that no attempt to show that a people exists can produce criteria adequate for defining the group's boundaries. As soon as you try to show the people to others, its edges dissolve before your eyes.

Conclusion

The problem is that we cannot show that there are, or could be, well-defined communities whose members all recognize one another as equal and free. It thus affects and indeed underpins most normative theories of liberal democracy. This claim of indeterminacy means different things depending on your original attitude toward liberal democratic theory. On the one hand, critics of liberal democracy may find in it a confirmation of their position. Identifying this problem will not surprise those who have long suspected that liberal democracy cannot make good on its promise to legitimize the state. But they may still find that the indeterminacy helps them spell out arguments for their criticism. On the other hand, for those of us who believe that the core ideas of liberal democracy remain good reasons for justifying and legitimizing the state, pinpointing this problem gives us an opportunity to continue working toward a better theory. When I insist on describing a problem in liberal democratic theory, I am not trying to undermine the entire theory; rather, I am trying to shore it up. I begin reinforcing the seawall in the next chapter, where I ask what concept of a democratic people we require in order to deal with the indeterminacy problem.

3

Mechanical and Teleological Conceptions of the People

Democratic theories presuppose a demos, a people. But what is a people? Only a few theorists have focused on the concept.[1] Yet democratic theory cannot afford to ignore the question of the people's nature—at least if it is serious about dealing with the problems I have highlighted in the prior chapters. Bringing to light implicit assumptions about the concept of the people helps us understand why traditional theories of popular sovereignty fail to legitimize the state. This examination can also help democratic theory determine what concept of the people—if any—can solve the indeterminacy problem.

In the previous chapter, I argued that by a "democratic people," political theorists generally mean a collection of individuals in a given territory *who agree,* or *would agree,* to organize ruling institutions according to liberal democratic principles. This definition reveals that there are two dominant conceptions of the democratic people in current liberal democratic theory. The first conceives of it as an actual group of individuals making a collective decision: *those individuals who agree.* The second conceives of the democratic people as the hypothetical outcome of a rational consensus: *those individuals who would agree.* At first glance, it seems that the indeterminacy problem I described in chapter 2 arises only for the first conception. If the actual composition of the people changes, then you cannot show empirically that the people is unified at any given time, and thus the state cannot be legitimate. So it might seem that the second conception can determine

---

1. Canovan, *The People;* Laclau, *On Populist Reason;* Näsström, "Legitimacy of the People"; Smith, *Stories of Peoplehood.*

hypothetically when the state is legitimate because it allows you to appeal to the people even if individuals do not reach a consensus. It is enough to determine rationally that they *would* do so. If this were the case, you could dismiss indeterminacy as a curiosity rather than a real problem for democratic theory. Yet a closer look reveals that even in this situation the indeterminacy problem still arises.

In this chapter, I argue that the indeterminacy problem besets both actual and hypothetical democratic theories, as well as the conceptions of the people they implicitly endorse. These two justificatory theories—actual and hypothetical—may seem very different, but I claim that they both suffer from the same problem: they require popular unification (as a goal or an origin), and thus they demand a unified people at a specific moment in time. For this reason, neither theory can accommodate change in the people or the lack of popular unification. But accommodating these shortfalls is necessary for tackling the indeterminacy problem and legitimizing the state. Thus the current dominant conceptions of the people are not useful for dealing with the problem. Solving it would require more than either institutional mechanisms for producing a unified people or a goal around which individuals could coalesce. Instead, democratic theory requires a people understood as an ongoing *process*, one propelled by mechanisms and aimed at goals, but fully present even if always incomplete.

I make this argument in three parts. In the first part, I examine the conceptions of the people that underlie democratic theories of actual and hypothetical consent, in order to show why they are beset by the same problem. The two conceptions are often held to be very different, since one is empirical while the other is normative. But I claim that both conceptions include normative and empirical elements. They are also held to differ because one is said to be organic (or natural) and the other designed (or artificial). I claim that this is not a good distinction either, because both share organic and designed traits. In the second part, I argue that a more accurate distinction between these two conceptions of the people is one between *mechanical* and *teleological* accounts of how a people comes into being. The first conception relies on a mechanism: constitutional and electoral rules that determine which individuals participate and how they stay together as a democratic people. The second conception depends on a teleological account of how the people comes about: it aims at the goal of consensus, or popular unification, which in turn defines what the people is and who could be part of it. In the third part, I claim that both mechanical and teleological accounts of the people suffer a common problem: they are deterministic. Hence they are incompatible with democratic justifications of rule, for such justifications must be able to incorporate individual freedom and the indeterminacy of nature. Finally, in the conclusion, I anticipate my solution to the indeterminacy problem: rather than conceiving of the people as the product of teleology or mechanism, we must conceive of the people *as a process* if we want to legitimize the state and embrace popular change. This conception, which I deal with in subsequent chapters, can better accommodate change and legitimize the state democratically. For unlike mechanisms and teleological systems, processes can create and alter themselves.

Two Conceptions of the People

What is a people? Surprisingly, political philosophy rarely asks this question. This is obvious in recent discussions of democratic legitimacy, which consider the conditions under which democracy makes the wielding of political power legitimate but take for granted the people over whom the power is wielded.[2] The question is also absent in debates on immigration and citizenship, which concentrate on what rights immigrants have but seldom discuss the nature of the sending and receiving political communities.[3] More broadly, discussions in political philosophy have usually ignored both the specific question of the nature of the people, and the more general issues of what Philip Pettit calls "political ontology."[4] True, in the last few years there has been some interest in examining tacit conceptions of the people, but this new research focuses on the question of membership[5] or on the history of the concept of the people.[6] Moreover, inquiries into who has a right to have a say in democratic decision-making processes,[7] or whether there can be global democracy,[8] take for granted that there are peoples and avoid the question of what precisely these are.

2. Buchanan, "Political Legitimacy and Democracy"; Christiano, "Authority of Democracy."

3. Carens, "Aliens and Citizens"; Miller, "Immigrants, Nations, and Citizenship." Miller does acknowledge that there may be multinational peoples. Yet the idea of the people or *demos*, as distinct from the nation, remains unexamined.

4. Pettit, "Rawls's Political Ontology."

5. Näsström, "Legitimacy of the People."

6. Canovan, *The People.*

7. Arrhenius, "Boundary Problem in Democratic Theory"; Goodin, "Enfranchising All Affected Interests"; Shapiro and Hacker-Cordón, *Democracy's Edges;* Whelan, "Democratic Theory and the Boundary Problem."

8. Benhabib, *Another Cosmopolitanism;* Bohman, *Democracy Across Borders;* Held, *Democracy and the Global Order.* An exception is Lea Ypi, who discusses the type of political

Yet democratic theory cannot afford to avoid the problem of the people's nature, particularly if it wants to deal with apparently intractable difficulties such as the indeterminacy of popular unification. In the sections that follow, I analyze the dual definition I extracted from the explicit definitions of the people proposed in the current literature (see chap. 2). According to these views, the people is the collection of all those individuals in a territory *who agree*, or *would agree*, to organize institutions of rule according to the principles of freedom and equality.

Empirical/Normative

As I have said, two common conceptions of a democratic people arise from two different versions of a public justification of the state.[9] The first such justification depends on actual agreement, while the second depends on hypothetical agreement.[10] An actual-agreement justification tells you that a state is justified if actual individuals with names and faces consent to be governed. The people legitimizes the state if these individuals consent, regardless of their existing beliefs and desires, their actual information, or their idiosyncratic ways of inference and decision. The hypothetical-agreement justification, by contrast, tells you that a state is justified if it conforms to principles of political obligation that an individual would accept under idealized conditions, including ideal access to information and full rationality. Could you also characterize different conceptions of the people in those terms?

In the first justification, rule is justified if individuals *actually* agree on a liberal democratic justification of government. Those who agree thus constitute the people. This conception makes sense not only in a robust conception of democracy, where individuals grant one another rights through a collective decision, but also in thinner versions, where democracy means only voting. In either case, rule is justified if there is generalized commitment to an institutional framework that allows for equal rights and fair competition among interests. On this conception, the people are flesh-and-blood individuals who agree. The limits of the people and the

communities that may be the best substratum for the development of cosmopolitanism. See Ypi, "Statist Cosmopolitanism."

9. D'Agostino, "Public Justification."

10. The main example of a contemporary theory of hypothetical consent is found in the work of John Rawls, while a theory of actual consent is found in the work of Robert Dahl. See Rawls, *Theory of Justice*, 10, and Dahl, *Democracy and Its Critics*, 106–18.

criteria for exclusion can, according to this conception, be traced to an original consensual agreement that established the state's democratic institutions. For this reason, this view of the people traditionally goes hand in hand with a historical rendering of the social contract.

This empirical conception of the people evokes a long tradition in political thought, as well as a corresponding set of images and narratives associated with the foundation of a state.[11] Think, for example, of the Oath of the Rütli: a group of men stand together by the bank of a river and all swear allegiance to one another.[12] You find the same image in other accounts of the signing of governing charters, like that of the Mayflower Compact. Perhaps the most powerful of all such images is the ratification of the U.S. Constitution.

But this empirical conception of the people cannot be accurate because one of its necessary conditions cannot be met: consensus. As I argued in chapter 3, there is no such thing as actual consensus at any given time among a population. Actual individuals have conflicting beliefs and desires, they seldom have accurate information for making rational decisions, and their patterns of reasoning are such that it is hard, and perhaps impossible, to find schemes of government that all would consider legitimate.

Moreover, the empirical conception also cannot meet a second condition: we cannot locate in actuality the group of individuals who are to agree. Any empirical analysis of the people would show that popular consent, if it exists, is majoritarian rather than consensual. And the citizens who consent are the majority of an *already existing* group. The definition of the group, then, must depend on something other than agreement. This problem is obvious even in the mythical images that accompany the historical versions of the social contract. When the Rütli give their oath, for example, they represent the majority of the already existing people of their Cantons. Likewise, the signatories of the U.S. Constitution represent the majority of the already existing people of their states.

While an empirical account of justification may be appropriate, an empirical conception of the democratic people is not. A definition of the people cannot depend solely on the actual agreement of a group of individuals because without consensus you cannot clearly define and empirically locate the group. A purely empirical definition thus has to depend on nondemocratic elements like territory or ethnicity. Moreover, if we do not

---

11. For a recent account of foundation narratives, see Bernal, "Concept of Founding."
12. Schiller, *Wilhelm Tell.*

appeal to these morally irrelevant characteristics, then identifying the boundaries of the group requires nonempirical criteria of demarcation, like the idea of a collective will. Hence a purely empirical conception of the democratic people is incomplete, in just the same way that the historical rendering of the social contract cannot provide what its mythical counterparts convey. The figures standing by the shores of Lake Lucerne, and the legendary gathering at Independence Hall, stand in for a consensus that never obtained in Switzerland or the United States. Just as the mythical element reinforces these historical accounts, so a normative aspect is necessary in any empirical rendering of the democratic people. In sum, there is no such thing as a purely empirical account of the people.

The second conception of the people emerges from a hypothetical justification of the state. Theories of hypothetical consent justify the state by appeal to principles on which individuals would agree if these citizens were ideally rational and found themselves in ideal circumstances. These theories claim that a state could be justified on the basis of these principles regardless of whether there is an actual consensus. Yet such legitimizations of the state cannot do without unification. Hence they cannot produce a more useful conception of the people than can the empirical conception.

The reason why they cannot produce a more useful conception is that hypothetical and counterfactual justifications of the state also assume that an actual people exists already.[13] In these justifications, the people in question is not itself an ideal people. An ideal people could only exist if flesh-and-blood individuals were ideally principled or virtuous; only such people could be unified, democratic, and just. But no democratic theory ever assumes such a people. All democratic theories presuppose real and very-much-flawed individuals—or as Rousseau put it, democracy does not assume a people of gods.[14] The theories that rely on hypothetical consent use this idealization as a guide in the search for appropriate principles to design institutions for *real communities*. Their counterfactual arguments give actual individuals ideal reasons to accept or reject actual governments.[15] Thus those who accept or reject the principles justified in ideal conditions are flesh-and-blood individuals—and the problem of determining who those flesh-and-blood individuals are, and whether they agree on the justification, remains pressing.

13. The boundaries of a Rawlsian "well-ordered society," for example, are those of a "self-contained national community." Rawls, *Theory of Justice*, 401. For analysis, see Pettit, "Rawls's Political Ontology."

14. Rousseau, *On the Social Contract*, 85.

15. Stark, "Hypothetical Consent and Justification," 314.

For this reason, the people presupposed by the theories of hypothetical consent is also an actual group of individuals. The theories in question assume a geographically bound, pre-theoretical people.[16] In short, hypothetical-consent theories do not rely on a hypothetical people, and they do not try to determine how actual peoples come together. The justification that arises from their hypothesized situations is a normative counterfactual designed to facilitate choices for actually existing peoples. In these theories, the people itself (the sum of those who ought to agree on the justification) is actual and subject to being described empirically. So the people as conceived in hypothetical justificatory theories is not a hypothetical people, and hence it, too, faces the problem of indeterminacy.

The normative/empirical distinction does not map well onto the differences between conceptions of the people posited by actual-consent theories and hypothetical-consent theories, for these two conceptions both have normative and empirical aspects. Although the two types of justification from which these conceptions spring are very different, the conceptions themselves are almost identical when set against the normative/empirical criteria of distinction. So what genuinely differentiates them? Some hold that the real difference lies in whether the people is conceived as organic (natural) or designed (artificial).

Designed/Organic

The designed/organic distinction is sometimes conveyed by other names. For example, it can be drawn as a contrast between civic and national conceptions of the people.[17] The first conception considers the people a product of human design held together by individual wills. The second considers the people to be a natural product of history and geography, coming together purely by chance.[18] Let us examine each in turn.

In the designed conception, a people is a collection of actual individuals who participate in shaping their polity through common decision making. This view requires that actual citizens engage with one another in a public sphere. Such a view is implicit in republican and patriotic theories of

16. The classic case is Rawls's "closed society" in *Political Liberalism*, whose citizens "enter it only by birth and leave it only by death" (12).

17. Habermas, "Citizenship and National Identity"; Habermas, "What Is a People?"; Yack, "Popular Sovereignty and Nationalism."

18. The best example is Jacob Grimm's account of the people (*Volk*). For him, the spirit of a people (*Volksgeist*) resides in its language. See Habermas, "What Is a People?" 6.

democracy, which envision a democratic people as a group of individuals engaged with one another, working toward common ideals or sorting out differences in public institutional settings.[19] The characteristic trait of this conception of the people is voluntary participation in public discussions where the acceptable positions are grounded on nondogmatic reasons.[20]

The organic conception of the people, in contrast, assumes that individuals "find" rather than "forge" a people. According to this viewpoint, the people must (at least) share a common culture. In this view, the individuals who constitute a people are born into institutions and social structures,[21] and they share traditions and common assumptions that evolve through history. This received culture creates "common sympathies," as John Stuart Mill called the affinity that binds the individuals in a national group.[22] Most liberal democratic theories presuppose this kind of prepolitical community. Rawlsian political liberalism, for example, assumes individuals who are members of given peoples.[23] A *democratic* organic people of this kind can form when the "common sympathies" in question arise from a democratic culture and a democratic history.

These two conceptions of the people thus correspond to a natural and an artificial view of affective attachments.[24] The designed conception of the people seems to have much to recommend it, particularly in light of ongoing episodes of nationalist xenophobia in response to immigration. It is even more desirable when you consider how organic views of political belonging have sometimes contributed to genocide or ethnic cleansing. The designed conception allows you to consciously choose attachments that arise from ethical obligations and moral duties, and to eschew those that may have undesirable moral aspects. A designed conception, then, is especially attractive for those who fear the violent side of nations and their

19. Pettit, *Republicanism*, 245.

20. Habermas calls this an "intentional democratic community" (*Willensgemeinschaft*). *Between Facts and Norms*, 494.

21. Miller, *Citizenship and National Identity*, 25.

22. Mill, *Considerations on Representative Government*, 229.

23. Rawls, *Political Liberalism*, 23.

24. It may seem that the "natural" conception of the people is equivalent to the idea of a nation, and thus contradicts what I said in chapter 2 regarding my dealing only with political conceptions of the people. It may be true that "organic" versions of the people may pass as nations in a constructivist sense. See Anderson, *Imagined Communities*. Given that, accounts of patriotism are often propped up by narratives of history and descent. See Smith, *Stories of Peoplehood*. Nonetheless, organic conceptions of a democratic people may be distinguished from a nation: peoples are political communities brought together by chance, whereas nations, according to the strongest or "primordialist" theories, are primarily ethnic or linguistic communities.

historical exclusions, and for those who want to make communal affect "safe for democracy."[25]

Yet voluntary association and civic duties are not sufficient to define a democratic people. Like the empirical conception of the people, the voluntary account must presuppose a previously unified group of individuals because, as discussed in chapter 2, this group cannot be defined by consensual agreement (for this agreement would require a prior agreement to define those who can agree). Thus the design conception reintroduces the problem of popular unification. Patriotism, for instance, assumes a people instead of defining one.[26] In order to exist, this conception must require something other than voluntary participation of individuals. It needs either voluntary limits imposed from outside the democratic process, or a natural source of sympathy such as a common history or geography. We could conclude, then, that this conception of the people must also include an organic aspect.

As was the case with the empirical/normative distinction, both of these conceptions have too many organic and designed aspects for the distinction to do any work. On the one hand, in so-called design conceptions of the people (such as that espoused by civic patriotism), the composition of the people cannot be voluntary and democratically chosen, lest you get caught in the dreaded vicious circle (in which the people must determine the people's boundaries). Hence, if you want to avoid an external imposition of limits, and the paternalism this entails, then you must rely on organic criteria to distinguish the people's limits. On the other hand, the label "organic" is also misleading. Unlike organisms, which are the product of natural evolution, the products of historical evolution—which include peoples—presuppose conscious decisions and some degree of artificial design. Any conception of a democratic people must, therefore, require voluntary participation and individual choice. At least some of the individuals who compose a democratic people must have consciously both accepted democratic practices and designed democratic institutions. Moreover, the narratives that foster affective attachments and common identities are not purely natural, but are very often part of deliberate attempts to create closely knit groups for political purposes. These attempts are often explicit programs of people building.[27]

25. Markell, "Making Affect Safe for Democracy."
26. Canovan, "Patriotism Is Not Enough," 422.
27. Smith, *Stories of Peoplehood*.

In sum, both currently dominant conceptions of the democratic people require conscious choice and organic development. So is there a real difference between those conceptions? And if there is, what does it consist of?

Mechanical and Teleological Conceptions

The distinction between a mechanical focus and a teleological focus better captures the real difference between the two dominant conceptions of the people. It also captures many of the distinctions that political scientists and political theorists try to make when talking about the people and how it legitimizes the state. The mechanical conception posits a mechanism of aggregation that is external to the democratic process and determines what counts as a people and who belongs to it. The teleological conception defines the people in relation to its internal goal. In the following sections, I explain what I mean by mechanism, what is teleology, and how to recognize the differences between teleological and mechanical accounts of the people.

Conforming to Facts: Mechanical Conceptions of the People

Mechanics is the study and application of mechanisms. And mechanisms are "entities and activities organized such that they are productive of regular changes from start or set-up conditions to finish or termination conditions."[28] In all cases a mechanism describes a regular causal pattern: "Mechanisms are regular in that they work always or for the most part in the same way under the same conditions. The regularity is exhibited in the typical way that the mechanism runs from beginning to end; what makes it regular is the *productive continuity* between the stages."[29] When you describe a mechanism, you show how a set of conditions that obtain at the beginning of a process produce another set of conditions, until you reach an end state. Mechanisms therefore describe or explain end states by citing their causes. Mechanical accounts try to explain events by means

---

28. Machamer, Darden, and Craver, "Thinking About Mechanisms," 3. See also Elster, *Nuts and Bolts for the Social Sciences,* 36. In Elster's view, mechanisms are "frequently occurring and easily recognizable causal patterns that are triggered under generally unknown conditions or with indeterminate consequences." The view that I discuss here is stronger than Elster's because it does not include indeterminacy.

29. Machamer, Darden, and Craver, "Thinking About Mechanisms," 3.

of efficient causation, which "usually and always ultimately . . . takes the form of citing an earlier event as the cause of the event we want to explain, together with some account of the causal mechanism connecting the two events."[30]

Thus you have a mechanical conception of the people when you think of the causes that bring the people about. The conception of the people as "those individuals who agree" is mechanical because it partially describes the causes of its production. On this conception, a people comes about through a series of continuous, causally implicated stages. A common mechanical view of the people is one that aggregates individuals through particular institutional mechanisms. We can distinguish what a people is by how the individuals it comprises come together. Hence the core of this conception of a democratic people is the mechanism of aggregation of individual preferences.

But what precisely is this mechanism? The most common mechanical concepts are those that describe the products of push-pull systems—that is, those that describe machines. It is true that not all mechanisms are mechanical systems, but all machines are driven by mechanisms. This may explain why the machine is the metaphor that often accompanies mechanical accounts. For example, you can talk about a war machine when describing an army, or say that an organization works "like a clock." In the case of a people, the mechanism that defines it need not be a designed machine, although it could be one. For instance, we often think of constitutional arrangements as complex machineries designed to obtain a specific political situation.[31] This is why mechanical accounts of the people are often associated with constitutional arrangements, electoral procedures, and other institutional mechanisms for aggregating individual preferences.

A mechanical conception may seem mostly "designed." But the advantage of this approach over the others I discussed in the previous sections is that it can coherently incorporate both designed and organic aspects, as well as normative and empirical elements. For example, there is a mechanical conception embedded in American constitutional thought. This may seem chiefly to be a design conception, but it also exemplifies organic traits if we focus on judicial development and common law. Bruce Ackerman espouses a mechanical conception of the people when he asks, "Is

---

30. Elster, *Nuts and Bolts for the Social Sciences*, 3.

31. In discussing one such view of the U.S. Constitution, Bruce Ackerman writes, "Our Enlightenment Founders gave us the machine that might tick-tock forever if only we followed the written instructions in the operations manual." Ackerman, "Living Constitution," 1793. See also Kammen, *A Machine That Would Go of Itself*.

the Constitution a machine or an organism?"[32] because both options focus on the causes that bring constitutional changes about. The metaphor of the organism, in particular, illustrates that a mechanical conception of the people can have organic elements. Just as biological mechanisms work within a cell, the organic or "natural" creation of a people works via antecedent causes. Similarly, any view of the people that focuses on laws and formal institutional mechanisms—and is therefore mechanical—also has normative elements, even though it may be described empirically.

A mechanical conception of the people, then, defines a people by the causes that bring it into being. The advantage of this conception is that it is always subject to empirical description—you *could* actually find its referent. The drawback is that you usually cannot find it. Even if the conditions (the machinery) could exist, the people described by mechanical conceptions never actually exists, due to the difficulties in aggregating individual wills. Moreover, actual individuals never come together as a people at any given moment in time because of the now familiar circularity between citizens and democratic institutions. In sum, the mechanical account of the people does not do well when it comes to dealing with the problem of indeterminacy of popular unification. Perhaps for this reason another conception recommends itself.

Reaching for Goals: Teleological Conceptions of the People

Hypothetical-consent theory provides another way of describing the people, and one that maps nicely onto the second dominant conception. Those who use this conception tend to agree that you cannot show empirically that the people are unified. Yet they hold that you can still refer indirectly to a democratic people by addressing its ideals. Mechanical conceptions of the people focus on the causes that bring it into being, and thus they presuppose an original unification that never occurred. But as an alternative, you can define the people by its aim. This second conception is teleological.

Teleology is the doctrine or study of ends or final causes. By an end or a final cause, philosophers usually mean "purpose," "design," or "goal."[33] Typical sentences that describe or explain things teleologically contain the clauses "in order to" or "for the sake of." For example, I swim in order not to drown, or I swim for the sake of my life. Those descriptions are teleological because a present state is described and explained by reference to a

32. Ackerman, "Living Constitution," 1793.
33. Woodfield, *Teleology*, 1.

second state: a goal, which is usually expressed as a desire, a purpose, or an end state of a system. In teleological conceptions of the people, the goal in question is democratic agreement or popular unification. A teleological conception of the people thus allows you to conceive of the people in democratic terms, even if the people is not yet actually there because it has not yet achieved its full potential.

But this conception is problematic because it requires an end state that *causes* the events that it follows. This means that the goal must "attract" or "pull" prior events toward it. If you claim that a series of events is teleologically directed toward a goal, you mean that there was a tendency of the events to occur in that direction such that the later event explains why the earlier events took place.[34] A teleological conception of the democratic people, for example, assumes that in society there is a tendency toward democracy, such that the coming of democracy can explain why individuals coalesce in groups. Many teleological conceptions of the people presume that there is a natural drive toward democracy within the society in question.

As a result, social scientists are often skeptical of teleological conceptions and theories. If the goal provides an understanding of the events that lead up to it, it seems that the goal itself is in some way a factor in its own production,[35] or that a behavior takes place due to the existence of a state of affairs that has not yet occurred. How could this be? Some teleology skeptics respond that these accounts only appear "teleological" in hindsight, when we can know that the later event did in fact account for the prior one. For example, you can say that the goal of emancipation produced a revolution, but only if emancipation actually occurs. Hence a meaningful teleological conception must be able to explain how a not-yet-existing goal produces effects on actual events. Skeptics rightly point out that the link between the previous event and the goal is mysterious.

In fact, a teleological conception does not require any mysterious links, although it does require a commitment to holism.[36] Teleological accounts of entities are not mysterious so long as we can establish a causal link between the goal and antecedent events. This link can be provided by *systems* with intrinsic goals, or with a natural tendency that explains the press of events. This means that for an event to occur, it is sufficient that the event is required within the system of which it is a part.[37] In other words,

---

34. Ibid., 16.
35. Ibid., 5.
36. Taylor, *Explanation of Behaviour*, 9–12.
37. Ibid., 17.

if you can establish that something happens "because the system needs it,"[38] then the explanation of the phenomenon or the entity in question need not be mysterious. But it is also true that this view commits you to a form of holistic metaphysics. As Charles Taylor says, "It is the force of the notion of 'power' or 'natural tendency,' not the *de facto* trend of events, but rather a press of events, which lies behind the view that order exhibited in the behaviour of living organisms does not come about by 'accident,' but it is somehow part of their 'essential nature.'"[39]

Thus teleological conceptions of the people make full sense if you accept that individuals and society have an "essential nature." Even if most political scientists view with suspicion all claims about the inevitable course of history, they frequently accept claims about human nature, so their case against teleology is not as strong as it may at first appear. In fact, teleological claims are not controversial since "human nature" may be simply a tendency to pursue our own conscious goals. Teleological conceptions need not read into the future because the telos is not a future state, but rather a present goal. Having a goal is not controversial. We often act in order to achieve some end. We try to change the world in pursuit of our goals. Most things we do consciously, we do with a purpose in mind. All this suggests that teleological accounts should not be problematic, especially if the purpose for which we act is something we know we can achieve. Nobody objects, for instance, if I say that I pedal the bike in order to move forward and not fall, or that I knead the dough in order to get fluffy bread. Teleological concepts and propositions are not controversial even in the case of more complicated purposes: I run every morning in order to get fit, or I try to be tolerant in order to have better family relations. Most conceptions of the people that derive from natural law and natural rights are teleological. This can be seen in the earliest teleological formulations of the people, as well as in formulations that define the goals of politics in the light of natural law. For example, since Cicero, natural law stands for the laws of an existing ideal order to which a good political system must conform. According to this viewpoint, constitutionalism is a valid enterprise to the extent that it seeks to conform to this higher law.[40] The individuals under law strive to attain this ideal standard, and thus the people can be defined by its tendency to become what it ought to be. In sum, a teleological account of the people is one where the goal of attaining

38. Hollis, *Philosophy of Social Science,* 96.
39. Taylor, *Explanation of Behaviour,* 24.
40. Lutz, *Principles of Constitutional Design,* 189.

a unified people causes the events that lead up to its unification. Specifically, a democratic people is an aggregation of individuals who come together for the sake of the freedom and equality of all, such that the search for consensual democratic rule causes popular unification. We know what a people is by discovering what it essentially strives to become.

Like the mechanical conception, a teleological conception of the people has advantages over those described in the previous section. This characterization better captures the idea of the people as "those who would agree to organize their institutions according to liberal democratic principles" than does either the design account or the normative account. The collection of individuals in question would unify if they unanimously consented to liberal democratic principles, but they could only do so if they had achieved their full potential as human beings.

These two conceptions of the people—mechanical and teleological—are commonly used in democratic theory. The first conception is used to refer to those individuals who actually participate in democratic processes. The second is often used to denote the hypothetical people that guides the design of institutions. Moreover, unlike the normative/empirical and designed/organic distinctions, the mechanical/teleological distinction is mutually exclusive. A people, understood as a collection of individuals, cannot be both mechanical and teleological at the same time. In the mechanical conception the people is actual but not unified. In the teleological conception the people is unified but not actual.

Determinism in Current Conceptions of the People

The mechanical and teleological conceptions of the people may seem very different from one another, but they share a common problem: they both require that the people unify at a given moment in time in order to ground the democratic justification of the state. Given that the moment never arrives, however, both conceptions commonly settle for the expectation of its arrival. That is, those who adopt the conception often assume that unification will follow the appropriate mechanism or the adoption of the goal. This expectation allows a group to represent the future people with the aid of institutional mechanisms condensed in a constitution. Yet representing the ideal people in the constitution requires that you represent something that does not yet exist. And this in turn implies what I have called constitutional paternalism (see chap. 1). Representing the ideal people in the constitution means that the available conceptions of the people prevent actual individuals from actively forging a democratic people through their own experience of political participation. I call this problem in the mechanical and teleological conceptions of the people "determinism."[41]

Determinism, as I use the term, is the view that it is sufficient to determine an institutional goal, or a mechanism to attain this goal, in order to justify the institution in question. The determinism in mechanical and teleological conceptions of the people is problematic because by focusing on the goal, it underplays the importance of the actual path to its attainment and closes off the possibility of unexpected alternatives. Eventually, it substitutes the expected abstract people to come for the actual experiences of those who participate in a democracy. Hence, when mechanical and teleological conceptions introduce an abstract, future-focused solution to the problem of how the people may govern themselves, they dispense with the actual processes by which individuals and natural forces together forge a people. By focusing on the abstract goal, or the abstract institutional mechanism that allows us to attain it, these conceptions of the people leave out the actual experience of indetermination that individuals experience when they participate in politics. This experience is valuable in itself, and a necessary condition for self-government. Unless individuals go through the experience, one could not claim that the people governs itself, and thus a mere future possibility is not enough to justify rule. For this reason, the theories that espouse these conceptions of the people cannot solve the problem of the indeterminacy of popular unification.

Determinism in Teleological Conceptions of the People

A teleological conception of the people holds that there is a press of events such that the goal of democracy causes the unification of a people. Teleological accounts of political phenomena are often controversial because they seem to read into the future. But this is not the main reason why teleological conceptions are objectionable in the context of democratic theory. The problem is that teleological conceptions of the people do not tell you how to relate the goal to the events that should bring it about. Without an explicit statement of this connection, the conception of the people introduces an unwarranted determinism and causes problems for the justificatory theories that use the conception.

41. It may seem at first that determinism is problematic because it claims that every event is necessitated by previous events and the laws of nature, and thus seems incompatible with freedom. But this is not why determinism is a problem for political theory, which, since Hobbes, Hume, and Locke, has accepted compatibilist solutions to the problem of free will.

Determinism is controversial in teleological accounts when it is not clear that we can attain the goal in question. For example, teleological accounts are problematic when they drive actions meant to reverse injustice, attain freedom, or achieve democracy. But why? Striving to unify the people in order to achieve democracy is controversial because unlike a goal we have previous experience of attaining, a perfect direct democracy has never been fully realized. The only experience we have of perfect popular sovereignty is its absence, such that there is always a discrepancy between the ideal people and the sum of individuals in a given territory. Thus it is not surprising that many flinch at the idea of fighting for democracy, spreading democracy, or pursuing a general will. They know that what is done in the pursuit of the goal often goes against the values from which the goal was derived. The authoritarian excesses to which Rousseau's ideal gave rise after the French Revolution, or the pursuit of perfect democracy under communist regimes in the twentieth century, are good examples of this distance between the values underlying the goal and the actions taken to achieve it.

But is this determinism unwarranted? One could still argue that those concerns are not sufficient to dismiss teleological views. A defender of teleological views could argue that the terrors in eighteenth-century France and in the twentieth-century Soviet Union were mistakes, but mistakes that were committed in the pursuit of a just goal. And that goal may be the true internal purpose of those societies. To put it differently, democracy may be the correct answer to the question of how individuals ought to live together. And this goal need not be a capricious individual wish. Unlike kneading dough in order to get fluffy bread, pursuing democracy may be a goal intrinsic to human practical rationality.[42] If this were true, it would warrant espousing a teleological view. In Rousseau's theory of popular sovereignty, for example, rationality defines the people. A people can govern according to its general will because all can see that each individual's best interest may accord with the best interest of everyone else. The general will that arises from the social contract is not only the goal to attain, but also the condition for "the act by which a people becomes a people."[43] The theory therefore conceives of the people teleologically. In this view, the general will is not a contingent arrangement, but rather the only possible arrangement that guarantees freedom for every member of a group, and therefore this goal brings the people about. But if the will of

42. For a defense of normative utopianism, see Estlund, *Democratic Authority*.
43. Rousseau, *On the Social Contract*, 52.

all is to coincide with the general will, every single citizen must accept that popular sovereignty is the legitimate goal. The attainment of the goal, then, depends on the existence of a purpose in nature or in history that is binding on everyone, to the extent that everyone ought to be able to recognize that the goal is good. This suggests that if everyone can do so, there must be a natural press of events taking that people toward that goal and constituting that people as a unified whole. Rousseau's seminal idea remains the political goal at which most democracies aim, and it is not hard to see why the teleological conception of the people retains its attraction.

But this determinism is in fact unwarranted, even though teleological conceptions of the people do not pose problems because of their goal. Rather, they pose problems because they assume that we may attain the goal but do not succeed in telling us how. For one, how do individual actions relate to the goal? In many cases, democratic theory takes it as given that there is a tendency that links individual actions to a social goal. In other cases, authors try to deduce this tendency from reason or induce it from social patterns of behavior. Often, these theories contain a mixture of three sources (assumptions, induction, and deduction) coexisting in a view of human nature: a teleological conception of the people presupposes that all human beings are born free, equal, and endowed with reason, and that they have a tendency to seek the actualization of these capacities (i.e., a tendency to seek freedom). This assumption is too vague, however, to link individual actions to the overarching goal.

So determinism is a problem in teleological conceptions of the people. The issue usually arises in theories where the unification of a democratic people is the purpose of humankind because that drive toward unification follows from rationality, considered to be the natural endowment of every human being.[44] Even among those who share this view, though, there is wide skepticism that there can be one single formulation of the rational purpose that drives human action. Moreover, even if you hold that there is one single formulation, it remains doubtful that we can know it with certainty. For this reason, many believe there is no guarantee that the goal can be achieved or that the path toward it may be traveled without deviation. The link among universal human traits, communication, and a specific form of social organization is so faint that most of us think there

44. It follows from instrumental, practical, or communicative rationality, depending on the theory in question. Instrumental theories tell us that it is in our own interest to recognize one another's freedom in order to remain free, practical theories tell us that we ought to recognize the moral law if we don't want to fall into a contradiction, and communicative theories hold that we ought to assume that when we communicate we expect to be understood.

is nothing inevitable about the development of humankind: no necessary progress in moral development, no single interpretation of what is practical reason, no obvious manifestation of the moral law, and no clear revelation of the purpose of nature or the will of God.

Now we can see more clearly why determinism in teleological conceptions of the people is problematic. Many justificatory theories embrace these conceptions where the goal is the common achievement of freedom or justice. They make the goal the source of ethical action in the state, and thus make the legitimacy of the state dependent on the pursuit of this goal. More frequently they make it dependent on the moral development of a citizenry that ought to recognize this goal and thus achieve the unification sought. But unless they could tell us why the goal is inevitable, and how current events relate to the goal in question, they cannot legitimize the existence of current institutional arrangements. How could they know that this is what all individuals would agree on? Without an obvious bridge from present actions to the stated goal, it is impossible to say that current individual actions have a tendency toward a particular moral objective.

The people is never unified in the present because individual plans diverge, the shape of the citizenry changes constantly, and unexpected events change institutions and ideals. The indeterminacy of popular unification poses a challenge to teleological conceptions of the people, and thus to hypothetical justifications of the state. This challenge, however, is not to the goal itself, but to the implicit determinism that it entails. Unless the theories can explain the mechanism that drives the system, or account for the legitimacy of the extra-systemic pull that drives people toward their goal, teleological conceptions of the people introduce an unjustified paternalism to democracy. Moreover, by emphasizing the goal, rather than the process for attaining that goal, the justificatory theories forgo an important detail: actual participation in the process to attain democracy has an intrinsic value. This is especially relevant when the democratic process deviates from the projected path to achieve the goal. Could a mechanical version of the people counterbalance this finalism and the undesirable consequences that it often implies?

Determinism in Mechanical Conceptions

A mechanical conception of a democratic people holds that the people are those individuals who agree to organize their political existence according to democratic principles; moreover, it presents an explicit mechanism that generates this agreement. In contrast to teleological conceptions, mechanical conceptions of the people posit a mechanism that explains the natural tendency toward unification by efficient causation. This approach yields a conception of the people that does not assume finalism. But it also introduces a problem—that of determinism—because it substitutes the lived experience of democracy for the abstract mechanism that *could* lead the people to the goal.

Mechanical conceptions of the people promise to solve a problem in teleological theories: that of mistaking unrelated events for the actualization of a teleological tendency. Imagine, for example, Lenin's position in 1917. The Russian Revolution could have been the beginning of a world revolution, the solution to the last antagonism between capital and labor, which would in its turn inaugurate communist freedom. Then again, it could have been a failed peasant revolt, buried in a previous stage of world history. How do you know that a telic tendency is, in fact, being expressed by certain events and facts? To justify Lenin's constitutional paternalism you need a precise mechanism that relates events to the goal.

According to mechanistic theories, a natural goal is already contained in the facts that manifest a teleological tendency. This means that you can embrace the goal without recourse to the future. You can account for the tendency by attending to the natural regularities that explain the system's functioning. With sufficient information about the system, mechanical theories argue, you can establish the precise mechanism that links the teleological effect to the goal. Hence mechanical conceptions of the people can improve on teleological conceptions by giving you the precise mechanism of how popular unification can come about, even if it has not yet occurred.

Mechanical thinkers hold that apparent teleological explanations can be reduced to efficient causal ones. Biological and nonorganic systems have feedback mechanisms that relate the goal to previous events, such that the purposive elements of human behavior can be incorporated into efficient causal explanations by transforming aims into beliefs or intentions. According to these thinkers, with enough information we can reduce the teleological rule of any system to an efficient causal mechanism, such that the teleological explanation is unnecessary.[45]

---

45. "The difference between a teleological explanation and its equivalent non-teleological formulation is thus comparable to the difference between saying that Y is an effect of X, and saying that X is a cause or condition of Y. In brief, the difference is one of selective attention, rather than of asserted content." Nagel, *Structure of Science*, 405.

In social science, the best and most commonly used example of this is market equilibrium. The invisible hand is not a mysterious force leading facts and events toward their goal, but rather the mechanism that links self-interest and rationality to the end state in the system. Mechanical theories hold that, just as gravitational forces explain the equilibrium in a planetary system, and just as natural selection can explain adaptation in evolution, so self-interest and maximization of utility can explain market equilibria without needing to posit final causes. Similarly, you can account for the unification of the people with a mechanism. A mechanical conception of the people turns the social contract into the strategic pursuit of self-interest, one that connects individual actions to the general will. This strips the idea of its finalism, portraying it as an efficient causality. For example, in "Games, Justice, and the General Will," Walter Runciman and Amartya Sen use the theory of non-zero-sum, non-cooperative games to account for a mechanism that links rationality to the notion of the general will. Using the game of the prisoner's dilemma, they present a mechanism that explains how the conflicting interests of the will of all find a source of unification in a general will. They do this without recourse to an unexplained entity that transforms the multiplicity into a whole. The mechanism links self-interest to the idea of the common good without an exterior goal. On the assumption that all the players want to maximize their utility, this mechanism is a game that explains to players that a contract can be made because it makes everybody better off, or at least not worse off. In short, these theories offer a mechanism explaining how there *could* be uncoerced political cooperation, which in turn leads to the constitution of a people.

But this solution reintroduces the problem implicit in teleological conceptions of the people—determinism—by making the unification of the people an abstract possibility rather than an actual phenomenon, such that it is sufficient to determine the goal in order to legitimize an actual state of affairs. This can be seen in the way the theory explains why it is this particular mechanism that prevails. For instance, economists and rational choice theorists seek to explain the emergence of a particular equilibrium through "social selection": if the desired equilibrium is not established, the firm goes out of the market. Similarly, if a people does not unify, it cannot survive as a democracy. But this view of "equilibrium" assumes that society is naturally prone to democracy. In the case of popular sovereignty, it assumes that there is a tendency toward unification, and teleology thus creeps back in. The mechanical conception of the people also leads to an abstract view of the people that tends to ignore, and maybe even suppress, all deviation from the tendency toward equilibrium because it assumes that the mechanism will lead to the goal, even if this goal has never been attained.

When you assume that there is an intrinsic tendency toward equilibrium, teleology and mechanism become fused such that the institutional mechanism itself becomes the goal: the people. Instituting electoral mechanisms, then, becomes tantamount to attaining a democratic people, and individuals can only be part of the people to the extent that they partake in these institutions. The danger with mechanical views in democratic theory is that the machinery introduces an unjustified determinism and opens the possibility of paternalism. Like other machines, this type of democratic machinery does not allow for adaptation to changing circumstances, and it does not admit deviations in the path toward its goal. This view of the people hence excludes all individuals and events that do not partake in the stipulated mechanism. Suppose, for example, that electoral institutions define the people. Then the experiences of those who are not legal citizens, of those who chose not to vote, and of those who question the institutional structure do not count as part of the people. In the end, then, the goal of obtaining an abstractly conceived electoral machinery replaces the process of creating a democratic people through the experiences of real individuals, experiences that can often be ones of trial and error.

Both mechanical and teleological conceptions of the people are deterministic because they posit popular agreement as a goal that in turn determines the boundaries of the people and justifies state institutions. This is problematic because the goal and the mechanisms to attain it may introduce constitutional paternalism. "The people" as currently conceived in democratic theory consequently distracts from the actual experience of self-governance and the actual process of political participation, both of which are part of the people in the making or unmaking. As a result, these conceptions threaten to curtail individual freedom, which requires not only the liberty and capacity to make a choice, but also the lived experience of this capacity as it obtains over time.

The People in Time

As I have argued, both teleological and mechanical theories hold that facts and events in the world are bound to one another through causal chains; further, both viewpoints posit that, with enough information, we can explain any event in the past or predict any event in the future. A posited "pull" or "push" is the ultimate explanation for the chain of events, and it matters little whether it is placed at the end or at the beginning.[46] Hence both theories are committed to determinism because they hold that it is sufficient to determine the goal that creates a people, or the mechanism to attain it, in order to justify democratic rule.

Determinism is problematic for these theories of the people because by focusing on the goal or mechanism of self-rule, they leave aside the experience of self-rule. We cannot abstract from these experiences because without them, we can never have enough information to know what the path to attain the goal *will be like*. Even if we had full information of all previous events, and we knew what precise path they draw out in the future, we still would not know what it was like to travel the path. But this is precisely what we need to know because legitimate democratic rule requires both the abstract justificatory principles and the experience and practice of political participation. Hence we should reject both theories' deterministic fixation on the goal.

But why, exactly, should our conception of the people be able to capture the actual experiences of individuals who coexist and try to govern collectively? These experiences are important, I suggest, because they are creative and may alter the course of events and the appropriateness of the plotted path. We need to capture them because they can help shape the goal we are trying to achieve. But how best to capture them? As I shall argue, a conception of the people drawn from a philosophy that embraces the lived experience of time and change can both capture them and deal with the indeterminacy problem.[47]

Let me say a bit more about why a people conception should capture the actual experiences of individuals who try to govern themselves collectively. For one thing, a necessary condition for obtaining a democratic people is self-government: a people or an individual cannot govern itself if the individuals are not consciously aware of doing so. That is, they must experience self-governance and must live through the experience if it is to be relevant in any meaningful way. Governing means directing and controlling affairs through relevant decisions, and you could not say that you govern yourself unless you participate in the making of these decisions. In order to feel that a decision is yours, you must experience the feeling of not having yet decided. Thus democratic governance requires the experience of indeterminacy in time.

---

46. Nagel argued that teleology is inverted mechanism; Bergson believed that mechanism is inverted teleology. Bergson, *Creative Evolution*, 37–39. See chapter 6, below.

47. The philosophies of Bergson, Whitehead, and Rescher are three such examples. See my discussion in chapters 6 and 7 of their thought and my use of it in building a processual theory of peoplehood.

This kind of indetermination, however, is not only the freedom to determine your own future, which has so puzzled the defenders and detractors of free will. Regardless of whether the action in question is determined or uncaused, *the feeling* of indetermination always obtains. This is the experience of uncertainty that accompanies every important action and decision. Specifically, this uncertainty is a necessary element in all *political* action. Experiencing open-endedness is a requisite for participating in politics, and this experience cannot be expressed in the abstract: it must be lived in real time. Abstract teleological and mechanical conceptions of the people cannot incorporate this experience because they presuppose an outcome independently of what participants may or may not experience. Yet the very feeling is necessary for attaining the goal of self-governance and the goal of democracy: the simultaneous attainment of collective and individual freedom and equality. Therefore, an accurate conception of the people must include and value the actual processes by which individuals seek to attain their goals, including the experience of failure, wrong turns, and dead ends. For this reason, democratic institutions and constitutional protection of individual rights cannot themselves create a democracy if the individuals who are governed do not participate in the making of this government and its institutions.

Let me illustrate this point with a hypothetical example. Imagine that the existing government of a given country organizes elections. The elections are held peacefully, but by midnight on Election Day it becomes clear that the contest is too close to call. After days of recounts, the authorities of the electoral institutions decide in favor of the candidate from the governing party, but the proof of her winning a majority is never conclusive. The challenger rejects the legitimacy of the electoral authority and the government, and launches massive protests. Both sides claim to represent "the people." The supporters of the ruling party's candidate claim that existing institutions are the true representatives of the people. The opposition candidate's supporters claim that the masses in the street are the actual people. The government calls the demonstrations a "mob led by a populist leader," while the opposition calls the government institutions a "tyrannical government that stole the elections."

If you held a mechanical conception of the people, you would say that the people are those individuals who agree to organize the state according to democratic principles. Thus, in this view, the moment the opposition rejected the existing institutions, they ceased to be part of the people. Those who disagree on constitutional procedures and institutions willingly

step out of the democratic people. Revolutions, secessions, and other political movements beyond the scope of existing institutions are also beyond
the scope of a mechanical conception of the people. According to this conception, then, those in the streets could be a new people, and the situation
would be conceived as a constitutional crisis and a budding civil war.
Hence this conception of the people does not allow you to establish continuity between the existing people and extralegal movements.

Similarly, if you hold a teleological conception of the people, you would
not be able to tell which group represents the people at the moment of a
constitutional crisis. A teleological conception holds that the people are
those who would agree to organize the state according to liberal democratic
principles if as individuals they had achieved their potential for rationality
and virtue. Yet in our example, the two groups disagree fundamentally on
the path but not on the goal. So, on this conception, both groups have an
equal claim to represent the people. This is a problem because democracies would always be threatened from within and they would have no argument to deter internal breakdown.

Both conceptions fail to account for the intuition that individuals in
both camps are part of the people, and they cannot say how the experience
of the confrontation adds something to the institutions that result from
such events. Mechanical and teleological conceptions of the people cannot
encompass the fruit of this experience, and they do not value the experiences of democratic participation beyond the institutionalized roles of
voter or civil servant. Any conception of the people that cannot incorporate
the possibility of conflict and failure, as well as the experience of individuals in political turmoil, is deterministic in the sense that I have used here.

The problem with mechanical and teleological determinism, then, is
that by focusing on an abstract conception of the goal or the mechanism,
you leave out what time adds to the process, including the experience of
indetermination, the feeling of expectation, and the fear before the uncertainty of the outcome. But if you leave these out, you risk leaving aside the
changes that over time occur in the goal and the mechanism. The actual
process adds so much that it may in fact change how you understand the
goal. Moreover, these changes could be so important that they may render
useless previous plans for attaining the goal. This is important if you consider that those plans may include electoral mechanisms and institutional
arrangements such as a written constitution. Yet these important changes
cannot be part of the people unless we take time into consideration when
we build a conception of the people.

Conclusion

The problem of indeterminacy of popular unification may seem at first a theoretical curiosity. After all, it only affects theories that expect consensual agreement. To many contemporary democratic theorists, this expectation may seem a remnant of Enlightenment ideals that have been proven wrong both in theory and practice. As I have argued, however, the requirement of popular unification remains central to any theory that seeks to justify state institutions in the name of individual and collective autonomy. Democratic rule presupposes a people, and majoritarian rule presupposes a whole; this whole is the unified people on which all liberal democratic theories rest.

Yet the currently dominant conceptions of the people are inadequate to justify the state. By substituting an abstract goal for the actual experience of democratic participation, these theories in the end undermine democracy. The feeling of indetermination that comes from the lived experience of politics is a necessary condition for self-government, which is in turn a sine qua non of democratic politics. And neither theory can capture this experience. It seems, then, that to develop a democratic theory able to cope with the indeterminacy of popular unification, we need a conception of the people that incorporates change and the experiences of those who participate in politics over time. Incorporating time and change, however, requires that we conceive of the people as existing over time, incorporating the changes that individual experiences add to the whole. In short, in order to solve the indeterminacy problem, the people must be conceived as a *process*, rather than as an aggregation of individuals at a given moment.

There do exist some conceptions of the people that have recognized that democratic theory must incorporate change and movement. Jürgen Habermas's conception, and his analysis of the indeterminacy problem in *Between Facts and Norms*, has been particularly influential in the last decade. In the next chapter, I deal with his analysis and with some of the problems that arise when you take seriously a view of the people as process.

4

Dynamic Constitutionalism and Historical Time

The indeterminacy of popular unification is a problem that arises when democratic and constitutional theories overlook change and movement. It becomes most salient when there is an incongruity between a constitution, which is said to represent the will of a people at a given moment, and the opinions of an actual, changing population. It is perhaps for this reason that the problem has been studied by constitutional scholars who examine the tension between democracy and constitutionalism.[1] In response to this tension, many such scholars have argued that a constitution must change synchronically with the population, and they conceive the democratic or self-governing people by institutional procedures that incorporate change within a historical process.

But do these theories solve the indeterminacy problem? How do they differ from other appeals to history in politics? After all, there is nothing new in appealing to a historical process that creates a people. In most nation-states, politicians and ideologues try to legitimize rule by invoking history. For example, you can probably recall either political speeches that appeal to a unified people to come, or patriotic versions of your national history that celebrate a unified people in the past. Political rhetoric, in dealing with popular indeterminacy, often entwines nostalgia and hope.

---

1. In American constitutional theory there are at least two debates on the tension between constitutionalism and democracy that overlap with the problem of indeterminacy of popular unification. The first deals with the tension in reference to the legitimacy of judicial review. The second deals with precommitment in constitutional law. See Alexander, *Constitutionalism;* Elster and Slagstad, *Constitutionalism and Democracy;* Holmes, *Passions and Constraint;* Michelman, "Human Rights and the Limits of Constitutional Theory"; Michelman, *Brennan and Democracy;* Post, *Constitutional Domains;* and Waldron, *Law and Disagreement.*

These rhetorical images can eventually construct a people when they are woven into a patriotic or national history. The resulting idea of a civic or ethnic nation provides a symbolic reference that occupies the place of the unified collection of individuals in democratic theory. But these rhetorical images do not solve the problem; at most, they contain it symbolically.[2]

Are appeals to history in political theory any different? Constitutional and democratic theories often evoke history when the elusive people is at issue. Since the eighteenth century, most theories of democratic legitimacy in the social contract tradition have held that a historical process can close the gap between the ideal unified people and the populace. These theories assume that popular will and reason ought to coincide, and that if they do not coincide in the present then they have coincided so in the past, or could do so in the future. In short, rather than solving the problem, these theories displace it in historical time.[3] Such displacement poses a dual problem. Suppose that, on the one hand, you displace the solution to the past by claiming that unification already occurred, or you displace it to the future, by guaranteeing that history will close the gap between the ideal standard and reality. In either case, you may deprive current individuals of their right to decide the course of political events, which endangers the present democratic legitimacy of the state.[4] If, on the other hand, you acknowledge that historical processes drift with no particular direction, then history cannot be a solution to the indeterminacy problem. Without the hope of a unified people at some point in history, the theory does not provide an actual ground on which to legitimize the state.[5] This dual problem, of course, does not arise if you believe in a preestablished harmony between human aspirations and the course of future events.[6] But if you have no good reason to believe that history is progressive or intrinsically rational, how can historical time bridge the gap between the unified people and scattered individuals?

It is partly in response to these concerns that a set of contemporary political theories holds that understanding the constitution as a dynamic process can solve the indeterminacy problem. Following Kevin Olson, I

2. For historical examples of these rhetorical images and symbolic references, see Morgan, *Inventing the People*; Palti, *La invención de una legitimidad*; Smith, *Stories of Peoplehood*; and Yack, "Popular Sovereignty and Nationalism." For a theoretical argument that shows functional equivalences between ethnic and civic patriotism, see Markell, "Making Affect Safe for Democracy."

3. Connolly, *Ethos of Pluralization*, 138; Honig, "Dead Rights, Live Futures."

4. Honig, "Dead Rights, Live Futures," 797.

5. K. Olson, "Paradoxes of Constitutional Democracy," 333.

6. Chiaromonte, *La paradoja de la historia*.

call the view shared by these theories "dynamic constitutionalism."[7] According to these theories, a dynamic process establishes mechanisms that link the present political moment to a set of goals. This, I hold, is a promising path to take in dealing with the problem of indeterminacy. As the theories are now formulated, however, they fail to solve the problem. For in the end, these theories do not really focus on the process itself. They instead rely on the present moment and the future goal. By emphasizing moments rather than continuous processes, these theories eventually reconstitute the problems that arose when traditional theories relied on historical time to solve (or displace) the problems of democratic theory.

In this chapter and the next, I specify the problems that arise when you conceive of the people in historical terms. I do this by analyzing two influential examples of dynamic conceptions of the constitution and the people. In this chapter, I deal with Jürgen Habermas's account of "popular sovereignty as procedure." In the next, I examine in detail the dynamic conception of the people presented by Bruce Ackerman's theory of dualist democracy. I shall argue that these solutions to the indeterminacy problem in constitutional theory have an effect similar to the one we find in practical politics: they introduce images of a unified people in the past, or the vision of a unified people to come in the future. But these images and visions do not solve the indeterminacy problem—they defer it. They substitute a static people we can never find in the present with another static people, albeit this one displaced in historical time. Hence, while these theories can justify an ideal end state or an original constitutional moment, they cannot justify the process itself. They still require a static unification of the people at a given time. I call those static historical images, which function within these theories as stand-ins for a unified people, "images of the past" and "visions of the future."

In this chapter, I evaluate Habermas's solution to the indeterminacy problem. I show that it displaces the problem in time through visions of the future and images of the past.[8] The visions and images depict the idealized moment of popular unification (the coincidence of abstract reason and common will), which Habermas's theory claims may take place

---

7. Olson describes dynamic constitutionalism as an "open-ended evolutionary approach" to constitutional lawmaking, which "allows you to make an illegitimate first step with hope that things could be worked out as time goes on." "Paradoxes of Constitutional Democracy," 331.

8. For other recent analyses, see Brettschneider, *Democratic Rights*, chap. 2, and Thomassen, *Deconstructing Habermas*, chap. 2.

in an undetermined moment in history. A first moment of this kind arises in Habermas's theory of moral progress. In this theory, progress is described as an open, ongoing process moving toward an ideal (the generalized consensus on political principles on which every democratic citizen ought to agree). As we shall see, however, Habermas's theory of the people blocks the openness of this process by requiring a static moment of unification. If the people is to legitimize the state, there must be sufficient moral progress among a population, and this can only be found at a given time. Hence, to keep the process open, the theory would need to show that moral progress is the natural outcome of any historical process. Because the theory cannot rely on a providential view of history, however, it turns to the past to fill the gap. With this move Habermas then relies on the historical traits of given populations. This allows him to transform the ideal goal into a real possibility, but it also sacrifices the dynamic aspect of his original proposal. In so doing the theory runs afoul of the indeterminacy problem. In sum, Habermas's theory of a constitution changing in time alongside the people is a promising step toward dealing with indeterminacy; yet, as the images of a past or future people show, his viewpoint still fails to make democratic theory coherent in its own terms.

The rest of the chapter is divided into two parts. The first part describes dynamic constitutionalism, the theory that emerges from Habermas's attempt to solve the problem of democratic self-constitution. I claim that this theory relies on images of the past and visions of the future. The second part argues that dynamic constitutionalism falls short because these images and visions ultimately reintroduce the indeterminacy problem.

Dynamic Constitutionalism

In recent years, there have been several attempts to solve the problem of the indeterminacy of popular unification. These solutions introduce a dynamic conception of the people into the liberal constitution in order to defuse the vicious circle that arises out of the self-founding of a democratic state. On this conception, the people need not be defined by the state, and the state need not be defined by the people. Instead, both can enable the self-definition of the other. But to solve the problem this way, these views must acknowledge that the people change. Hence they must introduce movement into the theory; put differently, they must acknowledge changes in the demos and allow the constitution to accommodate them. These solutions have been called theories of dynamic constitutionalism.[9]

Dynamic constitutionalism stems from Habermas's thesis of the co-originality of public and private autonomy in the democratic constitution, as defended in *Between Facts and Norms* and other writings from the 1990s and 2000s.[10] The co-originality thesis conceives of the liberal constitution as an ongoing self-correcting process that turns the vicious circle of liberal rights and popular will into a virtuous one. In this new circle, rights and popular will mutually institute and enhance each other dynamically, such that the constitution can legitimize the state democratically without demanding that the people unify. Dynamic constitutionalism thus acknowledges that a democratic constitution does not legitimize a state once and for all, while it also acknowledges the rift that emerges between a concrete, changing populace and the will of an ideal unified people. Moreover, it grants that the lack of fit is an important theoretical and practical problem, one that manifests itself in debates over constitutionalism, political identity, the boundaries of citizenship, and the universality of liberal democracy. In short, dynamic constitutionalism is worth taking into consideration because it promises to solve the problem of the indeterminacy of popular unification.

Unfortunately, dynamic constitutionalism ultimately cannot deliver on this promise, for it reintroduces on two fronts the need for static popular unification. First, it requires a particular set of sociocultural conditions in the population that self-constitutes (conditions enabled by collective moral development). Yet it cannot offer a moral or political justification for these conditions. For this reason, the proposals must assume that a people was there *already,* even though they cannot say precisely when or how the people came into being, or for that matter why it is legitimate or desirable. Second, dynamic constitutionalism requires that an actual group of individuals participate in politics and give specific content to a set of abstract normative ideals. Yet the way the theory states these requirements prevents it from incorporating indetermination into these ideals. To illustrate these problems, I show how dynamic constitutionalism relies either on images of a unified past people or on visions of a static people to come, and I show that these images of a past people and the visions of a future people

---

9. Benhabib, *Another Cosmopolitanism;* Habermas, "Constitutional Democracy"; K. Olson, "Paradoxes of Constitutional Democracy"; K. Olson, *Reflexive Democracy.*

10. Habermas, *Between Facts and Norms.* Parenthetical page numbers in the text will indicate subsequent quotations from this book. See also Habermas's "Constitutional Democracy," "What Is a People?" and "On Law and Disagreement."

cannot help solve the indeterminacy problem because they ultimately cannot accommodate the fact that the people (and its ideals) change. In what follows, I describe Habermas's attempt to solve the problem of democratic self-constitution in order to explain why his form of dynamic constitutionalism ultimately fails.

The Problem of Democratic Self-Constitution

As I argued in chapter 2, a vicious circle arises in any theory that posits the democratic self-constitution of the demos. This vicious circle reveals that there is a gap between individuals in a democracy and the institutions that represent them, but it also shows that there is a mutual dependence between individuals and these institutions. Without the people, the representative institutions lack legitimacy; yet without state institutions, the population cannot be constituted as a body of citizens. Institutions, as we saw, provide the exclusion rule that circumscribes individuals and turns them into a democratic people. This circular relation between the people and democratic institutions creates all sorts of problems in democratic theory, which political philosophy has addressed ever since the original formulation of the thesis of popular sovereignty. Specifically, since Kant reformulated Rousseau's theory of popular sovereignty, the development of the concept of popular sovereignty has gone hand in hand with constitutionalism.

Constitutionalism substitutes the sovereignty of the people, which is never available, with the sovereignty of an abstract state framed by law.[11] Through this substitution, democratic theory bridges the gap between the people and the rulers. Hence this substitution seems to solve the problem of leaving decisions to leaders who claim to speak in the name of the people but who cannot show that they represent the popular will. This solution, however, introduces a new tension between the liberal rights enshrined in the constitution and the legitimizing power of the mobilized population in a state. That is, it introduces the tension between constitutionalism and democracy. Since the 1990s, Jürgen Habermas has addressed this tension, arguing that a theoretical reconstruction of the modern constitution could undo the apparent conflict between liberal rights and popular sovereignty. If so, then this reconstruction could provide a public justification for contemporary states.

11. See Hinsley, *Sovereignty,* 155–57.

But what precisely is this tension between liberal rights and popular sovereignty that Habermas addresses? Liberal democratic theories justify state institutions by claiming that these institutions protect individual rights. Yet these theories cannot explain why the principle of individual rights has precedence over democratic law, unless they appeal to universal moral principles. That appeal, however, is problematic because it makes those principles external to the democratic process. As a result, the principles are not a fruit of democracy, and citizens do not publicly justify them. Consequently, the principles and their precise formulation in legal terms are often subject to public disagreement. Individuals living under a constitution they did not draft may regard these rights (or their precise formulation in the law) as a paternalistic imposition.

To avoid constitutional paternalism, you need to be able to justify these principles publicly. If instead of appealing to universal moral principles you appeal to a democratic process, however, then a new problem arises: a circularity between rights and their democratic justification, since the democratic process presupposes individual rights. Yet those rights must be a fruit of the democratic process. It would seem that rights are both the cause and consequence of democratic processes. But that is a vicious circle.

Habermas uses the argument of co-originality to dissolve this circle. The argument seeks, in his words, to "satisfactorily reconcile private and public autonomy at a fundamental conceptual level" (83). Habermas evades the circularity between rights and democratic processes because his argument does not give priority to either term. Instead, he reconstructs the circularity abstractly. This reconstruction ultimately allows him to claim that "the legal code and the mechanism for producing legitimate law are co-originally constituted" (122).

How does this work? Habermas grounds the co-originality thesis on the insights of his theory of communicative reason. According to Habermas, an internal connection between popular sovereignty and human rights resides in the human capacity to communicate: to give and accept reasons. What he calls "a use of language oriented to mutual understanding" (103) can thus explain how public and private autonomy mutually enable each other.

Habermas argues that discourse theory offers a general normative standpoint that simultaneously enables both private and public autonomy. This is the discourse principle, which states, "Just those action norms are valid to which all possibly affected persons could agree as participants in rational discourses" (107). The principle is not a legal or moral anchor alien to the democratic process because it does not state anything substantial regarding law or morality. It states only the formal criteria required for determining whether a norm could be justified (specifically to people willing to accept reasons that are nondogmatic).[12] Moreover, this general normative principle does not require further grounding because, when it is introduced to guide the original legislation, it is neither juridical nor moral. The principle determines neither the content of the law nor its form. It specifies only the conditions for the law's production. This means that democratic law need not be subordinated to a prior legal or moral imperative.

To illustrate the co-originality thesis, Habermas conducts a thought experiment common to the social contract tradition: he reconstructs current institutions using a hypothetical argument. Habermas envisions a situation where a group of individuals come together. They know that they want modern law to regulate their life in common, but they do not know exactly how. So they ask the following question: what rights must we grant one another if we want to legitimately regulate our common life by means of positive law?[13] According to Habermas, individuals who accept the discourse principle and aim to understand one another would give a similar answer to this question: they would all expect others to agree on a set of basic rights that they would elaborate in common and autonomously. These rights would accord freedom, equality, protection under law, and access to political participation. Such principles would make sense to these hypothetical individuals, or so the argument claims, because they would allow them to be authors of the law that binds them. Thus these principles would preserve the individuals' autonomy, something that the theory assumes is universally desirable (122–23). In this way, the hypothetical assumption of general agreement can ground an institutionalized system of rights.

Once in place, this system of rights simultaneously establishes and guarantees popular sovereignty. As I argued in chapter 2, we can interpret generalized agreement as popular sovereignty. Popular sovereignty as generalized agreement thus suggests that there can only be popular sovereignty under the assumption of rights, and conversely that rights must arise from popular sovereignty. Habermas's co-originality thesis does not

---

12. That is, "it expresses the meaning of post-conventional requirements of justification." Habermas, *Between Facts and Norms,* 107.

13. "This system should contain precisely the rights citizens must confer on one another if they want to legitimately regulate their interactions and life contexts by means of positive law." Ibid., 122.

favor one term over the other because its design is *purposely* circular. It allows us to see rights and popular sovereignty from both perspectives, depending on where we enter the virtuous circle, as it were. Whether we enter the circle from the side of popular sovereignty or that of individual rights, neither is sacrificed to the other. The two terms can thus be said to arise simultaneously in the original agreement.

This account of the democratic constitution is attractive because it preserves the democratic impetus that animates the constitution. It allows a changing people to participate in the creation of its own laws, for the agreement is not that of flesh-and-blood individuals drafting and approving a constitution, but rather a hypothetical assumption. This assumption does not restrict the freedom of a changing people. Rather, the hypothetical agreement sets in place the rules of lawmaking; as such, it allows actual individual citizens to deliberate, decide, and thus self-legislate using the language and form of law and their legal rights and protections. In this way, a changing people can always participate in the legislative process and thus appropriate its rights, meaning that real individuals can make the laws their own. In sum, law creation in modern liberal states is, according to Habermas, a reflective and self-correcting process, such that law and institutions can adapt to accommodate changes in the people. A constitution improves as individual citizens appropriate abstract principles and make them their own through actual democratic processes.

This account appears to lift the constraints that constitutionalism seems to place on democracy. Yet it introduces a new difficulty. This solution *reconstructs* the modern state to solve the apparent conflict between human rights and popular sovereignty. That is, it provides a tool for publicly justifying existing institutions to an existing population that would accept this justification as a valid reason. But the reconstruction, as I have thus far described, cannot tell us how to jump-start the democratic process. Can Habermas's formulation deal with the problem of the indeterminacy of popular unification?

Popular Sovereignty as Procedure

According to Habermas, you can solve the problem of the self-constitution of a democratic state using a revised conception of popular sovereignty. The people, he argues, need not be unified at any given time. The people is not a concrete subject, neither an individual nor a constituted popular body: it is a procedure. Habermas's theory turns popular sovereignty into a procedure to help us legitimize the state without the need for popular unification. In this section and the next, I argue that this solution may work, but not according to the design that Habermas and other dynamic constitutionalists propose. It is true that in an *already* constituted state popular sovereignty as procedure allows the people to participate and alter the legal process without needing a perfect agreement at any one moment. But it can do this only if a people is "already there." To see why Habermas's solution fails, let us take a step back and look at his reformulation of popular sovereignty.

In the traditional use of the concept, popular sovereignty means that in a state the unified will of the people is the supreme authority. This conception presupposes the possibility of generalized consent. Such a conception thus implies that there is, or was, a unified people, since generalized consent implies that all the members of a given group must agree on something. This "something" may be substantial, such as agreeing to found a state, or procedural, such as agreeing only on basic norms to settle disputes, or on rules to generate substantial decisions. Yet we know that a perfect agreement such as this is hard to find. Indeed, constitutionalism was introduced to solve this problem: it presupposes that actual individuals need not coincide on substance, but only on the principles of practical reason that ground a hypothetical contract.

But there is always a risk that a group of people, or an individual in the guise of being the group's "spokesperson," could usurp sovereignty in the name of the people. This would happen unless all individuals could understand the terms of the hypothetical contract and actively will that a democratic state come into being. If popular sovereignty is so conceived, there is always a risk of constitutional paternalism.[14] To avoid this problem, Habermas proposes a revised conception of popular sovereignty. In his view, sovereignty is not the actual coincidence of will and reason in a concrete collective body. Instead, in a modern constitutional state, reason is embedded in the legal and political procedures that channel popular will. Consequently, the coincidence of will and reason occurs when democratic institutions channel popular opinion. In his words, "[Sovereignty] is found in those subjectless forms of communication that regulate the flow of discursive opinion- and will-formation in such a way that their fallible outcomes have the presumption of practical reason on their side" (486).

In Habermas's view, a sovereign people need not be (and in fact ought not to be) a functional replacement for a sovereign prince. This view is fairly uncommon: most traditional conceptions of popular sovereignty

14. See chapter 1.

retain a unitary source of power and hence seek to substitute the sovereign prince for the sovereign people. This traditional view developed historically as parliaments wrestled with kings for governmental power,[15] and in this struggle "the people" became the repository of legitimacy.[16] The traditional view requires that, like the absolute prince, the unified sovereign people hold all power and authority in the state.[17] According to Habermas, however, modern popular sovereignty differs (and ought to differ) radically from traditional sovereignty. Traditional sovereignty presupposes personified unification; in traditional societies, for instance, religion or personal charisma legitimizes the ruler. Modern popular sovereignty, by contrast, legitimizes a liberal democratic state, a form of rule for which a unified source of authority is neither necessary nor desirable. The legitimacy of a modern liberal democratic state depends on consent and democratic participation (what Habermas calls "post-conventional conditions for justification").[18] In the modern liberal democratic state, individuals could grant their consent, but only on the condition that individual and collective autonomy are possible. That is, in modern democracies, legitimacy requires a public justification of the state that *all* citizens could understand, evaluate, and approve of. Hence the source of modern legitimacy is public, it depends on all citizens, and it is irreducibly plural.

For Habermas, then, popular sovereignty must be understood to be plural. It depends on the people: "The people . . . only appears in the plural, and *as* a people it is capable of neither decision nor action as a whole" (469). Rather, the authority of the people arises from thoroughly diffused political power. This type of political power emerges out of the autonomy and the capacity for communication of free and equal citizens acting together,[19] what he calls (following Hannah Arendt) "communicative power."[20] When law channels this communicative power, it becomes

15. Morgan, *Inventing the People*, 63–65, 288; Annino, "Soberanías en lucha."

16. Engster, *Divine Sovereignty*; Hont, "Permanent Crisis of a Divided Mankind"; Yack, "Popular Sovereignty and Nationalism."

17. For the historical evolution of the concept, see Bartelson, *Genealogy of Sovereignty*, and Hinsley, *Sovereignty*.

18. After the French Revolution, "the exercise of political domination could be legitimized neither religiously, by appeal to divine authority, nor metaphysically, by appeal to an ontologically grounded natural law." Habermas, *Between Facts and Norms*, 469.

19. Note, however, that this is contingent on there being post-conventional forms of justification: "After the canopy of sacred law had collapsed, leaving behind as ruins the two pillars of politically enacted law and instrumentally employed power, reason alone was supposed to provide a substitute for sacred, self-authorizing law, a substitute that could give back true authority to a political legislator who was pictured as a power holder. A very different perspective opens up with the discourse-theoretic concept of political autonomy." Ibid., 146.

20. The source of legitimacy emerges from the action of declaring the creation of a new political order, or from what Arendt calls the "act of foundation by virtue of the making and the keeping of promises." This combination of the "grammar of action" and the "syntax of

popular sovereignty. Popular sovereignty understood in terms of communicative power is for Habermas plural and public. When individuals act together to defend or institute the freedom and equality of persons, they generate political power. This power, in turn, can be institutionalized in the system of rights.

Communicative power is thus, for Habermas, the ultimate source of legitimacy in a democratic state because it sets a democratic process in motion. Eventually this process grounds institutions, and once institutionalized, communicative power can become administrative and executive power. A good example of this process is a democratic revolution: public mobilization generates communicative power that becomes institutionalized in a system of rights, and later, in governmental institutions created by democratic means. In this account, popular sovereignty is not one voice, but a diffuse procedure that begins with many voices and exchanges, becoming a definite opinion and will only when the voices pass through legal channels. On this account, there is no risk that popular sovereignty will turn into constitutional paternalism because democratic "processes of opinion- and will-formation" (146–50, 180) always check and control institutions and public officers. As a result, a democratic people can actively participate in government. The people can control institutions and keep government in check without the need for a concrete, decision-making popular sovereign.

Habermas's "popular sovereignty as procedure" thus explains how citizens can participate and alter the legal process without the need for popular unification at any given moment. But, we may still ask, how do you set up this procedure if you did not have a people to begin with? By this I do not mean to say that Habermas's theory could not tell us how to improve an already existing state.[21] I am concerned instead with how the theory relies on an already existing democratic state that draws legitimacy from a given people. The problem of indeterminacy of popular unification is not simply how to justify the state, but also how to legitimately define a new demos, a new people. In short, even if Habermas's theory could help us

---

power" makes the mutual relations of humans the source and ground of a new polity. Arendt, *On Revolution*, 175. See also Habermas, *Between Facts and Norms*, 147.

21. Drawing on Habermas's insights, Kevin Olson describes a "bootstrapping process to create legitimate law where none existed before," which he calls "reflexive agency." "Paradoxes of Constitutional Democracy," 334, 337–40. This process can legitimate existing state institutions in constitutional states, which means that it presupposes the existence of a people with precise boundaries and a post-conventional morality to whom the constitution is publicly justified. One cannot assume this, however, because the existence of such a people is precisely what is at stake in this discussion.

deal with the problem legitimizing an existing demos, it cannot tell us how to constitute it. We cannot simply assume that there already is a people that agrees to enact a constitution. As I argued in chapter 2, we cannot show that the people unify at any given time, and existing democratic theories do not offer normative criteria of exclusion.

Procedure and the Unified People

Popular sovereignty as procedure can solve the problem of popular unification only if a unified people already exists. By "reconstructing" the institutions of a given state as a way of legitimizing the state, the theory takes for granted that institutions are constructed and that there is a people to which institutions are to be justified. Moreover, this people must have been unified at some point, because we know that it has progressed to a stage of moral development where the society accepts post-conventional forms of justification. That is, the people as a whole forms a collectivity by agreeing to accept reasons that are not dogmatic. This much is revealed by two of the theory's main assumptions: first, that democratic constitutions come into being only in societies where a defined group of individuals recognizes the need for positive law; and second, that democracy is universally acceptable among a population.[22] In short, popular sovereignty as procedure assumes both (1) the existence of a preexisting and well-defined group of individuals whose members call themselves "us," and (2) that the members of this group share a commitment to regulate their common life by means of a democracy and positive law. The theory takes for granted a population with given boundaries and common cultural traits, a people who could agree on basic institutional arrangements.[23]

This people, Habermas has made clear, is not and should not be a nation. The theory does not require cultural homogeneity or demand a perfect consensus on any substantial matter. The theory does not require that leaders fabricate a national ideology to secure social integration.[24] In

22. See Habermas, "Constitutional Democracy," 772.

23. Compare this with Rocafuerte's argument in chapter 1. How could democracy emerge in a territory without a previous democratic culture? Like Habermas, Rocafuerte knew that he could not ask for civic virtue as the ground of legislation, given that this assumes the previous existence of the civic space. But he takes for granted that a group of people would evolve into democratic citizens. Although an ocean, a culture, and two hundred years separate these authors, their arguments share a similar structure. Both Rocafuerte and Habermas rely on (1) the assumption that the state is already constituted by a people and (2) the expectation that a political culture can meet the law halfway—that is, they both rely on an image of the past and a vision of the future.

24. Habermas, "Apologetic Tendencies," 224.

fact, it does not even require a unified *civic* nation.[25] But the theory does need a defined collection of individuals who would accept the public justification that the theory provides. Hence, while Habermas reformulates popular sovereignty, this reformulation requires the assumption of a modern demos or people. True, Habermas has argued that this people does not need to be a traditional *Volk*.[26] The people or demos may be bound by "universal value orientations," which "filter" the undesirable aspects of nationalist attachment.[27] But even this cleansed conception of a people does not do away with historical images that help to construct a collective identity among a population.[28] The problem in the theory does not arise from the *kind* of glue that binds the collection of individuals together, but rather in the very assumption of a historically bound collection of individuals that has the right to self-determination.

To constitute the democratic state, Habermas relies on the historical evolution of a democratic culture within a well-defined population. "Law," he writes, "is not a narcissistically self-enclosed system, but it is nourished by the 'democratic *Sittlichkeit*' of enfranchised citizens and a liberal political culture that meets it halfway" (461).[29] He emphasizes this democratic *Sittlichkeit* further, writing, "Naturally, even a proceduralized 'popular sovereignty' of this sort cannot operate without the support of an accommodating political culture, without the basic attitudes, mediated by tradition and socialization, of a population *accustomed* to political freedom: rational political will-formation cannot occur unless a rationalized lifeworld meets it halfway" (489).

Habermas abstracts the liberal political culture that must meet the law from the two-hundred-year history of democratic culture in the West. Therefore, the grounds of popular sovereignty as procedure are not solely the discourse principle and the democratic procedure that make legal

25. For this reason, this issue is not, strictly speaking, part of the debate on "constitutional patriotism" or the "historians' debate." On the debate over constitutional patriotism, see Markell, "Making Affect Safe for Democracy," and Müller, *Constitutional Patriotism*.

26. Habermas, "What Is a People?" 14–19.

27. Habermas, "Apologetic Tendencies," 227.

28. This is what Markell calls a "strategy of redirection" that tries to make the cultural substratum of a given people "safe for democracy." Markell, "Making Affect Safe for Democracy."

29. The same position can be found elsewhere in *Between Facts and Norms*: "The system of rights does not exist in transcendental purity. But two hundred years of European constitutional law have provided us with a sufficient number of models. . . . Democratic institutions of freedom disintegrate without the initiatives of a population accustomed to freedom. Their spontaneity cannot be compelled simply through law: it is regenerated from traditions and preserved in the associations of a liberal political culture" (131).

rights concrete. The co-originality thesis also presupposes that to constitute a democratic state requires a well-defined group of individuals who
agree or would agree to organize institutions under the assumptions of
rights. In short, Habermas's thesis assumes a well-defined democratic
people as the ground to the liberal constitution.

But this immediately leads to problems. It means that the thesis has
difficulty resolving the issue of the self-constitution of a democratic state.
What would happen if, for instance, we wanted to apply the theory where
individuals are not *already* a people (let alone a democratic people)? This
is not an uncommon situation. In chapter 1, I gave the example of Mexico
in the nineteenth century, but the problem is not specifically Mexican,
since it arose in all other Latin American republics. At the time of independence, these countries did not have well-defined boundaries or electorates.
Many similar examples can be drawn from successive waves of decolonization during the twentieth century. In all those cases, the boundaries of the
demos were not stable, and it was their new constitutions that determined
who would be participants in the democratic process. In these examples,
we cannot conceive of a legitimate democratic procedure unless there are
real individuals who understand the communicative origin of their rights
and want to regulate their common life by means of positive law. Without
such actual unification, the state would not be legitimate because legal
mechanisms would be undemocratically imposed on a population.[30] For
this reason, any constitutional arrangement based on hypothetical (rather
than actual) agreement risks falling into constitutional paternalism.

A deeper look shows that this is not a problem particular only to pre-
modern countries. When we seek the origin of *any* legal arrangement, we
must rely on preexisting boundaries and a common sense of belonging
within a clear institutional sphere grounded on a common culture. This
raises the question of the moral relevance of that culture. Is the common
culture the result of an accident in history? Is it the result of an ideal
aspiration? How can we legitimize either source?

As I argued in the previous chapters, contingencies of history or geography are not a legitimate exclusion rule for a democratic people. Further,
exclusion rules based on ideal aspirations are hard to defend for at least
two reasons. First, if the rules based on ideal aspirations arise from universal moral principles, we would expect them to apply to everyone in the

---

30. This is not solely a hypothetical example. Many actual populations did in fact resist
these democratic mechanisms throughout the nineteenth century in Latin America and in
the twentieth century in Asia and Africa.

world, which makes them bad candidates for excluding some individuals. Second, if the ideal-based exclusion rule is to be legitimate in procedural terms, the rule of exclusion that determines the boundaries of a people must itself be determined democratically, and this leads to a new vicious circle.

In the case of Habermas's account, if the common culture were a culture of participation and deliberation, it would have to presuppose democratic institutions. As such, it would reintroduce a vicious circle into the theory. The democratic process encounters a further problem when it finds its ground in a common culture. For one thing, how do you deal with deviations? Is there ever a homogenous democratic culture in a given territory? But if you introduce a set of socio-ethical conditions (a democratic common culture) as a condition to legitimize the state, you jeopardize the legitimacy of the democratic state and the soundness of the co-originality thesis.

Habermas's account of popular sovereignty as procedure relies on the previous existence of a democratic political culture among a given population. This democratic political culture breaks the vicious circle between institutions and participation by anchoring itself in a contingent history— that is, outside the democratic discursive process. This external ground, alas, is not itself democratic, and as a result the theory cannot legitimize the democratic state.[31]

The problems encountered by theories of popular sovereignty do not come only from difficulties with the traditional conception of sovereignty: they also arise from problems in the traditional definition of "the people." We cannot take the democratic people as given because we cannot show that the people are unified at any specific time; for this reason we cannot define the people democratically. That is, even though co-originality can solve the circularity between human rights and democracy, we cannot use "co-originality" to solve the problem of the self-constitution of the people. Hence the strategy does not help us deal with the self-constitution of the democratic state.[32]

To solve this problem, Habermas's theory of law emphasizes the dynamism of the democratic constitution. Habermas's discourse theory of law

31. Even if the culture were reconstructed according to moral norms implicit in forms of communication, this cultural ground would not be democratic in the political sense of the term. We could not construe the historical process as popular sovereignty unless there were democratic institutions already in place.

32. In other words, in order to sustain this theory we would have to offer an argument for why the people are legitimate. For two different expositions of this problem, see Honig, "Between Decision and Deliberation," and Näsström, "Legitimacy of the People."

acknowledges that the people are never actually unified in the present, but it argues that constitutionalism can justify the state because the people *may have been* unified in the past or *could* be unified in the future. This recourse to historical time generates and uses images of the past and visions of the future, and thus steers clear of the problem of self-constitution. In the next section, I will evaluate these images and visions, and specify why they are problematic.

Dynamic Constitutionalism and Legitimization Through Temporal Images

Dynamic constitutionalism is an important contribution to political thought. It helps theorists deal with the indeterminacy quandary and its associated practical problems. Dynamic constitutionalism helps you to know whether constitutions are democratic, who should be included in the demos,[33] what is the source of an authentically democratic political culture,[34] and whether and how political and social rights ought to be extended.[35] All these features of dynamic constitutionalism underscore the importance of change in constitutional and democratic theory. Dynamic constitutionalism acknowledges that you cannot legitimize the liberal state on democratic grounds unless you take into consideration, and actively seek to accommodate, changes in the composition of the people.

Yet all available dynamic constitutionalist approaches share a problem. They rely on images of the past and visions of the future. By so doing, they reintroduce a static people into the theory. By "images" and "visions" I mean a reference to a specific moment in time when a concrete event took or will take place. This event is visibly identifiable, so one could refer to the actual visual or narrative image. That is, grasping it requires pictures and stories. The types of event depicted by these images and visions is the actual or possible moment in which autonomous individuals come

33. Seyla Benhabib argues that successive iterations of universal principles embodied in rights can incorporate universal principles into democratic law, and thus can provide the demos with a morally justifiable exclusion rule. See *Another Cosmopolitanism*.

34. According to Patchen Markell, the search for a democratic political culture is part of an "ongoing, always incomplete, and often unpredictable project of universalization." "Making Affect Safe for Democracy," 58.

35. Kevin Olson says that we can find "future-oriented legitimacy . . . within the shifting sands of a dynamically changing constitution" in reflexive political agency and path dependence, which promote the expansion of political and social rights." "Paradoxes of Constitutional Democracy," 340.

together in common agreement, thus legitimizing the state.[36] These images therefore contain a source of political identification and tell a story of the origin and destination of legitimacy. But this story is itself neither a coherent argument nor a justification that an individual evaluating reasons could accept. In fact, these temporal images come instead of reasons, and thus they patch the theory at its weakest spots.

It is true that theorists of dynamic constitutionalism actively seek to avoid such images. Nevertheless, the theories tend to rely on them despite their author's best efforts, precisely because these writers take the people for granted. These images arise even if their encompassing theories present a "filtered" version of the people: a citizens' demos, rather than a cultural nation. Like other types of dynamic constitutionalism, Habermas's theory gestures to a moment when generalized agreement *could* occur or *may have* occurred. In this way, he adds temporal images to two abstract assumptions. First, the theory assumes an idealized form of historical evolution culminating in a founding moment. It does so when it describes the genesis of the conditions necessary to bring a democratic order into being. This assumption becomes explicit in *images of the past*. Second, the theory assumes that there is, fundamentally, progress toward an ideal. It places the burden of legitimization of existing practices on what Habermas calls the "future-oriented character" (471) of democracy. I call the images that depict such progress and give hope for its arrival "visions of the future."

But what precisely is the problem with these images? The first problem, as I have already argued, is that an image stands in for a set of reasons that a citizen could evaluate and accept as a ground for justification. True, the images could synthesize a set of good reasons that in fact legitimize the state. Yet were that the case, the images would then suspend the dynamism of the theory. But that dynamism was required to reconcile abstract reasons (summarized in liberal rights) with the actual political participation of individuals in a democracy. Past images, that is, suspend the political relevance of change because they anchor the political process in a concrete moment outside the democratic process. Images of the past point to a contingent historical fact (e.g., a group of people happened to be here at the moment of enacting a constitution) that is impossible to transform democratically from the standpoint of the present. Yet if the democratic

---

36. Habermas does not explicitly draw or endorse these visions. Yet he acknowledges that any construction of personal and collective identities requires such concrete, particular "images." See Habermas, "Limits of Neo-historicism," 239. This is quoted and discussed in Markell, "Making Affect Safe for Democracy," 61.

process depends on that moment, it binds the hands of those who seek to alter the process *now*. On the other hand, a vision of the future, or a specific goal to be attained, constrains the range of actions available to individuals. It limits them to those that we (today) believe will achieve the vision. This hinders individuals' creativity and each citizen's capacity for creating novel kinds of political organization. Eventually this puts individuals' freedom at risk, and wrecks the normative bases of democratic legitimization. In what follows, I will examine in more detail these images and visions of past and future.

Images of the Past

Imagine a moment in the history of your country. What comes to mind? Chances are that it is a distinct picture: a view of a popular uprising, or maybe the aftermath of a battle. Given the previous discussion, perhaps you thought of a constitutional convention. These are all images of the past that make sense within a larger narrative. They tie the present to the past of a given political group. But why precisely are these images—affective stops of a historical narrative—of interest to dynamic constitutionalism?

   Dynamic constitutionalism seeks to dissolve the vicious circle of the self-constitution of the democratic state. The circle can be avoided, these theories argue, if you conceive of the constitution as a procedure. They acknowledge that the still frame of a constitutional convention is not sufficient to legitimize a state, but they argue that this shortcoming is not fatal. Will and reason need not coincide at the state's foundation, so long as the ongoing practice of liberal rights improves existing institutions. If the procedure incorporates mechanisms for improving democratic practices, then the quality of democratic politics will improve over time. As democratic practices improve, they incorporate the opinions of more individuals and the citizen body becomes more inclusive. Correspondingly, changes in the institutions (and the constitution itself) reflect changes in the demos. This relation between practices and institutions generates constant improvement in democratic practices. An appropriate democratic procedure progressively narrows the distance to generalized agreement— that is, to consensus. According to Habermas, you can "break out of the circle of a polity's groundless discursive self-constitution" on the condition that "this process—which is not immune to contingent interruptions and historical regressions—can be understood in the long run as a self-correcting learning process."[37] In sum, dynamic constitutionalism argues that the

37. Habermas, "Constitutional Democracy," 774.

possibility of future change justifies the institutional project, even though the people are not unified at any given time. Yet this justification merely restates the problem. To get the process going, you need preexisting democratic conditions in a given population, such that individuals can recognize the project as their own.

Dynamic constitutionalism does not explain or justify the origin of these conditions. Instead, it assumes that they are the fruit of the long history of a group. This history is itself contained in the moment in which a democratic culture adopts the constitution. If you capture that moment in a single snapshot, the resulting image encapsulates the long series of events that made the group democratic. This is an image of the past, and it becomes indispensable for dynamic constitutionalism. In a dynamic constitutionalist theory, the images of the past are those references that allow you to jump-start a democratic process. These references are part of a historical narrative, and they define the people in the mechanical terms described in the previous chapter. The references specify and describe those people whose commitment is necessary to set a democratic project going, to keep it alive, and to make it coherent. Without these images, a constitutional project falls into the philosophical regress that I called the problem of constituting the demos.

But if such a theory cannot explain or justify the constitution without appealing to these images, then it is clear that the political culture does not meet deliberative democracy "halfway," as Habermas claims. In fact, a receptive culture must go "all the way." Hence the project of dynamic constitutionalism relies fully on the historical development of an appropriate cultural ground where democracy can take root.[38] Yet that ground's emergence is a contingent historical fact: it depends on luck rather than on moral or political will. For this reason, it ties the hands of those who were not lucky enough to be born in an appropriate context. In sum, the images of the past stand in for a theoretical justification of democracy within this ground, and they work by patching the theory at its weakest spots.

For example, an image of the past ties specific cultures to the universal principles at the core of dynamic constitutionalism. In Habermas's version of the theory, the justification of the state relies on democratic principles derived from communicative reason, yet these principles are universal,

---

38. According to Ferrara, the role of "D" (the discourse principle) becomes unclear when Habermas introduces the past to give specificity to popular sovereignty as procedure. See "Of Boats and Principles."

always the same in every society. But if the discourse principle is the same everywhere, then it cannot tell us how to distinguish one democratic project from another. It cannot justify the allegiance to a democratic process that arises within particular sociohistorical conditions. Habermas must thus appeal to an image of the past, such as the moment of the enactment of a constitution. Without an image of the past, you cannot explain why the process is specific to some particular group in a given time and place. You cannot justify our being in "the same boat" as our forebears, as Habermas calls the common allegiance that sustains a particular democratic process.[39]

Yet introducing images of the past also poses problems. Appealing to such images to stop the regress of political self-foundation only moves the regress to a different place. Instead of accounting for the self-foundation of the state, you must account for the self-foundation of the democratic culture that binds a people. Unless you do this, you lack a normative justification of democracy. It is not a good justification to claim, as images of the past do, that democracy ought to be this way just because it has been this way in the places where it has existed.

These images, then, can only justify democracy in those places where history has actually followed the precise path that takes it to constitutionalism. Yet this happens only where society has become steadily rationalized (i.e., where rational discourse substitutes for religious sanction as the ground of legitimization of rule), because rationalization is the condition for the emergence of the form and language of modern constitutional-democratic law. That is, democracy requires positive law and a clear differentiation between the spheres of law and morality. Unless a society is rationalized or a democratic culture is *already* in place, the constitutional democratic project cannot begin. For example, as I discussed in chapter 1, the incipient Mexican state could not ground institutions because in 1821 there were no geographic, political, or demographic borders in the territory we now call Mexico. The government could not present the constitution as a viable project because the individuals in that territory were members of hierarchical corporations and did not fully understand the requirements of modern law. Nor is this example an archaic relic; it could arise today in a thoroughly religious country.[40] You could not offer a democratic project as a normative ideal in a country where the majority of the population

---

39. Habermas, "Constitutional Democracy," 772.
40. A place where, in Habermas's terms, the sacred has not been "linguistified." *Theory of Communicative Action*, 2:77–113.

believes in the authority of revelation. Nor could you offer such a project among peoples who do not consider themselves as composed of fully individuated beings. In these cases, there are no images of the past to prop up a normative demand for modern constitutional law and to set a democratic process in motion. If you are committed to the normative aspects of constitutional democracy and you believe that a democratic project is the only way to legitimize the state, then you need democratic institutions to found the state democratically. This ultimately takes you back to the vicious circle that the reconstruction of constitutionalism was supposed to break.

But instead of appealing to an image of the past, perhaps you could appeal to a vision of the future. Habermas, for example, proposes "that we understand the regress itself as the understandable expression of the future-oriented character, or openness of the democratic constitution."[41] The dissolution of the tension through co-originality translates the circularity between individual rights and democratic institutions into a regress that Habermas avoids by substituting the future for the past. Let see how this other option works.

Visions of the Future

Imagine the day when you finish your current project. Some of the things you did today were probably done for the sake of finishing it. When you look ahead to the moment of finishing, you have a vision of the future. You are familiar with these visions; indeed, most people live with an orientation toward the future. We can conceive of a democratic constitution in terms of these visions, as a project in the making, one whose future orientation keeps it alive and going. But could a vision of an improved constitution in the future *justify* the project today? In this section, I argue that a dynamic constitutionalism oriented toward the future returns Habermas to the same port from which he set sail: the theory reintroduces a unified people, and by so doing, it resurrects the problem of the indeterminacy of popular unification. It does so because it cannot justify the democratic process itself, but only the goal of individual and collective autonomy. It tells us that we ought to pursue an ideal, but it doesn't say why we ought to pursue it in *this way*. The ideal thus reintroduces into the theory a unified people as a vision of the future.

Why does this vision of a unified people enter into the picture? To answer this question we must first understand what is a vision of the

41. Habermas, "Constitutional Democracy," 774.

future in the context of dynamic constitutionalism. Dynamic constitutionalism, as I have shown, strives for a vision of collective and individual freedom. This could be attained in a society perfectly organized under principles of democratic will formation and universalistic principles of law.[42] Yet such a vision, and such a society, does not exist anywhere. To deal with this, the project of dynamic constitutionalism builds an ever-narrowing bridge between democratic institutions, crafted from abstract universal principles, and the ethics of a real society. The goal is a vision of the future, and the striving to attain it is a future orientation. In Habermas's view, one of the happy consequences of this future orientation is that you don't need a unified people to justify the state. The constitution itself can justify the state because its principles beget an ideal model. The ideal model may guide political action because it is an example of the perfect application of rules. It allows citizens to compare actual occurrences and judge them as progress or regress. In this way, Habermas's model resembles a Kantian regulative ideal.[43]

Habermas's vision of the future, however, differs from a Kantian ideal of reason since the practical power of these two ideals comes from very different sources. According to Kant, ideals may guide action because in its ideals "reason aims at complete and perfect determination according to a priori rules."[44] Thus an ideal of reason in politics derives from a priori moral principles. Given that moral principles are universal, ideals of reason are unchanging, and in this sense the Kantian ideal is closed to the future. For example, in politics, a Kantian ideal of reason is closed because it takes the following form: if you accept that all human beings have an innate right to freedom, and that the Kantian categorical imperative is a rule for political action, then you must agree on the universality of such principles as "No law ought to be enacted which a whole people could not possibly give its consent to."[45] The *idea* of freedom provides this rule. If we could imagine a political order perfectly determined by the rule, it could become the *ideal*, an archetypical model of legal and political order. By definition, the ideal is complete and unchanging. It stays the same regardless of the social contexts or the empirical account of what actual individuals believe. Thus, in any political order that incorporates this ideal, the goal

---

42. Habermas, *Theory of Communicative Action*, 2:106.
43. "The idea as an individual thing, determined and determinable by the idea alone. . . . As the idea provides a rule, so the ideal serves as an archetype for the perfect and complete determination of the copy." Thus wisdom is an idea, but the wise man of the Stoics is an ideal. Kant, *Critique of Pure Reason*, 319.
44. Ibid., 320.
45. Kant, "On the Common Saying," 297.

is always already there. So, rather than a vision of the future, the Kantian ideal of a unified people resembles an image of the past contained in the founding moment of the constitution.

By contrast, Habermas claims that the regulative ideal of dynamic constitutionalism is open to the future because the practical power of the political ideal is not given a priori. It is important for him to avoid a classical Kantian view because if the principles are given a priori, there is a risk of falling into constitutional paternalism or unjustified finalism. Unlike the Kantian sovereign, dynamic constitutionalism does not introduce paternalism because the constitution is democratic in its very principles. In a dynamic constitutional order, the ideal to be pursued itself depends on democratic approval; hence it is a function of the assent of individuals in a particular ethical context. The normative force of Habermas's vision, unlike that of a transcendent Kantian ideal, comes from within the society that adopts it. The model itself may change over time because it is the fallible outcome of an ongoing process of deliberation. Each generation can give substance to the project that began when a group established a democratic framework. For this reason, dynamic constitutionalism should not require a unified people once and for all.

A second reason to adopt this project, rather than a Kantian ideal of reason, is that the process contains within itself the mechanisms for its own improvement. Once set into motion, the process corrects itself. For this reason, the process is not aimless wandering: when there is a vision of the future, the people can change and grow toward this vision. Over time the process may improve institutions, allow more individuals to participate, and progressively break the vicious circle between democratic rights and popular sovereignty that we find in the democratic founding. Thus it would appear that dynamic constitutionalism can in fact solve the indeterminacy problem without reintroducing a static ideal.

But I claim that Habermas's version of dynamic constitutionalism cannot avoid the requirement of an ideal unified people, since without it the theory cannot justify the concrete political processes of states grounded on a specific set of historical institutions. Dynamic constitutionalism cannot show that every society ought to work toward the ideal according to a particular set of ideal institutions, because what matters is the goal, not the process itself. Dynamic constitutionalists can claim that the ideal (as a moral insight) is universal, yet they cannot establish that the *process* is also universal. The theory, however, seems to demand *this* path, a specific kind of process that institutionalizes liberal democratic ideals according to liberal rights and the rule of law, under the umbrella of a written constitution.

But the demand to follow this specific path is unjustified. The path itself does not emerge solely from abstract principles, but also from the reconstruction of a network of discourses particular to a society. This happens because dynamic constitutionalism does not rely on a transcendent moral ground to sustain the claim that a country ought to pursue an ideal. Instead, it relies on communicative rationality. This means that to acquire normative force, a claim must have been discussed and evaluated within a specific society. Hence a specific path can only be justified as an archetype if it can be shown that every society ought to engage in an identical process.[46] Without this justification, the ideal is not an abstract goal; rather, it is a reference to a specific moment in time within a concrete historical narrative. That is, the ideal turns into a vision of the future.

Is it possible to show that this is the adequate path for every society and every time? You could justify the democratizing process itself (and finally do without a unified people) if you could show that there is a set path for the evolution of human societies that leads to rationalized modernity. This would show that communicative rationality is an internal propellant that lends the same normative force to every process. This is why in *The Theory of Communicative Action* and earlier works, Habermas outlines a path toward attaining the decentering and self-reflectiveness of societies. This is important not only for the theory of communicative action but also for dynamic constitutionalism. If it could be shown that there is a natural tendency toward this type of society, we could then understand why the process toward the normative ideal is desirable. This in turn would allow us to show why a democratic constitution is a proper path toward attaining a normative goal, and it would give an aim to a democratic process that would otherwise be adrift.[47]

In *Between Facts and Norms,* Habermas describes the path of moral development that creates a progressive disenchantment of society as leading to the rationalization of the basis of law (137–44). In other works he justifies the claim that this path is inherent to humanity by drawing a parallel between the modes of learning in different societies and the development of the child proposed in theories of developmental psychology (particularly those of Kohlberg,[48] Piaget,[49] and G. H. Mead[50]). In this way,

46. Ferrara suggests that the "exemplary" character of constitutional history could be itself a normative aspiration. See "Of Boats and Principles," 789.
47. For an analysis of these ideas, see Schmid, "Habermas's Theory of Social Evolution," 180.
48. Kohlberg's *Philosophy of Moral Development* and *Psychology of Moral Development.* For a critical discussion, see Modgil and Modgil, *Lawrence Kohlberg.*
49. Habermas, *Communication and the Evolution of Society,* 71.
50. Habermas, *Moral Consciousness and Communicative Action,* 119.

Habermas's model of the process draws normative force from the analogy between the development of the ego in individuals and the evolution of worldviews in societies.[51] In this view, the path of development is progressive: it leads to an improvement, just as the moral development of individuals leads to an improvement in their moral capacity.

This analogy also illustrates the social changes required to make law positive and post-conventional, such that a rationalized society is analogous to a fully developed individual. For example, the forms of social organization that rely on "spellbinding" authority are analogous to lower forms of individual moral development, like those common among children. In contrast, those societies that tend toward autonomization, universalization, decentering, and self-reflectiveness resemble individuals with fully developed moral characters. They are the social equivalent of a moral adult. The analogy, then, turns the process of social rationalization into a process of social optimization. For this reason, the analogy is aimed at justifying the very process toward the ideal of individual and collective autonomy. In light of a theory of development, the process would have as much normative force as the goal. To this extent, the analogy could solve the problem that arises when you try to dissolve the vicious circle of democratic founding with a hypothetical version of the social contract.

Yet the analogy also implies that historical transformations are neither contingent nor value-neutral. The theory turns historical events into progress or regress along a path of linear moral development, and it is difficult to justify the existence of such a path without a full philosophy of history. The path poses at least two problems in the context of dynamic constitutionalism. First, if it is justified as necessary for attaining the conditions that support a democratic constitution, one would have to establish the historical trajectory and the social mechanisms that yield these conditions. But Habermas does not make an empirical case for either trajectory or destination: he does not study the progressive rationalization and secularization of society and the source of law in light of facts. On the contrary, the rationalization remains a theoretical presupposition.[52] Second, the assumption of moral development through superseding stages of social development has methodological inconsistencies. Habermas establishes a parallel between stages of psychological development of the individual and

---

51. Habermas, *Communication and the Evolution of Society*, 102–3; Habermas, *Theory of Communicative Action*, 1:68.

52. Habermas's only empirical ground can be found in *Structural Transformation of the Public Sphere*. See also Dryzek, "Critical Theory as Research Program."

historical stages of collective consciousness, yet he gives no detailed argument for thinking the connection exists.[53] Why should we think that a society develops like a person? What is the theoretical ground of this analogy?[54]

If the process cannot be justified by appeal to a philosophy of history, or to an empirical account of the evolution of societies, then the rationalization of the basis of law in a given society becomes itself an ideal, though this time an unjustified one. Habermas projects the idealizations of discourse theory to all societies, including those societies to come. Unlike a normative ideal of reason, however, this ideal of universalization is just an expectation that a moment will come. The hope that this expectation will be realized gets projected into the future of the state. But this projection lacks justification or normative force.

Habermas legitimates constitutional democracy through a vision of the future, but this vision does not depend on the democratic process or the contingencies of history; it is already determined through a set of idealized conditions. But if those conditions do not obtain at the beginning, there is no reason to hold high hopes for the future; and if the conditions are imposed on a given society, then the burden of paternalism falls on the theory. The goal could impose through the constitution and the state an order deemed desirable by a group, rather than one justified by the democratic process itself. Thus, unless we could count on a philosophy of history, the vision of the future jeopardizes the democratic agency of those to whom the constitution was given because it presupposes a set of conditions that were *already* there. In the end, this vision reintroduces the vicious circle. In order to have a democratic constitution, we need a concrete people with a democratic culture. But only the democratic constitution can bring democratic culture and make the people concrete.

Habermas's theory of law addresses many traditional difficulties in philosophy and reenergizes how we think about traditional problems, including the paradoxes of legality and legitimacy. But it cannot deal with the problem of the indeterminacy of popular unification. The theory still requires a unified people to justify the state, but it cannot show how the

53. In *Theory of Communicative Action*, the connection is at best vague. Habermas argues, "Piaget distinguishes among stages of cognitive development that are characterized not in terms of new contents but in terms of structurally described levels of learning ability. It might be a matter of something similar in the case of the emergence of new structures of world views" (1:68).

54. For a critique of this connection, see Whitton, "Universal Pragmatics and the Formation of Western Civilization."

people unify at any given time. In order to deal with the problem, it resorts to static images of the past and equally static visions of the future. Dynamic constitutionalism thus displaces the indeterminacy of popular unification in historical time and prevents constitutional theory from seriously grappling with indeterminacy and change.

Conclusion

The theories of dynamic constitutionalism, as they are formulated nowadays, fail to solve the indeterminacy problem. Dynamic constitutionalism tries to correct the problems of legitimating democratic constitutions by making constitutional government more democratic. For this purpose it conceives of democratic law and government as a self-correcting process. This process is the key to solving the indeterminacy problem because according to dynamic constitutionalism the state cannot be legitimized once and for all in the moment of an original pact. Thus, by conceiving of the people as a process, dynamic constitutionalism recognizes changes in the people, and accommodates them to make the constitution compatible with democracy. Yet, in the end, the theory fails; while it justifies the aim of this self-correcting process, it cannot justify the process itself.

Dynamic constitutionalism does not tell us why the process itself is valuable; it only justifies the process's goal. Hence it reintroduces the need for static popular unification on two temporal fronts: past and future. On the one hand, dynamic constitutionalism reintroduces the indeterminacy problem when it reconstructs existing institutions and discourses. Reconstruction shows how moral insights can have normative standing, but this method presupposes a shared set of moral insights, as well as a particular set of sociocultural conditions in the self-constituting population. In short, such reconstruction requires a unified people to set in motion the democratic process. Yet this reference to an original past moment and a historical set of practices jeopardizes the democratic process because it may perpetuate the nondemocratic character of the status quo. Moreover, while the reconstructive approach makes the past experience of current democracies (particularly those in western Europe and the United States) a model for all democracies, it cannot tell us why this precise historical path is best. Hence, in dynamic constitutionalist arguments that seek to legitimize the state, all references to this original moment become static images of the past.

On the other hand, dynamic constitutionalism also needs a unified people in the future. Democratic constitutionalism is a particular historical model, which cannot itself be a general ground for moral and political action. Hence, to justify the state, we must rely on procedures that may not have the necessary normative force. Actual political processes may evolve away from widely held moral insights, and they may also become *less* democratic as time goes by. There is no guarantee that popular elections produce good rulers, or that elected legislatures produce good law. The only way to insure that the process improves in time is to give direction to the project by seeking collective and individual freedom. Because by design it lacks the normative force of Kantian a priori moral principles, however, this becomes a weak vision of the future rather than a regulative ideal. In this way, dynamic constitutionalism reintroduces the unified people as a vision of the future.

In sum, dynamic constitutionalism cannot accommodate the people (and its ideals) changing because it cannot say why the political process is itself desirable. It can tell us why the goal is good, but it does not say much about how to get there. Most important, the theory cannot tell us why the process is desirable unless it approaches the goal progressively, yet dynamic constitutionalism is too tightly bound with images of the origin and goal of a unified democratic people to do this. Its orientation toward the past and toward the future illustrates that it accepts one of two versions of how democracy could be achieved. The one returns to the mechanical version of the people: it deals with the causal mechanisms required to aggregate individual wills into a collective whole. The second focuses on the goal to be reached. In short, dynamic constitutionalism is tightly bound to teleology and mechanism. As I showed in the previous chapter, teleological and mechanical conceptions of the people are problematic because they are static and hence restate the problem of popular unification. They do this because they do not take seriously the value of the process of democracy and of the *experience* of democratic participation. This poses a new challenge for dynamic constitutionalism: can it open up the assumption of a static people and frame it instead as a live process? In the following chapters, I consider the view that a people is a process rather than a collection of individuals coming together at a given time.

5

The People Between Change and Stability

The conflict between popular change and legal stability generates important problems in democratic and constitutional theory. For example, should the constitution contain clauses banning popular movements that challenge the basic laws of the state? May people vote to secede or adopt a new constitution? Could the people make decisions that do not involve established procedures or institutions? In response to this conflict, some theorists resort to the idea of process. They depict the accumulation of judicial precedents and legal transformations as ongoing processes that respond to changes in the people that legitimizes the state. In their view, the constitution is a process: it incorporates changes but preserves its authority and identity over time.[1] In this chapter, I am particularly interested in an unexplored assumption of these theories. Those who conceive of the constitution as a process implicitly assume that the people is also a process. They assume that the people changes but also that it retains its identity and persists over time.

Constitutional scholars care about the unity and continuity of a changing people over time—or the people as process—because assuming identity over time eases the tension between constitutionalism and democracy.[2] They also care about the people as process because this conception of the people can solve the logical problem of self-constitution. It solves the

---

1. Ackerman, *Transformations*, 187; Habermas, "Constitutional Democracy," 774–75; Post, *Constitutional Domains*, 196; Rubenfeld, *Freedom and Time*, 145–59; Rubenfeld, *Revolution by Judiciary*, 135–41.

2. Elster and Slagstad, *Constitutionalism and Democracy*; Holmes, *Passions and Constraint*, chap. 5; Michelman, *Brennan and Democracy*.

vicious circle that arises when institutions grant rights and citizens create institutions. The conception breaks the circle by incorporating one term into the other over time.[3] Moreover, conceiving of the people as a process makes space for popular self-renewal. As the people changes, it may become more inclusive and hence fertilize the soil of institutional legitimacy.[4]

But conceiving of the people as a process within a democratic constitution brings problems of its own. Any view of a changing constitution that allows for a progressive extension of rights assumes the legitimacy of the original boundaries of the people, even when it expands those boundaries to include others.[5] Yet we cannot take that legitimacy for granted. In fact, doing so may obscure a fundamental illegitimacy in the constitution of the sate. Such views of a changing constitution also assume the legitimacy of the original institutional commitments in the polity—that is, they take for granted the popular legitimacy of the state that *grants* rights. Thus the people's continuity depends on those institutions that grant rights to individuals.

For example, according to most Americans, "the people" are always the "We the People" of the U.S. Constitution. The problem with this view is evident once you consider that, first, the people never unify, and second, the people often acts *outside* or *against* these institutions, particularly during revolutions or popular movements involving civil disobedience.[6] When individuals act without institutional sanction, this implicit view cannot consider their actions as part of the people, even if these actions strengthen democracy. Eventually, legal institutions and political action drift apart. In that case, the people and its institutions do not coincide, and the problem of the indeterminacy of popular unification arises anew.[7] How, then, can the people legitimize the state democratically if the people constantly changes in composition?

Some constitutional theorists have tried to solve this problem by conceiving of the democratic process as a dualistic interplay between change and stability.[8] On this conception, the people transforms the law of the

---

3. Habermas, "Constitutional Democracy"; K. Olson, "Paradoxes of Constitutional Democracy." See also my discussion in chapter 4.
4. Benhabib, *Another Cosmopolitanism*, 47–51.
5. Honig, "Between Decision and Deliberation"; Näsström, "Legitimacy of the People."
6. For a recent analysis of counter-institutional political movements, see Rosanvallon, *La contre-démocratie.*
7. See chapter 2 for the definition of this problem.
8. I am thinking primarily of Ackerman's "dualist democracy," discussed in *Foundations.* But a dualist view of the people as process also includes those interpretations that focus on complete constitutional rupture or suspension, notably Carl Schmitt's in his *Constitutional*

state in exceptional constitutional moments, also referred to as moments of "higher lawmaking." These moments are, in this view, followed by periods of relative institutional calm. This dualistic approach to constitutional change rests on the old idea that a population has two distinct political modes, one in which it is an active lawmaker, and a second in which it is the passive subject of the law.[9] On the dualist approach, the interplay between these two modes generates a political and legal process that allows you to sustain the law (and thus the rights of citizenship), as well as to incorporate political changes, while retaining both the people's unity and continuity and the state's legitimacy over time.

This conception of the people as process seems promising, for it confronts change while preserving the people's unity and continuity. Yet envisioning the people progressing in time by leaps between exceptional and regular politics is not as fruitful as it may seem at first. In this chapter, I will argue that a dualist people as process cannot solve the indeterminacy problem, and thus it cannot mediate between constitutionalism and democracy.

In the first part, I examine the juridical view of the people as a constitutional process. I argue that this conception of the people fails to legitimize the state because it reduces the people and its action to law. In the second part, I examine the view of the people as the pre-legal subject of collective action, arguing that it also fails because a sovereign people without legal mediation is incomprehensible. In the third part, I evaluate the conception of the people as a dualist process, focusing on Bruce Ackerman's "dualist democracy." I argue that by replacing a sovereign with a process, this conception initially moves toward a solution to the indeterminacy problem. Yet, in the end, dualism cannot ultimately reconcile change and stability because it relies on the exceptionalism of a traditional conception of sovereignty. Hence it cannot establish the continuity of legitimacy in the temporal breaks between "higher" and normal lawmaking. As a result, rather

---

Theory. For an analysis of Schmittian constitutive power, see Kalyvas, *Democracy and the Politics of the Extraordinary.*

9. The old idea of an active and passive mode of the people is the basis of the notion of popular sovereignty. In its modern version it goes back, at least, to Locke. He writes in the *Second Treatise of Civil Government,* "There can be but *one Supream Power,* which is *the Legislative,* to which all the rest are and must be subordinate; yet the Legislative being only a Fiduciary Power to act for certain ends, there remains still *in the People a Supream Power to remove or alter the Legislative,* when they find *the Legislative* act contrary to the trust reposed in them." Locke, *Two Treatises of Government,* 366–67. Popular sovereignty so conceived figures prominently in Rousseau's *On the Social Contract,* where the people is composed of subjects and citizens at the same time, and also in the Abbé Sièyes's distinction between *pouvoir constituant* and *pouvoir constitué.* For a contemporary take on this problem, see Kalyvas, "Popular Sovereignty, Democracy, and Constituent Power."

than a process, it demands static moments of popular unification, over and over again, but this just lands it back squarely into the indeterminacy problem.

The Promises of Stability (and Its Legal Trammels)

Constitutionalism promises the stability of the rule of law. In this account, a group comes together by a decision to grant rights to one another. These rights ground the basis of law and allow citizens to create the "laws of lawmaking."[10] In this traditional view, the group of individuals transcends itself to create a people in the legitimate state. The group "transcends itself" because it creates its own supreme law, which stands as a guarantor of rights and a producer of lesser laws. In this sense, it is the constitution that makes the people. The constitution grants each individual a right to membership, as well as the stability necessary for the group's life in common as a people.

But the law that allows for a stable collective life can subsequently hinder democracy, tying citizens to a fixed set of laws and procedures and eventually constraining their individual autonomy. One of the central problems of constitutional democracy is how to solve this tension. How can you identify your autonomy with the decisions of lawmaking institutions so that those institutions do not become fetters on democracy and on individual autonomy? The legal people as process tries to provide an answer.

The People as Process and the Need for Stability

There is a tug-of-war between two important values in constitutional politics: on the one hand, individual and collective autonomy; on the other hand, individual security and social stability. This struggle generates a tension between democracy and the rule of law. Most constitutional scholars, however, claim that the tension between these two is misleading: law and democratic politics can, and must, go hand in hand. Hence the question for them is how to maintain the precarious balance between the two terms.

In the last few decades, constitutional scholars who lean toward the side of democracy have pointed out that rigid constitutional rules may constrain collective freedom and unnecessarily limit the scope of democratic

---

10. Michelman, *Brennan and Democracy*, 48.

politics. This criticism is particularly relevant in the debates over "precommitment" and constitutional entrenchment.[11] In these debates, some argue that the constitution ought to have immutable, or at least hard-to-change, laws that protect individual rights and keep in place fundamental norms that guarantee fair procedures. Others argue that rigid constitutions constrain the capacity of legislatures to alter fundamental laws. These debates thus often circle whether it is the courts or the legislature that are better suited to interpret the law and change it in relation to popular opinion. But the discussions about institutions occur in the shadow of a bigger question: can individuals really be self-governing if they are bound by laws and institutions that they did not personally choose and cannot radically transform?

Most constitutional scholars would answer this question in the affirmative. They assume that there can be an accommodation between law and democracy because constitutional democratic politics posits that the two terms can coexist harmoniously as long as there is a popular agreement on fundamentals. Law and democracy coexist because when all individuals agree on a basic, supreme law, the people may rule as a collective—that is, democratically. But democracy is not dangerous to individuals because it is constrained by higher law, that which both guarantees the stability of the agreed-on principles and institutions and secures individual rights. This arrangement guarantees individual security. It also allows for collective autonomy within the bounds of the rule of law, since it gives space for democratic politics to renovate the constitution through legal means. Thus, for most constitutional scholars, the premises of contractualism coupled with a historical moment of founding are sufficient to legitimize the state democratically and to guarantee legal stability.

But some of these scholars invest more importance in the democratic ideal than in the constitutional constraints. They believe that to harmonize the rule of the people and the rule of law, it is not sufficient to create a legal framework once and for all. For that, you also need to ensure that the constitution stays in synchronicity with the people, such that succeeding generations and new citizens can also consider the laws as their own. These scholars hold that at any given time the actual population must be able to evaluate and approve the existing fundamental laws, such that the subjects of the law can at the same time consider themselves its authors.

11. Elster, *Ulysses and the Sirens*; Elster, *Ulysses Unbound*; Habermas, "On Law and Disagreement"; Holmes, *Passions and Constraint*, chap. 5; Rubenfeld, *Revolution by Judiciary*; Schwartzberg, *Democracy and Legal Change*; Waldron, *Law and Disagreement*.

Only when this condition is met can an individual be truly invested in the law, because it is only then that she can see it as the product of a political process in which she participates. At that point, and only that point, the law is rightfully hers.[12]

Thus a legal and political *process* of active participation by citizens within the bounds of a constitution promises the harmony of democracy and the rule of law. The product and the ground of this ongoing process is a democratic people. According to Michelman, "One possible way of making sense [of how the law and the people relate to each other] is by conceiving of politics as a process in which private-regarding 'men' become public-regarding citizens and thus members of a people. It would be by virtue of that people-making quality that the process would confer upon its law-like issue the character of law binding upon all as self-given."[13]

In this view, politics not only produces law, it also produces citizens subject to the law; the political process thus produces a legal people. For this reason, the legal people is itself part of the process, and thus we may say that in this view the people itself can be conceived of as a process. This legal people as process changes the constitution as it changes itself, and consequently it may add to or transform written law. Because it is a process, it can do so without ever declaring the constitution perfect and unamendable, thus reconciling change and stability within democracy and legitimizing the democratic state.

The legal people as process seems promising because it can explain why an original commitment binds successive generations and guarantees stability. At the same time, it provides enough flexibility to alter the law as the people changes. As we shall see, however, built into the terms of the process is a demand for stability that may hinder a people's capacity to act.[14]

12. This is the core of a republican reading of the liberal constitutional order. See, for example, Michelman, "Law's Republic." This view shares many points in common with Habermas (see chap. 4) and Ackerman (below).

13. Michelman follows this quotation by saying, "A political process having such a quality is one that, adapting a term of Robert Cover's, we may call jurisgenerative." "Law's Republic," 1502.

14. In recent years there have been several proposals for negotiating the tension, all of which in one way or another use the image of the legal people as process. Michelman proposes the "normative tinkering" through judicial review. Ibid., 1495. Benhabib talks of "democratic iterations." *Another Cosmopolitanism*, 47–51. Post resorts to "responsive democracy." *Constitutional Domains*, chap. 5. And Olson proposes "reflexive citizenship." *Reflexive Democracy*, 135–37. In different ways, all these authors try to fold the democratic process into the constitution, in order to guarantee popular participation and stability. For this reason, they have problems similar to those that afflict Habermas's dynamic constitutionalism.

Democracy in Legal Fetters

According to constitutional scholars, the people can rule itself, but it can only do so on the condition that it remain bound by law. This means that a people may change laws according to changing mores and ideological trends, but popular action cannot deviate fundamentally from principles stated in the constitution. This may seem healthy for a liberal democracy, but it eventually tilts the balance too far toward the liberal side of the equation. The law can confine popular action such that any fundamental challenge to the constitution becomes impossible.

Challenging the constitution becomes impossible because the people is here conceived primarily as a *legal* process. Therefore, the people cannot challenge the constitution if it wishes to remain a people. The legal conception of a people as process thus banishes the possibility of popular action before or against the sovereign state. It cannot award the label "popular" to any protest, revolutionary activity, or civil disobedience. In this view, the law makes the people rather than the other way around. For example, in the words of Jed Rubenfeld, "What makes persons a people is simply this: co-existence, over time, under the rule of a given legal and political order. A people, for the purposes of democratic self-government, is the set of persons co-existing under the rule of a particular political order."[15]

In this view, aggregations of individuals cannot make collective decisions without the aid of structured governments and laws. The process thus turns the people into an appendix of the legal order. This view is problematic, as can be seen in its conclusion: if the people is the ultimate source of legitimacy in the state, and it is not independent of existing rule, then there cannot be standards of legitimacy independent of existing rule. Hence the stability of the existing state becomes an ultimate normative goal. When legitimacy is necessarily anchored in established law, stability is the only guarantee of both legality and legitimacy. Yet by the theory's own lights, was it not supposed to be the other way around? The theory set out by claiming that the people bestows authority on the law. If the people are supposed to be the law's authors, but are ultimately a function of the law, then the dreaded circularity of constitutional founding arises once again.

The vicious circle between the law and the people results when you cannot justify the state by appeal to objective morality, natural law, or independent standards of rationality. For this reason, the idea of the people as

15. Rubenfeld, *Freedom and Time*, 153.

a legal and political process does not work unless you assume that the democratic process carries an independent standard of legitimacy within itself. That is, you must assume that in any democratic community there is a tacit agreement on the "laws of lawmaking," or a "higher law." There must be a popular unification. This assumption, of course, would not be a problem if all could rationally agree on what is the moral ground of the law. But as I argued in chapter 2, this consensus (actual or hypothetical) cannot be taken for granted. The people are always indeterminate and the law's legitimacy can come only from the procedure itself, thereby making the process circular.

The lack of popular unification thus breaks the delicate balance between law and democracy that the legal people as process promised to solve. As I argued in the previous section, the people as process could exercise collective freedom under law only because individuals together created the laws of lawmaking. A problem arises, however, if we cannot appeal to consensus, since the legal people as process view must assume that there will have been some*body* who lays down the fundamental law. Since this fundamental law also determines the people's boundaries, we would have to conclude that some*body* also determines who gets to participate in the legal and democratic process.[16] In the end, the people cannot be self-legislating and self-creating because a prior decision of an individual or a group must create the legal order, and therefore the democratic people with it.[17]

The people, however, cannot claim the law as its own, and it cannot disturb the legal order. This fact, of course, curtails individual and collective autonomy, even if existing laws are fair and the political order just. Hence, when the authority to decide who gets to participate in the legal process does not form part of the process, you compromise autonomy. In fact, you may render it impossible.[18] Yet a democratic people must be able to rule itself. If the people are a function of the law, however, they come to the democratic process bound by legal fetters.

We thus come back full circle to the limitations that rule by law places on collective autonomy. If the people is a function of the law, all political

16. This is the problem of the legislator in Rousseau's *On the Social Contract*. For an interpretation that sees a creative tension in this external moment, see Honig, *Democracy and the Foreigner*.

17. This view of popular sovereignty has become associated with Carl Schmitt, for whom "a constitution is not based on a norm. . . . It is based on a political decision. . . . In contrast to any dependence on a normative or abstract justice, the word 'will' denotes the essentially existential character of this ground of validity." *Constitutional Theory*, 125. A sovereign will constitutes both the state and the people.

18. Carl Schmitt's view is that liberalism and democracy are mutually exclusive. See *Crisis of Parliamentary Democracy*, 10.

processes require constitutional commitments; courts and judges to interpret those commitments; and executive institutions to apply those commitments. In the view of Stephen Holmes,

> To say that "the people" of a modern constitutional state, while . . .
> unbound by law, can spontaneously choose a political order, is unre-
> alistic. It is unrealistic even if we put aside the democratically unan-
> swerable question of who is a member of the community. For a
> society with millions of citizens, even where the membership ques-
> tion is uncontestedly resolved, there is no such thing as a collective
> choice outside of all prechosen procedures and institutions. Both
> elections . . . and public discussions depend upon the entrenchment
> of liberal constitutionalism.[19]

Most constitutional and political theorists agree that in a modern legal
context, democracy depends on the constitutional entrenchment of rights.
So a political movement that opposes the constitution is evidence of state
breakdown. But not all these theorists conclude that you are "unrealistic"
if you do not support established procedures and institutions. For many
political theorists, just because a political movement that challenges the
bounds of the legal state cannot be called "a people" does not mean we
should be suspicious of the destabilizing movement. Rather, it means we
should be suspicious of the stable state and its law.

The Promise and Danger of Democratic Change

Even in conditions of popular indeterminacy, stability is not the only
source of political value. Many radical democrats value the experience of
individual and collective autonomy. For them, the experience of political
action trumps the value of stability within the rule of law. Some scholars
also value the pursuit of collective freedom over stability. I will call them
"fugitive democrats," borrowing a term from Sheldon Wolin.[20] Though
they, too, believe that the people can be described as a process, they hold
that it is a different kind of process than that theorized by constitutional
scholars. In their view, the democratic people[21] arises only from the lived

19. Holmes, *Passions and Constraint,* 9.
20. Wolin, "Fugitive Democracy."
21. For reasons that I will discuss below, some theorists doubt that "a people" could
ever be democratic. They prefer to call the subject of collective action "a supplement," "the
multitude," or "the trace," or "a remnant" of democracy.

experiences of participation in political collective action.[22] These experiences can exist beyond the law because they are not confined to voting or to other civic activities defined by pre-chosen state institutions. They also include political actions that are not legal *yet*, such as revolutionary activity and the creation of new rights and new laws.

The promise of this people conception is that it may be able to restore collective freedom to constitutional democracy. Its danger is that it does not produce established means of determining whether the disruptive action will enhance self-government or will prove too dangerous for democracy. Ultimately, the popular movement in question can only define itself *against* institutions. Hence it may put out of reach the very ideals it tries to foster.

The Promise of Change

According to fugitive democrats, the people may also be conceived as a process, even if they do not define it explicitly in those terms. Unlike the legal process conception, where the aim is to issue legitimate law, this version does not require a concrete product. Rather, in this context we may interpret the word "process" as the course of becoming. In this view, process is the experience of political action over the course of time, rather than the series of steps by which a group of consociates produces the law of the state.[23] Thus, in this view, the people as process exists only as the transitory experience of political action. For this reason, change (and even disorder) is promising. The main promise of the fugitive experience of the people as process is to release collective freedom from the arbitrary power of state institutions.

According to most constitutional scholars, the rule of law keeps in check the power of the democratic state. According to fugitive democrats, however, the rule of law tends to be equivalent to the power of the state. Hence it may also thwart collective autonomy. This conception of democracy decouples the people and the legal state, and seeks to restore the possibility of a pre- or extra-legal people. In this view, the people is prior to or

22. For Wolin, "democracy is not about where the political is located but how it is experienced." "Fugitive Democracy," 18. See also Arendt's "lost treasure" in *On Revolution* and the preface to *Between Past and Future*.

23. Wolin contrasts the view of democracy held by contract theory with his own idea of "politicalness," which is historical and must be both experienced and actively produced. See Wolin, *Presence of the Past*, 139–41.

independent of institutions. According to Wolin, political freedom "cannot be co-opted."[24]

But given that on their view the people does not depend on any institutional mechanisms, fugitive democracy cannot answer the question of who precisely this people is, or how precisely they act. These theorists can only affirm the ambiguous nature of politics. In their view, democracy can never be perfectly legitimate; this is its plight and its promise.[25] Hence democracy cannot be a mode of government. It is, at most, an experience of political renewal that resists any attempt at institutionalization.[26]

In sum, for fugitive democrats the people is occasional, fugitive, even evanescent.[27] Yet democratic action can be liberating, even though it resists institutional forms, laws, and predictable patterns. Fugitive democrats emphasize the processes of experience that create the people, which include acting in the face of uncertainty, failure, taking wrong turns, and running into dead ends. These processes also include the awareness of the many roads not taken.[28] These fugitive experiences together add up to create the political processes we call "the people," but these processes cannot, according to fugitive democrats, be the ground of collective decisions, for they lack clarity, universality, and homogeneity.

For this reason, say the fugitive democrats, the people as a process of experience may renovate political life, but it cannot legitimize the state. For fugitive democracy, a legitimate democratic state is a contradiction in terms. According to Bonnie Honig, for example, the logical impasses implicit in the justification of the state make democratic legitimization impossible. The people exists always in the tension between less-than-legitimate paternalistic institutions, and forms of popular mobilization that lack a precise voice or well-defined edges.[29] This position presupposes that any conception of a democratic people will land you in a logical paradox. It embraces this fact, and in so doing it seeks to affirm and disrupt democracy at the same time.[30]

24. Ibid., 149.
25. Honig, "Between Decision and Deliberation," 9.
26. Wolin, "Fugitive Democracy," 23; Wolin, *Presence of the Past*, 150.
27. Wolin, "Fugitive Democracy," 19, 24.
28. Honig, "Between Decision and Deliberation," 14.
29. According to Bonnie Honig, Rousseau's paradox of politics "points to alternative domains of political work by depriving us of the postulated points of origin (landing us in the conundrum of which comes first, good law or the wisdom of self-governance?) and inviting us to see how . . . law and its authors/subjects fundamentally fail to intersect in the present in ways that satisfy independent standards of legitimation." "Between Decision and Deliberation," 15.
30. Similar views can be found in Keenan, *Democracy in Question;* Markell, "Rule of the People"; and Rancière, *Dis-agreement.*

But this indeterminacy may also be a shortcoming. If democratic politics cannot count on the clarity of collective decisions, and if political movements are beyond the law (and perhaps they *must be* beyond the law), then the people may also threaten collective freedom. Hence accepting the people as a function of change requires that you embrace the risks of instability for the sake of the experience of collective action.

The Dangers of Disruption

Fugitive democrats embrace a conception of the people that emphasizes the ambiguities of politics. In their view, the people is the subject of collective action, but in acting it must always deal with state institutions, and these may pose dangers to individual and collective freedom. Fugitive democracy consciously presses the problem of the indeterminacy of popular unification, disclosing the logical paradoxes in those arguments that try to legitimize the democratic state. This can be productive in situations where the state is already constituted. But it cannot tell us how to proceed when we are looking for either a conception of the people that allows us to legitimize rule, or for a type of political order that averts disaster better than others. Fugitive democracy, then, cannot tell us how to embrace novelty and change without losing the desirable aspects of institutional stability. It tells us to accept uncertainty and risk for the sake of collective action, but it does not tell us how to avert the danger that the "ever-changing people" turns into populist politics.

This danger is particularly clear in a strand of political thought similar to fugitive democracy, one that sees the people in perpetual motion. For Michael Hardt and Antonio Negri, the indeterminacy of popular unification is also the condition that disturbs any claim to legitimacy in the state. In their view, there cannot be a people as the heirs of Locke, Rousseau, and Kant envision that concept. Such a people must be homogenous enough to arrive at the consensus that allows it to make collective decisions. Yet individuals never unify, and hence there cannot be a legitimate popular ground in a legal state. Nonetheless, these authors remain committed to the collective freedom that may emerge among mobile populations, a freedom that, in their words, forms "constellations of singularities and events."[31]

For Hardt and Negri, the people tends toward uniformity and homogeneity, while the "multitude," which they embrace, is an ever-changing and

31. Hardt and Negri, *Empire*, 60.

inconclusive set of relations.[32] Though the multitude, as they see it, cannot legitimize the state, it can realize a version of fugitive democracy. Like others who cherish the idea of collective freedom without institutions, these authors envision democratic political action as naturally harmonious.[33] Without recourse to the traditional resources of a common will crafted by reason, positive law, or a common culture, however, it is hard to determine what precisely coordinates collective action. Whence the harmony? Here it is helpful to examine the parallels between musicians playing in a concert and politically active individuals engaging in collective action. Just as in a concert hall, I argue, political action may need sheet music. Hardt and Negri, by contrast, offer an image of collective participation without sheet music, something like the free-flowing spontaneity of jazz. But even jazz requires common frameworks: good jazz musicians often share years of training, much rehearsal, and the well-known patterns of a musical culture. In the same way, a political community, or a transnational multitude conceived of as a process, must have some common traits. Without any commonalities, the people ends up being defined *against* legal institutions. In the end, what Hardt and Negri see as defining the desirable multitude is its opposition to the sovereign state (or "the empire"). Yet for this very reason, their view of the people as an ever-changing process of open relations cannot legitimize democratic institutions, and it cannot reconcile change and stability.

There is, then, an unresolved tension between change and stability in democratic theory. This tension generates the now familiar dilemma that all scholars who seek to understand and describe the people face: if you try to describe the people as a process, you are torn between the images of the people bound by its legal framework, and of the people as the source of unruly alteration. One extreme works as a foil for the other, such that the two positions become caricatures. On the one hand, the critics of creativity and spontaneity focus on how their rival picture leads to disruption and reinforces the indeterminacy problem. They caricature fugitive democracy as being incompatible with established order. On the other hand, the fugitive critics of constitutionalism focus on how that viewpoint obsesses over problems of stability and exalts unification, which the fugitives claim is anathema to individual freedom. Yet all those who conceive of the people as a process seek to have both change within stability, and stability within change. Why not, then, embrace each in turn?

32. Ibid., 103.
33. Hardt and Negri, *Multitude*, 338–40.

The People in Dualist Democracy

A democratic people grants legitimacy to the state. Yet popular participation in politics does not guarantee the benefits of a stable liberal rule of law, and the law's stability does not always allow for collective freedom. Hence, in order to legitimize the state by appealing to the people, you must conceive of the people in a way that allows both for the development of individual and collective freedom over time, and for change beyond established institutions. Moreover, popular change and stability must remain within the bounds of liberal democratic principles, even if loosely defined.

In this section, I examine Bruce Ackerman's conception of the people in the context of "dualist democracy," because his definition of the people as process has the features described above. But I will argue that his conception of the people as process cannot solve the problem of the indeterminacy of popular unification because it does not fully commit to process. Ackerman's definition trades on the sovereign rupture between norm and exception in a constitutional order, rather than on the transitions between change and stability in a people independent of the sovereign state. Thus, rather than dissolving the problem of popular unification, those legal ruptures actually reproduce it, time and time again.

An Extended Process of Interaction

The main aim of the theory of "dualist democracy," which Ackerman presents in the two volumes of *We the People,* is to provide a framework by which to interpret constitutional changes in the United States. Here, however, I do not discuss the historical aspects of Ackerman's framework, the legitimacy of judicial review, or specific changes to the U.S. Constitution, for I am primarily concerned with the theory's definition of "the people."

Ackerman's definition may look like an afterthought given that it appears first on page 187 of volume 2 of his project. But it is in fact a critical part of his constitutional theory because it gives normative support to the constitutional changes he describes and to which he is committed. Ackerman claims that at historical turning points an energized, proactive population took the political lead and changed the institutional structure of the United States. This view may not seem special: many other scholars attribute agency and responsibility to the people. What makes Ackerman's definition worthy of our attention is the type of entity the definition specifies. In most other political and juridical theories, the people is a collection of individuals. But in Ackerman's "dualist democracy," the people is a process: "'The People' is not the name of a superhuman being, but the name of an extended process of interaction between political elites and ordinary citizens. It is a special process because, during constitutional moments, most ordinary Americans are spending extraordinary amounts of time and energy on the project of citizenship, paying attention to the goings-on in Washington with much greater concern than usual."[34]

The aim of the people ("an extended process of interaction between political elites and ordinary citizens") is thus the transformation of existing institutions. The people authorizes moments of "higher lawmaking," which eventually redefine the constitution by way of institutional actions and juridical decisions. Unlike other changes that occur in the normal course of governing, the changes correlated with periods of popular mobilization are special because they fundamentally reshape institutions. Hence, on Ackerman's account, existing law does not fetter the people.

The people transcends existing institutional frameworks, and thus it may redefine them without completely breaking the state's legal continuity. This means that the people can, in effect, act. Nevertheless, given that the people is not a unified "superhuman being," it does not have reason, will, or voice in the traditional sense. The popular will and its sovereign decisions can only be discerned after the extended process is over, though this may require that judges and legal scholars posses special interpretative abilities. Regardless of what precisely the people said, anyone would be able to tell whether the people is in the process of speaking.

You can recognize the processes that compose the people because they typically follow a series of political events, or what Ackerman calls "phases."[35] These phases consist of the events by which a group demanding change formulates a proposal. The proposal may be approved or rejected in consecutive elections, after extended periods of acute debate and remarkable public awareness. Eventually, the proposal may become law, even if it never becomes a formal constitutional amendment. The process is recognizable because it follows a pattern that has occurred on several occasions throughout U.S. history.[36] According to Ackerman, recognizing the phases in the process allows you to say that "the People spoke."[37]

34. Ackerman's capitalization. Ackerman, *Transformations*, 187.

35. According to Ackerman, the phases of a successful movement are signaling, proposing, triggering, ratifying, and consolidating. See Ackerman's *Foundations*, 266–67, and *Transformations*, 23–25, 66.

36. Most historians would agree that there are "hot" periods in which the public becomes much more involved in politics, but they disagree on which, precisely, these periods are and what the juridical consequences are of the mobilization. Ackerman now recognizes eight cycles of popular mobilization. See "Living Constitution," 1758.

37. Ackerman, *Transformations*, 187.

Thus the people may express its will and voice, and this allows for the development of individual and collective freedom over time. The people produces change without being unduly constrained by institutions. Yet once the process of "higher lawmaking" is over, the people falls back into the shadows. During times of normal politics, politicians make decisions according to established legal procedures. In this way, the people remains within the bounds of liberal democratic principles, as defined by the constitution that frames the changes.

In sum, this conception claims that the people has two modes: at some moments, the people actively forges institutions, while at others it is the passive recipient of legislation, even as it remains a source of collective action in reserve. These two modes incorporate stability and change into Ackerman's theory of constitutional democracy. Hence this conception of the people allows Ackerman to explain how there can be legitimate change within the continuity of the state. It also allows him to explain how there can be normative ground to support the constitution.

As compelling as this conception may at first seem, however, Ackerman's "People" raises difficult questions. If the people is a process, how can individuals rule without the popular unification that initiates the process?

Change and Stability as Norm and Exception

In a liberal democracy the state is legitimate if the people authorizes basic or "higher law." In that case, all can participate in the creation of laws and institutions and thus govern themselves in a meaningful way. That is, they can be autonomous. This means that it is a condition for democracy that the people exist prior to the institutions, or at least be "co-original" with them.[38] This is a problem, however, because a democratic people can exist prior to a constitution only if it is unified, but as I have argued so far, the people cannot unify at any given time. How can Ackerman's conception of the people ground the state's legitimacy even if the people does not unify?

At first it might seem that Ackerman cannot solve this problem, since he appeals to a vision of the past: a pre-political community from which new democratic institutions receive their legitimacy. In this view, this community emerged as a fully formed people from the ashes of the colonial order. He writes, for example, that the "disintegration of the old legality did not reveal a political vacuum. . . . It revealed *a People*, capable of

---

38. I discussed Habermas's argument of co-originality in chapter 4.

organizing their own political affairs."[39] If you think that the original people is the free association of consociates under law that sustains the creation of a radically new government, however, then you will run headfirst into the problem of legitimization and the vicious circle of self-constitution. You will then have to ask where the Founders got the legitimacy to enact the U.S. Constitution. And the answer is, as readers will by now expect, circular.

Ackerman, however, is not tripped up by this problem. He argues that legitimacy does not come from the pre-political people, but rather from the process of deliberation that led up to the constitution's ratification. You may object that this process presupposes the legitimacy of the institutions that enabled deliberation. This is, of course, problematic in the American case, since those institutions were not democratic. They included harsh restrictions on the franchise (only some white males had a right to vote), nondemocratic means of designating constitutional delegates, and the nondemocratic origin of territorial demarcations. Those individuals who created the new government did not constitute the association of all free and equal individuals that Enlightenment philosophy required. Rather, they were a people in the ancient sense: a corporate body with deep roots in the colonies' institutional structure, propped up by a robust collective imaginary and homogenous cultural practices and beliefs.

This objection against the original legitimacy of Ackerman's people seems to have clout because the revolutionaries used images of the past to legitimize the state. They appealed to the imaginary of the English Revolution and to those legal institutions that they envisioned as going back to Magna Carta. Moreover, to the extent that the people had to break away from these grounds of legitimacy, the Founders were in danger of contradiction. If they had relied solely on freedom, equality, and contract, they would have had to deal with the vicious circle of self-constitution. In sum, Ackerman's people cannot be a pre-political ground that enables the creation of legitimate institutions, because it always presupposes the legitimacy of the institutions it destroys.

The persistence of this contradiction, you might think, restates the logical difficulties in any legitimization of democracy. More specifically, you might think that it reveals the strategic (or ideological) value of the concept of "the people" in the project of creating the modern state. The people is "strategic," you may think, because it functions as a conceptual tool to stop the philosophical regress that occurs when you search for a normative

39. Ackerman, *Foundations*, 215.

ground of democratic law. For instance, you need a higher law to legitimize the higher law. You could also argue that the people functions as a device for interrupting the vicious circle of self-constitution that arises in any democratic political order. In short, you might maintain that the people occupies the function of the sovereign, the mystical unified source of legitimate authority in the state. In fact, Ackerman acknowledges as much: "The Federalists brilliantly saw that Radical Whig ideology permitted [the following] answer, . . . in America, the only legitimate sovereign was *the People*, who could delegate different powers to different governments in any way that would serve the common good."[40]

But Ackerman can genuinely avoid the difficulties intrinsic to the concept of sovereignty because in his theory the people is dual. Like medieval European kings, who could be inside the legal order as subjects and outside the legal order as sovereigns because they were both "human by nature and divine by grace,"[41] Ackerman's people can be both inside the legal order as an aggregation of citizens and outside the legal order as a popular sovereign. Ackerman's dualism solves the problems of unified sovereignty just like these medieval theories and classical democratic theories do. Further, it echoes the distinction between the people as constitutive power and constituted power. As constitutive power, the sovereign people is unrestrained by law and its decisions are ultimate. In this view, the sovereign people is the highest source of power and the depositary of the state's authority. Tapping into this power source gives the law legitimacy because this power is the exceptional ground that undergirds juridical normality. In times of judicial normality, one can always justify the law's authority by appealing to the depositary of authority in the people. Hence the constitutive power is the logical requirement of normality and continuity: the anchor for the philosophical regress of authority or self-foundation. For example, the people stops the regress and vicious circle because it remains the unified, ultimate source of authority and last instance of appeal, and it makes decisions in exceptional circumstances. Yet its will is not arbitrary because it remains bound by law at other moments, as constituted power.[42] The people is not only the revolutionary force that sustains the internal coherence of institutions; it is also the subject of those laws given from an exceptional place outside the state. The

---

40. Ibid., 217.
41. Kantorowicz, *The King's Two Bodies*, 52.
42. Even Schmitt's sovereign, who is the product of arbitrary will, remains bound by law because the sovereign is a logical part of the legal order. See Cristi, "Metaphysics of Constituent Power."

duality of the people allows Ackerman to say that there is an inside and an outside of the state (to which the people always belongs), and thus allows him to distinguish juridical normality from constitutional breakdown. Ackerman's dualism can mediate between constitutionalism and democracy because it offers the people as the constitution's ground and unifier.

You might further object that if Ackerman's solution relies on the notion of popular sovereignty, then why is it not liable to exactly the same problems described in chapter 2? I argued there that the divine sovereign cannot solve the difficulties surrounding the creation of the legal order precisely because a rational argument cannot appeal to divine grace to make the sovereign dual. As soon as you dismantle the religious (or mystical) structure of the general will, the problems reemerge.[43] How can Ackerman avoid this problem?

Unlike classical theories of popular sovereignty, Ackerman's dualist democracy holds that no*body* expresses sovereign decisions in the people's name. In his account, sovereignty is not some*body's* exceptional decision; rather the sovereign is the people as process.[44] When the sovereign is a process, the logical difficulties that haunt other theories do not arise. For example, you do not need to bend the laws of logic or introduce other mystical subterfuges to claim that a *process* is both inside and outside the legal order. If different stages of a process occur at different times without severing the process's continuity, it makes perfect sense to say that the people is both legislator and subject of the law. Once you introduce the notion of process, sovereignty loses the rigidity and the coercive arbitrariness often associated with it. And yet sovereignty retains the capacity to solve the logical problems associated with the state's foundation and legitimization. The people as process can solve the paradoxes of sovereignty without stripping individuals of their autonomy because the decisions of creating, changing, and governing institutions occur within the process itself, thus allowing genuine self-government. The people as process governs itself over time, and therefore the people does not depend on a founding moment or on the legitimate association of the original group. In this view, the people accompanies the institutions as they both extend through time.

A Distinct Popular Voice and the Problem of Closure

Ackerman's people as process promises to solve the problems that arise in the traditional theory of the sovereign state. On this theory, there can be

43. For an argument showing the links between the social contract's sovereign and the traditional, religiously sanctioned sovereign, see Riley, *General Will Before Rousseau*, and Riley, *Will and Political Legitimacy*.

44. As I argue in the next section, however, this cannot be a closed process.

sovereignty without coercion because the people is not a "superhuman being," and thus the people can be sovereign even if it is never unified. Yet dualist democracy does not fully embrace process. In Ackerman's view, the people is a closed process that finishes after it speaks. Rather than having a continuous identity open to time and the contingency of the future, Ackerman's people progresses by determinate jumps and complete cycles. The people consists of discrete periods of mobilization, each of which demands closure in order to determine what the people has said. And with this closure comes the need for a decisive sovereign will.

To this objection, Ackerman might reply that he is not offering a normative theory, but rather an empirical one: a historical account of events as they occurred. It is true that Ackerman's idea of discrete periods of popular mobilization fits historical experience. There have been moments of exceptional political effervescence in American history, where wide sectors of the population shared a specific agenda. Yet while such moments recur periodically, they cannot be shown to be closed or self-contained as Ackerman would have them be.[45] Ackerman requires that these moments have clear beginnings and endings, and that they follow the phases he describes, because he is mostly concerned with the outcome of the process (i.e., with specific legislation that can be considered an amendment to the constitution). For this reason, he also requires that the people speak with a unified voice.

But what Ackerman does when he introduces the people as process, he undoes by requiring closed cycles with a determinate outcome. Introducing the indeterminacy of time into the people can tell us how the people rules without the need for consensus at a given moment. The demand that we know precisely what the people said and when the cycle began and ended, however, is tantamount to demanding a decision at an exceptional moment. The determinacy required to establish the outcome of the process requires a commanding will that overrides conflicting opinions and ongoing debate.

Time could solve the problem of how to legitimize the state as the people's composition changes. Ackerman's cycles, however, complicate the problem rather than ease it. In his view, time is not continuous. Instead, it consists of independent moments. Between each cycle there are radical breaks, both in the symbolic sense and in the actual organization of political relations in the state. The problem is that when processes proceed by

---

45. There have been eight "turns of the wheel," or complete cycles of popular sovereignty: "whatever the fate of particular movements, the cyclical pattern recurs and recurs." Ackerman, "Living Constitution," 1758.

jumps between change and stability, they multiply the instances wherein you require such precise determination. These moments become identical with a moment of popular unification. For example, as I argued in the previous section, in the original moment of constitutional founding the difficulty consists in determining whether there is a people with the authority to found a state. If the people is a collection of individuals, we can only know if they have legitimacy when they are unified in their consent. If instead the people is a process, then we do not have to find a single moment of agreement on a single issue. This agreement can occur over time, as people debate and one opinion becomes more accepted than others.

By contrast, if, like Ackerman, you need to find out what precisely was said in a cycle of popular sovereignty, then you demand a final decision and a closure to the cycle. For all practical matters, this demand reproduces the indeterminacy problem. Rather than having to determine whether the people has the authority to found the state in the time of origin, you must determine whether the people has authority to make decisions during each of many moments of "higher lawmaking." In dualist democracy, you still require moments of unification, but rather than needing one moment of foundation that gives legitimacy once and for all, you have many over history. The problem is that without a collection of individuals to give closure through a consensus, now we need a sovereign decision that determines the people's will. Neither option, however, can bring legitimacy to the state.

This problem may be easier to convey with an image. Imagine, for the sake of this argument, that the popular consent that legitimizes the constitution is an instance of unified popular will. Now, symbolize this moment with a perfect solid sphere, a round pearl. In traditional theories of constitutional founding, this pearl is the starting point of historical legitimacy and continuity (imagine this continuity as a tight string extending through time). The temporal string extends from the moment of foundation to the future. Hence those constitutional theories that derive legitimacy from the moment of founding look like a single pearl pierced by a string that itself extends far into the future. In contrast, constitutional dualism looks like a long string of pearls: each moment of unification is represented by a pearl linked by shorter or longer pieces of string (representing periods of normal politics). In this theory, instead of having one intractable moment of popular unification, you have as many moments of popular unification as there are pearls in the string.

Why this need for closure? Ackerman's demand to know the precise phases and outcome of the cycle follows from the intricacies of his constitutional theory. Particularly, it follows from his need to give an authoritative voice and a precise formulation to those illegal acts and unwritten laws that acquire the status of constitutional amendments, as well as from the need to give meaning, direction, and normative content to a process that otherwise would be morally random. To give meaning to the process, the exceptional moments must be surrounded by long periods of stability of codified law and buttressed by the legitimacy of the constitution. Without these moments and this authoritative voice, the population within Ackerman's theory could never enjoy the normal politics that guarantees stability and continuity. Unfortunately, those moments remain instances of unjustified will: the will of the interpreter of the constitution, or of the scholar who claims to know when the popular movement ended.

Dualist democracy introduces the idea of process, but ultimately it resembles those theories that ground the state's legitimacy in a unified people. The problem, I believe, is that the theory does not take the idea of process seriously enough. On Ackerman's view, the interplay between change and stability is dualistic rather than processual. Instead of a continuous progression of relations and events that influence one another, Ackerman's view of the people is still one of a chain of moments wherein partial aggregation of individual wills occur.

All constitutional theories I considered here acknowledge that they must take change seriously if the people is to legitimize the state. But they do not state what precisely is a process, and they do not specify why the people as process (rather than a people conceived as an aggregation of individual wills) should be conceived as a normative foundation for democracy. In the end, these theories embrace the standard account of popular sovereignty: they ultimately hold that the people must have one voice at a given time.

Conclusion

The tension between change and stability remains a problem not only for constitutional theory but also for those theories that conceive of the people as a process in order to legitimize the state. Those theorists who demand stability cannot appeal to the people as a source of legitimacy, for the people changes constantly. Conversely, those theorists who demand pure change cannot tell you how changing, creative individuals find the means to coordinate their actions without the help of stable institutional structures. Moreover, those theorists who, like Ackerman, want to preserve both change and stability end up preserving the problems on both ends.

Constitutional theories find it very difficult to reconcile change and stability. They treat change as equivalent to chaos and make stability a synonym for order. They find it difficult to see that there are stable disorders, just as they find it difficult to envision harmonic change. Dualist democracy, in turn, cannot solve the problem of popular unification because its commitment to process is lukewarm. Rather than embracing continuous change, dualist democracy posits a series of breaks. Instead of dissolving the problem, dualist democracy makes things such that each individual instance of popular sovereignty reproduces the paradoxes of legitimacy over and over again. Dualist constitutional theories try to conceive of the people as a collective identity extending over time, but they ultimately retain the traditional view of the people as a collection of individual wills. Hence they likewise retain the prejudices about change that plague the traditional view of the people.

Given all this, it seems that we need to recover the people as the agent of self-organization. To do this, however, we cannot define the people via the law. That is, we cannot define it as within the law or as the law's abstract negation. A self-organizing people must encompass change and stability without breaks. It needs to include both legality and changes that transcend law, all in one thrust of continuous, coordinated development. To do this we need a full-fledged theory of the people as a process.

A full commitment to process promises to bring together change and stability in a single idea of harmonic development. This idea accounts for both acceleration and deceleration of the rates of change. As I shall show in chapter 6, we can realize this promise and legitimize the state by appeal to a thoroughly processual theory. But we can only do this by determining what precisely is a process, why the people is a process, and why a democratic process is desirable in its own right, independent of its outcome or that which it denies. Hence, in the next chapter, I turn to process philosophy in order to show how process provides harmonic development and avoids the dilemma of change and stability. I also consider how processes can be self-creative. Finally, in chapter 7, I show how a democratic process can provide a normative ground that arises from the process itself, rather than from aggregate consent at a particular moment in time or from commitment to a written document.

6

Creative Freedom and the People as Process

As I have argued throughout this book, you cannot legitimize the state by relying on the unified will of a people. The people and its will never unify: the people conceived as a collection of individuals is always indeterminate. This indeterminacy is clear in the unified-will legitimizations of democracy, since these attempts to legitimize democracy produce a vicious circle between the unified people that should create institutions, and the legitimate institutions that bring the people about. But indeterminacy also plagues the unified-will theory's very conception of the people because unless you find an original unification, you cannot determine the people's boundaries or understand its continuity in time. This raises the following question: could you dissolve the logical problems surrounding democratic legitimization if you had a more accurate conception of the people?

As I argued in the previous chapter, conceiving of the people as a process promises to do just that. Intuitively, it makes sense to appeal to process in order to dissolve the vicious circle between citizens and institutions. The circularity dissolves as soon as you consider that the people evolves over time. After all, a chicken-and-egg problem disappears when you bring time to bear on it, and indeed, even *the* chicken-and-egg problem vanishes entirely. No one expects to find an original chicken or an original egg in the process of the evolution of species because the two terms dissolve into the organic forms that preceded them. But let us not take this analogy too far. In the case of the real chicken-and-egg problem, we have a coherent evolutionary theory at our disposal. In our case, by contrast, there is no processual theory of the democratic people ready at hand.

This all suggests that we need a processual theory of peoplehood. In chapter 4, I looked to Habermas's theory of dynamic constitutionalism for a solution to the indeterminacy problem, but I found that his theory fails in this regard. Habermas's dynamic view still relies on popular unification, albeit displaced in historical time. Dynamic constitutionalism, like most other versions of liberal democratic theory, relies either on images of a people unified by cultural traits emerging from a misty past, or on the promise of a universally agreed-on democracy to come at an unspecified moment in the future. These images of the past and visions of the future still demand a moment of popular unification. In chapter 5, I examined Ackerman's view of the people as an institutionalized process occurring between ordinary citizens and governing elites. This view of the people as process does solve the problem of a static origin in the constitutional state. But it also introduces a sharp duality between change and stability, wherein each moment of higher lawmaking is made equivalent to a new beginning. As a result, this view reintroduces all the difficulties of popular unification.

In this chapter I propose a different, full-blooded theory of the people as process. A people, according to this theory, is *an unfolding series of events coordinated by the practices of constituting, governing, and changing a set of institutions. These institutions are the highest authority for all those individuals intensely affected by these events and these institutions.* Within this process, there exists what I call "creative freedom": the aim that partly coordinates the becoming of such a people. I then argue that this definition of the people as process can help us individuate different peoples. In the next chapter, I show that this conception of the people can solve the problem of how to legitimize the state democratically as the people's composition changes.

I develop my argument for this theory of the people as process in two parts. In the first part, I examine the nature of processes and explain how process philosophy can help us develop a theory of peoplehood. To do this I develop the insights of Henri Bergson, Alfred North Whitehead, and Nicholas Rescher. I argue that a process is a series of events unfolding in coordination, where this coordination is a self-creative aim. I call the self-creative aim that coordinates events in specific types of processes, such as persons and peoples, creative freedom. In the second part, I present my theory of the people as process, describing the main constituents of peoples and specifying how to tell one people from another. I discuss the origin and the end of peoples as process, as well as where their boundaries lie.

Process

Many contemporary theories claim that the people is a process. This is true of the dynamic constitutionalism I discussed in chapter 4 and of the dualist democracy I discussed in chapter 5. But how can the interaction among ordinary citizens and elites, or between free-floating discourses and institutions, claim legitimacy without an original moment of unity? How can there be citizens before there is a state? How can this process tell us who counts as the "we" in "We the People"? Theories of dynamic constitutional change leave us wondering what precisely a process is, how one process differs from another, what the limits of a given process are, and why a process can avoid the indeterminacy problem. The notion of a people as process provided by these theories seems promising, but it does not answer these questions.

The theories that describe the people as a process adopt this view partly to ease the fears of critics of popular sovereignty. These critics envision the sovereign as the image in the frontispiece of Hobbes's *Leviathan:* a monstrous person towering over all individuals as ultimate and absolute ruler. These critics, such as Stephen Holmes, often fear the power of majorities, worry about collectivism, and doubt that the people can exist at all if it is not created and constrained by external procedures and institutions.[1] They are particularly wary of a people that endangers individual rights, which they construe as a superhuman with absolute power.[2] The people as process dissolves these fears by appeal to the pacific interplay and sustained deliberation of individuals engaged in politics.

But even if describing the people as a process can help to ease the fears of those who imagine the sovereign people as a many- or single-headed monster absorbing millions of individual wills, we are still left wondering what precisely is this "people as process." In this respect, even the most elaborate processual accounts of the people in time are sadly wanting. For example, in *Freedom and Time,* Jed Rubenfeld espouses an account of the people as an agent existing continuously over time. In defending this account, however, he does not give us anything more than an argument from the negative. All he tells us is that individualist theories are also quite lost when it comes to defining a free individual, the basic metaphysical assumption of their theories. In defense of his view, Rubenfeld can say only that alternative theories suffer the same difficulty he does: it is hard

---

1. Holmes, *Passions and Constraint,* 9.
2. Ackerman, *Transformations,* 187.

to justify a metaphysical claim. "To recognize a people as a subject persisting over time, despite the heterogeneity of its composition," says Rubenfeld, "is ultimately no more mystical than recognizing individuals as subjects persisting over time despite the heterogeneity of their composition."[3] But an appeal to the equally mystical crutches of the opponent's argument hardly amounts to a strong defense of one's claim. A defense of agency over time requires that constitutional and political theorists take identity over time seriously, metaphysical grounds and all.[4] Process philosophy provides these grounds.[5]

It makes sense to take process seriously if you wish to uphold the value of creative change. This is particularly true if you seek a theory of state legitimacy that is compatible with popular consent, with each individual's lived experience of time, and with the incomplete determinacy of nature. But in order to cash in on the promises of process, you cannot simply repeat a static moment over and over again, expecting all the while that the difficulties will vanish. This strategy only succeeds in displacing in historical time the problem of popular indeterminacy. Rather than conceiving of process as a string of static moments, and thus multiplying the problems in the present by as many occasions as there are moments on your temporal string, processual thinking requires that you reorder some

---

3. Rubenfeld, *Freedom and Time*, 158.

4. This incursion into metaphysics, of course, stands in sharp contrast with John Rawls's view of what is required from a political philosophy. See Rawls, "Justice as Fairness." For Rawls, the formulation of a conception of justice does not need a prior discussion of controversial metaphysical claims. His conception is political and "freestanding," for it claims not to rely on controversial philosophical or religious views about universal truth, or about the nature and identity of persons. But Rawls can only afford to bracket these difficult questions because he relies on an implicit overlapping consensus in a given people. Rawls acknowledges that the metaphysical discussions of personal identity that bear on his political philosophy pose "profound questions on which past and current philosophical views widely differ, and surely will continue to differ. For this reason it is important to try to develop a political conception of justice which avoids this problem as far as possible" (406). But what happens when the principles embedded in the public culture undermine the legitimacy of the state and the very people? Or when the principles are not already embedded in this public culture? My view is that when you reach the problem of popular unification, it is *impossible* to develop adequate political conceptions without incursions into metaphysics. Under such conditions, a theoretical solution to the problem of the state's legitimacy cannot be freestanding. It will have to acknowledge its metaphysical grounds. Thus a discussion of the nature of the people is necessarily metaphysical rather than just political. Rawls's political liberalism cannot guide us here. Hence it is better to make these metaphysical incursions as clear as possible rather than hiding them in the background.

5. Process is only one among many metaphysical doctrines of material, personal, and collective identity over time (i.e., persistence). In fact, the most common doctrines are not process but rather perdurantism and endurantism, which, unlike process, presuppose the doctrine of "temporal parts." See Haslanger and Kurtz, *Persistence*.

basic metaphysical categories. Specifically, you have to make the ideas of "relation" and "event" central. To do this well, however, requires help from process philosophy.

Process philosophy is "a system of general ideas in terms of which every element of our experience can be interpreted."[6] In short, it is a general theory of the basic structure of reality. Such a philosophy can help to produce specific theories about different aspects of experience, and it allows us to give a more precise account of what it means to persist in time, and of how a people (or an individual) may preserve their identity as time goes by. It can also provide grounds for other philosophical views, including those that tell you how you ought to behave or how you ought to organize political life. In sum, I claim that adopting process philosophy can do much for political philosophy. But to make good on this promise I cannot personally argue for all aspects of processualism. In the following pages, therefore, I will rely on the insights of a tradition that encompasses Leibniz, Hegel, Nietzsche, Peirce, Bergson, James, Whitehead, Deleuze, and Rescher,[7] though I lean mostly on Bergson,[8] Whitehead,[9] and particularly Rescher.[10] To be clear, I do not attempt to summarize their systems of thought or to offer a critical analysis of their theories. Instead, in what follows I reconstruct some of their arguments so as to explain why the people is better conceived as a process rather than as a thing (an aggregation of individuals), and why conceiving the people as a process can solve some of the problems caused by the indeterminacy of popular unification.

Process Philosophy

Process philosophy makes time, creativity, and change the basic categories of metaphysics.[11] This viewpoint stands in sharp contrast with the dominant metaphysical viewpoint, which begins from the substance of static

6. Whitehead, *Process and Reality*, 3. For interpretations of Whitehead's views, see Schilpp, *Philosophy of Alfred North Whitehead*, and Weber, *Whitehead's Pancreativism*.

7. We may in fact be talking about two traditions: a Continental European tradition that includes Leibniz, Hegel, Nietzsche, Bergson, and Deleuze, and culminates in contemporary accounts of reality as becoming; and an Anglo-American tradition, beginning with the pragmatists Peirce and James and moving on to Whitehead, Hartshorne, Rescher, and contemporary process philosophy. (Of course, the two traditions overlap and crisscross.)

8. See Bergson's *Creative Evolution, Time and Free Will, The Creative Mind, The Two Sources of Morality and Religion*, and *Matter and Memory*.

9. See Whitehead's *Adventures of Ideas, Modes of Thought, Process and Reality*, and *Science and the Modern World*.

10. Rescher, *Process Metaphysics*; Rescher, *Process Philosophy*; Weber, *After Whitehead*.

11. This section is broadly taken from Rescher's accounts of process philosophy in *Process Metaphysics* and "Replies."

things. Those who hold that process is basic come to this position after realizing that there are many real phenomena that cannot be reduced to physical things, like waves, droughts, storms, loud noises, or cold seasons.[12] It is easy to pick out "things" when itemizing the contents of a cupboard, but it is much harder to do so when talking about global warming, personal relations, or ideologies. Indeed, the need for tools for describing these parts of reality is particularly obvious in the social world, where processes, events, and occurrences are more common, and more important, than physical things.

Processes are not unique to process philosophy, of course. Many other theories and doctrines also recognize their importance. But in process philosophy, processes are as basic as, and perhaps even more basic than, things. It emphasizes such terms and categories as creativity, activity, relation, alteration, striving, novelty, emergence, and becoming. It holds that these are fundamental to understanding and explaining the world. Hence one of the main characteristics of process philosophy is that it is precise about specifying relations but imprecise about specifying limits, beginnings, and endings. The items it deals with are often fuzzy and best grasped as probabilities rather than generalizations. As a result, process metaphysics is well suited for dealing with entities in statistical terms, and it harmonizes with many contemporary theories in psychology, the social sciences, evolutionary biology, and physics.[13]

The degree to which process philosophy can encompass and undergird these other theories, however, depends on how you envision the changes that make up processes. Some process philosophers see such changes as products of the nature of cognition (e.g., William James), others, as provided by the nature of life (e.g., Darwin), and yet others, as products of the nature of matter (e.g., quantum physicists). A full-blooded processualist view, like Whitehead's or Bergson's, commits to all these claims. In that view, all matter, life, and cognition are related in nesting and crisscrossing processes that extend through time.

To develop a processualist political philosophy, and more specifically a processualist theory of the people, I need not argue that processes are a product of cognition, the nature of life, or the nature of all material reality. I need only claim that processes are fundamental entities of social life. The changes in the social world may well be a function of other, more fundamental processes in life and nature (a view shared by many of the

12. Rescher, Process Metaphysics.
13. See Decock, "Taming of Change."

philosophers mentioned above). Nevertheless, my own claim is more modest. I will argue, with the help of process philosophy, that a people is a process, by which I mean that a people is a series of events unfolding in coordination, where the coordination involves a self-creative aim.

The terms used here to define the idea of "process" themselves need clarification. In what follows, I will explain them, approaching it backward by first describing what process is not.

What Process Is Not

The most common objection to process thinking is that if everything is in flux, then identity is impossible. But a process, as I construe it here, is not the constant, boundless flux of nature associated with Heraclitus's view that everything flows (*panta rhei*). Holding that the world is in eternal flux denies the stability of anything: nothing ever persists, and nothing can be expected or predicted. This view goes against common sense and scientific practice, and also against the views of most process philosophers. This has not stopped critics of process philosophy, however, from saddling processualism with this caricature.

Perhaps the most important such caricature is Plato's, since he was the most famous opponent of process thought. This is the view that Socrates mocks in Plato's *Cratylus*[14] and ascribes to Protagoras, Heraclitus, Empedocles, and Homer in Plato's *Theaetetus*.[15] In this latter dialogue, Socrates summarizes the philosophy of flux thus: "I am about to speak of a high argument, in which all things are said to be relative; you cannot rightly call anything by any name, such as great or small, heavy or light, for the great will be small and the heavy light—there is no single thing or quality, but out of motion and change and admixture all things are becoming relatively to one another, which 'becoming' is by us incorrectly called being, but is really becoming, for nothing ever is, but all things are becoming."[16]

Unlike the thinkers in Socrates's caricature, however, those who embrace process do not deny being, stability, or the possibility of self-identity. For one thing, becoming can explain being, but the reverse is not true. According to Whitehead, for example, "*How* an actual entity *becomes*

14. "No man of sense will . . . be confident in any knowledge which condemns himself and other existences to an unhealthy state of unreality; he will not believe that all things leak like a pot, or imagine that the world is a man who has a running at the nose." Plato, *Cratylus*, 338.

15. Plato, *Theaetetus*, 206.

16. Ibid.

constitutes *what* that actual entity *is,* so that the two descriptions of an actual entity are not independent. Its 'being' its constituted by its 'becoming.'"[17] Process philosophy thus allows you to interpret entities from the standpoint of change as well as from the standpoint of stability. For example, process philosophy would not deny that the people *is* recognizable as a people at different moments in time, if you accept that an entity like the people may be changing constantly. According to processualism, we can hold that there *is* a people while also holding that the people changes in relation to other external entities, and in relation to the entities it comprises. These changes may arise when the individuals in the group change, but also because there are changes among and within individuals. In any case, to hold that these changes are more basic than the people is not to deny that the people is real and persists as a single entity over time.

Moreover, process philosophy does not deny self-identity. It recognizes that some entities, such as numbers, are eternally perduring objects. These are fixed and always self-identical. But many entities we encounter in everyday life are better conceived of as ever-changing processes rather than fixed, self-identical things. This is apparent in most things that undergo decay and change through time, and it is certainly true of those entities we encounter in politics, like the people. Yet this does not mean that we cannot recognize these processes as one entity for as long as they last. Processes have an internal structure that coordinates the events that occur within them. Hence we can recognize and individuate changing entities like persons and institutions as time passes, even if they do not resemble their former selves. Processes, then, may be individuated.

A philosophy of pure flux would be as useless for political theory as one requiring that political entities always be perfectly identical to themselves. In political philosophy, a view that denies being, stability, or self-identity could not help you solve the problems generated by the people's lack of determinate boundaries, by the lack of fit between the constitution and the people's current opinion, or by the vicious circle of self-foundation. Those problems would simply not arise in a Heraclitean philosophy. We would not be able to see continuity in a people, boundaries among peoples, or the founding of a people because such a philosophy could not account for the idea of a people at all. In sum, a philosophy of pure flux is not a useful metaphysical basis for political philosophy, and I want to make clear that process philosophy is *not* such a view.

There is a second distinction to be made: process is not procedure. A procedure specifies a method by which an actor may obtain a type of

17. Whitehead, *Process and Reality,* 23.

result—in other words, it is an algorithm. In contrast, the type of process we seek to explore, and which is the main concern of the social sciences, is different from applied procedure; the processes that interest us here are *self-creative*. A procedure's result is the purpose of following the procedure. A procedure thus requires a determinate outcome. The social processes that concern us, in contrast, are processes whose futures are indeterminate. In these processes, the coordination (or structure) arises from the constraints set by previous events and an aim set internally. But the final product of these processes cannot be known in advance because the very circumstances that constitute the process change as it unfolds. Good examples are organic growth and social development: these are processes, not procedures.

In political theory, the distinction between a process and a procedure matters; while positing that the people is a procedure may help us define the people, this cannot help us to solve the problems associated with this concept. If a process were solely a procedure, it could not help us legitimize the democratic state. A justificatory theory of democracy based on the idea of people as a procedure would claim that a state is legitimate when it is defined by a particular method for producing an outcome. The outcome in this case is self-rule or democracy. This view would then assume that a democratic procedure provides the necessary steps for obtaining democratic political decisions. Establishing a constitution and installing democratic procedures through which individuals could express their opinions and aggregate them would count as democratic legitimization. But such a procedure would strip the people of their capacity to decide on matters *of* the method. That is, a procedural account could not justify democratic procedures democratically, given that the goal is set in advance and is external to the individuals who undergo the procedure. To this extent, proceduralism could not show that there is popular consent on the basic assumptions (the procedure), and hence it could not show that the government is legitimate in democratic terms. Taking the people as the product of a procedure thus takes for granted the legitimacy of the procedure itself, and thereby restates the indeterminacy problem.

Definition of Process and Its Constituent Parts

In the previous section I explained what a process is not. In this section and the next I specify three key features of processes before presenting my processual theory of the people. If a process is a dynamic entity constituted by a series of events unfolding in coordination, where what does the coordinating is a self-creative aim, it is useful to sort out what process philosophy means by the terms "events," "coordination," and "self-creation."

An event is an occurrence, a happening.[18] Given that an event occupies a particular time and place, it is a concrete entity. But it is only identical to itself if it happens at the same place and time; hence events are one of a kind. Yet even though they are concrete, events are not like things, because their spatiotemporal locations are fuzzy. For example, it is clear that my cup (a thing) is now sitting next to my computer monitor. It has a clear spatiotemporal location. But when something occurs, the boundaries of the event are not so clear. For example, consider an event in which an election takes place and a candidate becomes president-elect. Where precisely does this happen? Saying that it occurs in the country in question cannot compare in precision to stating the coordinates of my cup.[19] And when does the election happen? When the first candidate began thinking about launching his campaign? When all votes are finally counted, one by one? The limits of this event are not well defined, and in this it is like most social events (e.g., a wedding, the ending of a war, or the founding of a state).

Yet what we lose in spatiotemporal precision, we can gain in clarity when using events to describe or analyze the social world. The concept of event allows us to describe social facts as activities and relations rather than substances or essences, and hence allows us to be more precise. Substances and essences are often too abstract and vague to describe concrete cases. Consider the case of personal identity: if a person is a series of events, rather than a thing, you can understand who this person *is* by *what* she *does, how* she does it, *where* she does it, and *whom* she does it *with*. On this conception, her identity is a set of characteristic activities and relations. On processual principles, what we do defines who we are.[20]

For instance, according to the philosophy of being, I would define my identity in terms of being. I *am* a Mexican woman. But the problem with this is that if I say I *am* a Mexican woman, I am not saying much about myself. There are about fifty-five million people scattered all over the world

18. A processual social ontology like the one I develop here does not require a nuanced definition of the concept of event. But it is worth noting that among metaphysicians there are discussions of whether we should consider events as abstract entities (having propositional form) or as four-dimensional objects. See Casati and Varzi, *Events*.

19. See Kim, "Causation, Nomic Subsumption, and the Concept of Event."

20. Rescher, *Process Metaphysics*, 111; Whitehead, *Process and Reality*, 23. Perhaps Gilles Deleuze's dissolution of identity into difference and repetition could be interpreted this way as well. See Deleuze, *Difference and Repetition*.

who satisfy that description, and these individuals have little in common. But if I tell you, instead, that I did and saw certain things in particular company and in a particular place as I was growing up, that I learned certain facts and habits, and I played certain games, then you have more precise information about me.[21] In general, describing events or sets of events in somebody's life gives more precise information about them than enouncing their identity. After all, what tells us more about a person is what this person *has done*. We know someone if we know about their career, their habits, and their relations. (That we gain in precision by focusing on activity rather than essence is well known by politicians and marketing experts, who prefer to think of individuals by their activities rather than their set identities. For example, "soccer moms" are defined by what they do rather than by who they *are*. Saying that a person is a Volvo driver, churchgoer, charity giver, or martini drinker is more precise than saying that he is middle-class, black, young, or a Republican.)

But how do the events that constitute a process relate to one another such that one can use them instead of identity? They are related in this manner because they are coordinated. In general, coordination means harmonious adjustment, or more precisely, the harmonious adjustment of the events within a process. That events are coordinated means that a series of events does not unfold randomly: recurring events establish a pattern over time. This pattern allows us to individuate different kinds of processes and concrete instantiations thereof. For example, the sun's appearance on the horizon is an event, normally followed by a sequence of appearances of the sun, which is a series of events. The predictable pattern of ever-rising appearances above the horizon coordinates the series. The coordinated series of events is a process: the sunrise I observe. There are different kinds of patterns corresponding to types of processes, such as processes of development where predictable successive stages occur over a period of time (chickens becoming hens), or homogeneous processes where there is a stable frequency in repetition (water continuously flowing under a bridge). The type of pattern allows you to establish what kind of process you encounter (say, a wedding), while the concrete

---

21. Take another example: I could also say that I *am* a processualist political theorist. But that description is misleading, since I *am* as much of a Latin American historian as I am a processualist political theorist. Moreover, somebody might object that, given the quality of my work, I *am* neither. I could reply that I *am*, too! Both! Then the discussion would turn on what counts as being one or the other, and eventually on a discussion of the essence of the theorist or the historian. By contrast, I could also tell you that I have written about processes in political theory and researched topics in Mexican history. Because I gave this last bit of information in terms of *events*, it is more precise and less controversial.

instantiation and specific characteristics of the series of events allow you to individuate specific processes (our wedding in Vermont on June 23, 2007). In sum, each pattern, and hence each actual process, is the function of a particular coordination of events.

But where does this coordination come from? At first, it might seem that processes have an intrinsic abstract form that a series of events together actualize, and so there must be some static universal form that predates the events. One could thus object that if the form of the people is a static reference preceding the actual events that constitute the people as process, then the people must actualize this static reference in a way that gives little room to individual agency. Thus such a people as process would not differ much from a people driven by an image of the past or a vision of the future, similar to those I discussed in chapter 4. Yet coordination is not a cause for concern when defining a people as process because the coordination (the form of the process) does not predate the events in question. The coordination is not an eternal or static form waiting to be actualized; rather, it is always the result of concrete occurrences.[22]

The coordination of a process can come from three sources: conceptual goals, causal constraints, and randomness. Think of the process of getting fit. You go running every morning and go on a diet. Every running session and meager meal constitutes one in a series of nonrandom events: they are coordinated by your goal of getting fit. A conceptual goal is an aim a person who initiates a process tries to attain. So "getting fit" is a conceptual goal, but concepts are not static: they themselves are conceptual processes that change over time. (Your idea of fitness is probably not the same as your mother's, or your own idea of fitness before you actually tried to exercise.) Moreover, your goal and your willingness to attain it are not the only links between events. Other events that occurred in the past also constrain the process. These are causal constraints. For example, you were in terrible shape before beginning, and you came up with the idea of fitness because you are a particular kind of person, surrounded by other people, living in particular circumstances. Finally, random events, such as

---

22. According to Whitehead, the coordination of events within a process allows you to say that processual entities have form, but this is just "a possible way in which process can be actualized, conditioned by that which occurred before." *Science and the Modern World,* 19. This can be interpreted in at least two different ways. You could say that coordination comes from the static form of a general process that predates individual processes. In that case you need something like a static form or Platonic universal. Alternatively, you could say that the general process of which this concrete process is an instantiation is itself a conceptual process occurring over time and therefore subject to change. I favor the second interpretation.

twisting an ankle or finding a great coach, may frustrate or enhance the unfolding of the process.

It is also worth considering that the main source of coordination need not be a conscious goal. Individual processes, for instance, can be coordinated by unconscious drives, external conscious aims, or physical constraints. This is particularly clear in natural and physical processes. For example, only physical forces coordinate a hurricane. But the coordination in an animal life is a life cycle, which is constrained by genetic information, physical surroundings, social pressures, individual choices, and death. Likewise, social events or social processes may occur without the direction of a conscious aim. Yet they are also not disordered, but rather follow discernible patterns. Think, for example, of the movement of a mob, the spread of a rumor, or the harmonizing of fashion trends. The best examples of coordination without a conscious goal are market tendencies. In markets, the series of events that lead to economic depressions or boom periods follow the constraints of the events that have taken place before, as well as trends determined by the correlation of countless individual aims (some more dominant than others). Hence the events that constitute a process can be distinguished as instances of longer tendencies driven by aims and determined by past constraints. In short, if you think of conceptual goals as a final causal constraint, then coordination amounts to causal constraints, both efficient and final, as well as randomness.

The third key feature of processes is the idea of self-creative aim, or self-coordination. I discuss this idea in the next section.

Creativity and Novelty

To explain how a process can be self-creative, we first have to explain a general feature of process philosophy: creativity. Creativity is what drives processes and produces change. For Whitehead and Bergson, whose arguments I follow here, creativity is the foundation of all processes. It presupposes the incomplete determinacy of nature as well as the emergence of novelty as time goes by.[23] In their view, as time passes, novel events always occur, and hence processes cannot be completely determined by past events. Processes create novelty as they occur, and thus they are not yet complete as they unfold. In this sense processes are unlike things, which

---

23. Bergson, *Creative Evolution*, 141–49; Whitehead, *Adventures of Ideas*, 177–80; Whitehead, *Process and Reality*, 21. For recent analyses of Bergson's views, see Marrati, "Time, Life, Concepts," and Widder, *Reflections on Time and Politics*. For analysis of Whitehead's views, see Weber, *Whitehead's Pancreativism*.

are supposed to be completely determined because they are complete at any given moment.

But how can there be incomplete determinacy if present events are a function of the past? Couldn't we predict exactly how a process will unfold if we had complete information of what occurred before?[24] According to process philosophers, an event is never completely determined because it is not only a function of the past; as part of an ongoing process, an event also depends on the undetermined future. Within a process, any given event is (to a large extent) determined, but the process itself is not completely determined because subsequent events within the series are yet to come. And when they do occur, they may alter the general character of the process. But since events are part of the process, a change to the whole process can also change its constituent events. Hence any given event within a process is never completely determined. Current events within the process are not completely closed to the future because subsequent events in the series may alter them retrospectively.[25]

The possibility of altering something that has already occurred may seem strange, for it amounts to changing the past from the standpoint of the future. Yet it is not strange if you think of change within an extended, continuous process. Consider, for example, how the last word of a sentence you utter can change the meaning of the first word, even though the event of uttering the first word has already occurred and is in all other respects gone. For instance, if you hear me utter the word "United," and in a subsequent event I enounce the word "States," the second event will affect the previous events differently than if I had said the word "Nations" instead. The first event was to a large extent, though not totally, determined by previous events. In other words, in an event "everything that is determinable is determined, but not everything is determined."[26] We could say, with Whitehead, that in any given event, prior causal determination does not exhaust the causes of a subsequent event. There is always a remainder for a decision, either a conscious decision or one by inherent tendencies in nature.[27] This tendency is creativity, "the throbbing emotion

---

24. As Bergson says, "The essence of mechanical explanation, in fact, is to regard the future and the past as calculable functions of the present, and thus to claim that *all is given*. On this hypothesis, past, present and future would be open at a glance to a superhuman intellect capable of making the calculation." *Creative Evolution*, 37.

25. This characteristic will be especially relevant when we seek to solve the problem of founding a democratic state within a democratic process (chap. 7).

26. Pols, *Whitehead's Metaphysics*, 11.

27. "There is always a remainder for the decision of the subject-superject of that concrescence." Whitehead, *Process and Reality*, 42.

of the past hurling itself into a new transcendent fact."[28] We could also say, with Bergson, that the "future [of a process] overflows its present, and cannot be sketched out therein in an idea."[29] The remainder between what is determined and what is left to be determined is what process thinkers call "novelty."

Because there is genuine novelty in the world, process philosophy holds that the universe is neither complete nor completable. Novelty may seem mysterious, and it is indeed difficult to argue for its existence. For that reason, process philosophers often argue for its existence by appealing to intuition or personal experience.[30] For example, as you experience it, each moment is not completely determined by the past; there is always a feeling of uncertainty. Because of this experience, we can say that every moment in our lives is different, and that the coming moment is always novel. Given that no lived moment is exactly equal to another, we could also say that at every moment, there is something new in the world. Time brings with it new experiences, and hence new (mental) events correlated with them. These new events, and the experience of them, effectively add something to the world. Moreover, these new events influence others. Therefore, we can say that novelty exists, and that it is effective because it may change other events.[31] In sum, because of the passing of time (the coming of new moments), there are new things in the world. As Bergson claimed, time does things:[32] it ushers novelty into the world, and it is creative.

Now you might object that just because there is difference in the world, that does not necessarily mean there is creativity or novelty. True, the experience of each event is different. But does this mean that each experience is novel? After all, differences are not necessarily novel; even though no two grains of sand or two drops of water are the same, no creativity is linked to this difference.[33] This is true. Creativity requires not only that there be different events, or different actualizations of the same process, but also that there be new *kinds* of events, new *kinds* of processes. That is, novelty in the world requires the emergence of new types of processes, or

28. Whitehead, *Adventures of Ideas*, 177.

29. Bergson, *Creative Evolution*, 103.

30. This is what Bergson calls "supra-intellectual intuition" (ibid., 160) and Whitehead calls "non-sensuous perception" (*Adventures of Ideas*, 180–81).

31. As Bergson put it, "The thread attaching [the son] to the rest of the universe is doubtless very tenuous. Nevertheless it is along this thread that is transmitted down to the smallest particle of the world in which we live the duration immanent to the whole of the universe." *Creative Evolution*, 10–11.

32. Bergson: "If [time] *does* nothing, it *is* nothing." Ibid., 39.

33. This is an actual objection offered by an anonymous reviewer. I thank him or her for the point.

new natural laws that determine their existence. In other words, novelty requires there be new possibilities, rather than realizations of already existing possibilities. (This feature of novelty and creativity is important for political theory because it allows us to expect the emergence of new goals or political possibilities that have not yet been envisioned. It also allows us to question those views that espouse a hypothetical unification of reason and will as the only possibility worth pursuing within a democratic state.)

The objector might insist that the idea of novelty as the emergence of new possibilities does not answer the main question: how can there be a truly new kind of process that was not already embedded in the past? It is true that a new kind of process opens up a new range of possibilities: different instantiations of this new kind of process can now exist. But that these new possibilities now exist entails that they must have been possible in the past. If they had been impossible, then they wouldn't exist now. Hence, if the processes were possible in the past, then the new type of process cannot be truly new. So, how, the objector asks, can there be real novelty?[34] The answer lies in the distinction between logical possibility and physical possibility. For example, human flying was always logically possible, though it was not physically possible until the creative technical innovations of the nineteenth and twentieth centuries. In these terms, we can say that human flying was a new type of event that came into being in the twentieth century. So there can be real novelty. Hence novelty and creativity can exist, and we can understand them as the ground of processes.

Creativity, moreover, is not only the ground of processes, but also the origin of self-creation. Self-creation occurs in a process because the coordination of any event is never completely external to the process: it is partially determined by the changes within the process itself. For example, in a personal process, previous events constrain what could happen, and conscious and unconscious aims drive the process's direction. Yet these two sources do not determine the process in its totality. While previous occurrences and goals partially determine future events, there is always some space for novelty. Causes do play a role in process, of course. A series of events is never completely free from causal determination. But whether it is the product of a mind or the very creativity of nature (or randomness), any process incorporates creativity.

We can thus say that a process is self-creative when it is at least partially determined by a creative synthesis that occurs within the process itself,

---

34. Whitehead's answer to this question is similar to Leibniz's: pure possibilities exist eternally in God's mind. Whitehead, *Process and Reality*, 20, 22, 44–46.

rather than being wholly determined by antecedent causes or external circumstances. So, for example, the process of writing this paragraph consists of a series of events (my drafting, reading, deleting, and drafting again). Some of these events were determined in advance by external circumstances (my waking up this morning and coming to the office), others were determined in advance by my judgment and conscious decisions, and yet others were determined by unconscious drives (fear, tendency to bite my nails) and by luck (isn't it fortunate that the computer didn't crash as I typed?). But a remainder of these events was determined by the very process of writing the paragraph. Therefore, the process of writing this paragraph is self-creative to the extent that some features of the process that did not exist before I started typing determined other aspects of the process. For example, the precise formulation of the first sentence determined the shape of further sentences, and these gave me new ideas, which subsequently got written down. As any writer knows, even the most precise outline cannot wholly determine the paragraph in advance. Something new occurs as you write. This example illustrates self-creation, an organization of events by which a process creatively generates some of its constituent events. (To use language that may be more familiar to some readers, self-creation is a matter of emergent properties arising in complex systems.)[35]

To sum up, creativity ushers novelty into the world and is the condition for self-creation.[36] In the next section, I describe creative freedom, a source of creativity that coordinates personal and social processes.

Creative Freedom

What I call creative freedom is a source of creativity that pertains to persons. As I argued in the previous section, creativity requires the existence

35. By emergent properties, I mean genuinely novel properties that were not possessed by the simpler constituents of a given system. These emerge when the system reaches a given level of complexity. See Kim, "Emergence," 458, and O'Connor and Wong, "Metaphysics of Emergence," 664.

36. This account of the creativity or partial indeterminacy of nature is intuitively attractive because it conforms better than do other accounts of reality to the experience of novelty in life. For example, it is intuitively more accurate than a hard determinism that denies freedom and the openness of the future. But if you doubt the soundness of process philosophy, you will perhaps object that my description of a personal experience is not a sufficiently good reason for espousing such a view. I am afraid I cannot counter this objection. A better argument for creativity lies beyond the concerns of political philosophy, and I cannot refer you to other arguments within process philosophy because for most process philosophers, creativity is a basic assumption. According to Whitehead, for instance, creativity is the basic fact of the world, "the universal of universals characterizing the ultimate matter of fact." *Process and Reality*, 31. There is always novelty, and at any moment the world is different

of emergent properties in processes. This is a controversial claim. It is also the type of basic assumption that is not normally discussed in political theory. Yet I think discussion of the matter is important for at least two reasons. First, laying out the metaphysical assumptions of a political theory—even of a limited theory, such as this processualist theory of the people—clarifies its structure and makes it easier to understand. Second, given that metaphysical assumptions are necessary but often controversial, it is better to present them for all to see. This makes any theory easier to criticize and facilitates comparisons. (Notice that rather than offering this claim as a self-evident truth, or taking it off the table for discussion, I offer it as a provisional hypothesis open to revision and criticism.)

Creative freedom partially coordinates the processes constituting individual persons.[37] According to process philosophy, persons can be conceived as the conjunction of the developmental sequence of a biological life cycle with a mental life process that integrates experiences. This conjunction obtains within an order of social relations (a supra-process) and a given physical environment (another supra-process). Thus the process that constitutes a person is coordinated by biology and culture—but it is not completely determined by them. Persons are also self-creative processes, such that individuals have a say over, and can partially coordinate, the processes that they comprise. That is, they are creative and free. This is the most basic assumption of a political theory that takes process seriously, and it is compatible with any other view of agency or personhood worth having. Hence it occupies a place analogous to individual freedom in liberal and democratic theories, and constitutes the basis for political rights, political legitimacy, and political obligation.[38] Creative freedom presupposes that individual persons can choose, that they are responsible, that they can judge, and that their consent to government requires reasons they can evaluate. In sum, creative freedom gives a ground for the claim that "a human community is a collectivity of free beings."[39] It makes the theory of democracy intelligible and explains why the principles of freedom and equality can justify the state. As I will argue, however, creative freedom also differs in important ways from the liberal view of individual freedom.

from how it was in the previous instant. For Bergson, creativity is also basic, something that cannot itself be explained by theory.

37. According to Whitehead, a subject is "a determinant of its own concrescence." *Process and Reality*, 135. For Bergson, "The outward manifestation of this inner state will be just what is called a free act, since the self alone will have been the author of it and since it will express the whole of the self." *Time and Free Will*, 166.

38. See Waldron, "Theoretical Foundations of Liberalism," 129.

39. Bergson, *Two Sources*, 3.

Liberal theories use the idea of freedom to establish the intrinsic value, and thus the equal worth, of persons. They then use these ideas to legitimize the state by appealing to the individual obligations that these ideas generate. For example, they legitimize the state by appeal to the obligation that free and equal individuals have to recognize one another's worth, to keep one's promises, or to be consistent. Liberal democratic theory thus legitimizes the state by appealing to categorical norms obligating individuals. As I argued in the previous chapters, however, the problem with categorical norms of this type is that in order to preserve autonomy, the norms would have to be recognized by each individual, either actually or hypothetically. This recognition presupposes the possibility of popular unification, which, as I argued in chapter 2, is in fact impossible.

In contrast to this traditional liberal democratic view, a political theory based on creative freedom does not seek to first establish the absolute intrinsic worth of persons, and then derive individual obligations and legitimacy from it. Rather, a processual political theory relies on creative freedom to exemplify and espouse the value of creativity itself—which is neither intrinsic to nor exclusive of individual persons. For Whitehead and his heirs, "the value of every entity resides in its power of self-creativity."[40] This is also true for Bergson and for other proponents of process thought, such as those influenced by Nietzsche.[41] The main consequence of this view, for our purposes, is that *not all* individual human processes, and *not only* individual human processes, have intrinsic value. There is intrinsic value in any self-creating process, which may include many entities, such as individuals and human collectives (families, communities, societies), but also physical, vegetable, and animal processes, and the processes of which they form a part (ecosystems). These are valuable entities that most liberal political theories do not take into consideration as subjects of their theories.[42] For process theory, determining and sustaining the value of these crisscrossing processes is the aim that partially coordinates a political process worth upholding.

Creative freedom also differs from the liberal democratic views criticized in previous chapters because it emphasizes relatedness. The worth of individuals is not absolute and self-sufficient. According to Rescher, "Every process—be it physical or biological, meteorological or agricultural, personal or social, theoretical or practical—exists in a larger context of

---

40. Morris, *Process Philosophy and Political Ideology*, 123.
41. See Connolly, *Pluralism*, 10, and Deleuze, *Difference and Repetition*.
42. A notable exception is the work of Jane Bennett. See *Vibrant Matter*.

further processes. No process is isolated and self-sufficient unto itself: every process has sub-processes that form parts of it, and macro-processes of which it itself forms a part."[43] Thus the value of any process, including persons, is relative to other processes. Given that no process is isolated or self-sufficient, we cannot claim that the worth of persons is absolute. The value of each process (including persons) depends on its relations, especially on its relation to a valuer. For example, according to Whitehead it is a moral wrong to "ignore the true relation of each organism to its environment, [and] the intrinsic worth of the environment which must be allowed its weight in any consideration of final ends."[44] Processes are open to the contexts in which they occur, and individuals as processes have an irreducible social aspect. This means that persons have moral worth only in the context of social and environmental relations. Their interactions establish a world of value through the medium of language. Moreover, in a processual view, values are themselves subject to change. Freedom, as a value, changes in respect to individual and social processes. This is a common position among process thinkers, including the American pragmatists, for whom universal values, and truth in general, must be construed in dynamic terms.[45] The values used to justify a state and grant legitimacy are social and dynamic, as are many of the theories that describe such values.

Moreover, creative freedom differs from the freedom emphasized by liberal democratic theories because it need not be associated only with personal liberty or free will. As I discussed above, novelty and creativity can be ascribed to nonconscious processes, organic and inorganic. We can see creativity at work in organic syntheses produced by random variation, like the ones occurring in evolutionary processes. We can also see it in inorganic processes that generate emergent attributes and show signs of self-organization. Thus there can be self-creativity in animals and plants, as well as in such complex physical systems as hurricanes and artificial intelligence. Yet none of these processes, obviously, has personal liberty or free will. Although I reserved the term "creative freedom" for the novelty in *personal* processes, it is worth noting that unlike human persons, personal processes can include other nonhuman entities (such as higher animals or collective persons). In sum, creative freedom is different from personal liberty in that creative freedom is not exclusive to individual

43. Rescher, "Replies," 307.
44. Whitehead, *Science and the Modern World*, 196.
45. See Hausman, *Charles S. Peirce's Evolutionary Philosophy*, and Rescher, *Process Metaphysics*, 14.

human persons. Moreover, all personal processes are partially constituted by their relations to other processes, including many nonconscious organic and physical processes.

Finally, most theories that put individual personal freedom and rationality at the forefront often associate the diffusion of freedom with progress. Creative freedom, however, is not inherently good and need not produce progress. All I have claimed so far is that creative freedom presupposes some causal indeterminacy in personal processes, as well as the real possibility of personal decisions and the introduction of new possibilities in the world. Creativity does have intrinsic worth, in the sense that it is not valuable only as an instrument for the satisfaction of particular desires. But the consequences of this creativity may not be to our liking. For example, we all want a world in which there is some causal indeterminacy, such that we can innovate in order to improve, but such indeterminacy also implies risk. The products of creative freedom are not always good. It is true that many process philosophers (James, Peirce, Bergson, Whitehead) were optimistic and believed that the outcomes of true creativity were inherently good. For Bergson, the best example of such optimism, creativity alone produces moral and political progress in society. Unlike Bergson, I hold that while creative freedom guarantees an open future, it does not guarantee anything else. Creative freedom allows for the creation of processes that I consider good, and others that I consider bad: technical innovation and environmental destruction; institutions that further equality and peace, as well as those that promote exploitation and war. It allowed for the spread of democracy, as well as the advent of Nazism. In sum, creative freedom is the condition of possibility for a political order worth upholding. But it is not sufficient to explain that order, or to bring it into being. Creative freedom may make the world more complex, better, and more beautiful—but it also may not.

The People as Process

After discussing what process is, we are now in a position to describe the people as a process. As I mentioned earlier, I hold that a people is an unfolding series of events coordinated by the practices of constituting, governing, or changing a set of institutions. These institutions are the highest authority for all those individuals intensely affected by these events and these institutions.

In the next sections, I explicate this definition in more detail; I clarify the elements constituting the people as process; and I show how we can distinguish one people from other peoples, and where their boundaries lie.

Constituents of the People as Process

If the people is not an aggregation of individuals, then what are its constituents? If you conceive of a people as a process—that is, as a series of events unfolding in coordination—the constituents of the people are just those sequentially structured events. As I argued above, an event is an occurrence, which suggests that a people is constituted by occurrences rather than by individuals. This may sound strange at first, particularly if you consider the whole range of possible events. An event, for example, is the crash of a tractor trailer. The collision and the consequent interstate traffic jam are sequentially structured events, and so are many other processes that you may encounter every day. But, of course, not all events that occur in a polity are constituents of its people. Peoples are constituted by the *political* events I call "people events." They are also partly constituted by individuals, in that you see people events from the perspective of events in the lives of individuals. Let us first examine people events.

The people, as I have examined it so far, is a political—rather than a cultural, ethnic, or religious—entity. From this perspective, only political events figure in the constitution of the people. According to this view, Paul Revere's crossing of the Charles River, the bombing of Pearl Harbor, and a 2000 decision by the U.S. Supreme Court are political events that make up the American people. In the same way, Hidalgo's calling his parishioners to revolt in the town of Dolores and starting the insurrection that culminated in independence from Spain, the Battle of Chapultepec during the Mexican-American War, and the 1938 nationalization of Mexican oil are all political events that make up the Mexican people. A people is constituted by myriad such political events in a coordinated series.

Now, you may ask, precisely which political events go into making up a people? How about less momentous events than the ones I just mentioned? What is the status of events that seem less important but have political aspects, such as the private conversation I had this morning about presidential candidates, or the arrival of a new illegal immigrant in a country? Indeed, almost any event can be described as political. Nevertheless, events that appear insignificant may have a bearing on important political matters like the election of leaders, the creation and destruction of public opinion, and the birth and death of social and political institutions. Other seemingly irrelevant events, like a person watching the evening news, or coworkers exchanging political views over the water fountain, can be part of a process culminating in political unrest, or one that cements periods of calm civic participation. To decide which of these events constitute a people, however, we need a criterion for deciding whether the event is a people event. This criterion is the *coordination* of the process.

In this view, what makes some political events people events depends on the coordination that structures the series. This morning's conversation, for example, is a political event that should be considered part of the people because what coordinates this particular series (the people as process) is the practices of constituting, governing, or changing a set of institutions, which are the highest authority for all those individuals intensely affected by these events and these institutions. The conversation is an event that forms part of the practices of electoral politics, which in turn are part of the wider practices of governing and changing institutions with the highest authority. The arrival of an illegal immigrant changes the face of the population, and eventually (but not immediately, and not necessarily) could alter the practices by which the people constitutes, governs, and changes its institutions. Thus a coordination by these practices constitutes a *type of process:* a people.

In this view, people events are those events that are part of the practices of constituting, governing, or changing the institutions that are the *highest* authority for those affected by the institutions in question. So political events restricted to your club, your city block, or your province don't count. Institutions range from forms of greeting and table manners to the rules governing churches and sports clubs. And yet the members of churches and sports clubs, just like the sum total of polite eaters, don't seem to constitute a people. The mobilized citizens of a neighborhood, a city block, or a political club are also engaged in the business of changing institutions, and yet you would probably hesitate to call them a people.[46] In most modern countries, the institutions that are the highest authority are those of the sovereign state.[47]

46. This view has the advantage of keeping the referents of the concept of the people fairly close to that traditional people conception. Contrast this view to that of Rogers Smith, who holds that the people are best conceived in terms of the strengths of obligations. On Smith's view, the collection of individuals in a neighborhood, city block, or sports club could be considered a people. See Smith, *Stories of Peoplehood,* 20–29.

47. Other political configurations have different institutions. For example, the emperor is the highest authority within the empire, while a chieftain may be the highest instance of authority governing a confederation of tribes. Other loose, supranational confederations, such as the European Union or the United States before the ratification of the Constitution, have mixed higher sources of authority.

The final and perhaps most important question regarding the constituents of the people is, *Who precisely* participates in constituting, changing, and governing those institutions? Which individuals or which group? I claim that the persons participating in peoplehood are all those individuals intensely affected by the supremely authoritative institutions and by the events that modify the institutions. A person is intensely affected by those institutions when they can coerce her and there are no alternative institutions that would allow her to continue her normal life. For example, I am not a citizen of the United States, but I have lived in the United States for more than nine years. I often consider myself a part of the American people because many events in my life are coordinated by the political practices that affect the supremely authoritative American institutions. Moreover, these institutions regulate my work, my family, and my health, and they can coerce me. I cannot detach myself from these institutions without it affecting my normal life. Hence these institutions intensely affect me.

None of this implies that those individuals intensely affected by the institutions in question constitute the people. My definition of the people differs in two ways from another people conception that builds the demos on the basis of the "all affected interests" principle.[48] First, on my definition, it is not the individual members who make up the people, but rather the events and relations in which individuals participate; the people is a series of events, not a collection of individuals. Second, just because institutions intensely affect an individual does not grant her a right to citizenship. My definition does not constitute a normative or legal theory that tells you *who* is entitled to have which legal rights. Rather, it is part of an ontological argument that tells you *what* is a people. My claim is not the normative one that all these individuals are entitled to citizenship. On the contrary, it is the ontological claim that they partake of the people *because* they are intensely affected. The occasions in which these individuals are intensely affected are some of the events that *make* the people as process.[49]

Now, even if a people is composed of events rather than individuals, these events are *also* part of the lives of individuals. Your life, for example,

48. Those versions of the "all affected interests" principle affirm that the persons affected by the decisions of a demos should be included in that demos. For defenses of this normative version of the principle, see Goodin, "Enfranchising All Affected Interests," and Dahl, *Democracy and Its Critics*, 119–31. Yet the definition of the people that depends on "enfranchising all affected interests" denies the possibility of a legitimate democratic state because the people then presupposes the institutions that ought to be created by the people. I discuss the importance of the different uses of this principle in the next chapter.

49. I believe these theoretical claims may be the ground of normative claims, but I am not making the normative arguments in these pages.

is partly constituted by people events: you participate in discussions about national politics, you vote in countrywide elections, you were moved by the images on television on September 11, 2001. Elections and other grand-scale political events occur in public, but they also take place at home: they are part of your life as well as part of the people. Yet the converse is not true: not all events in your life are part of the people. For example, you, an American citizen, may now be in the Swiss Alps, setting out a picnic while your children gather daisies. This event in your life is not part of the American people, just as your decision about whether to grill or broil chicken for tonight's dinner is an event in your life but not a people event.[50]

So what precisely are the conditions under which a person partakes of a given people? Remember that a whole individual person does not count as a *member* of a people because peoples are not collections of individuals. But if the events in an individual's life overlap with people events, and if her interests are intensely affected by those people events, then she partakes of this people. Moreover, when an individual's life and interests are so affected by some people events, and when she recognizes those events as part of her life, and when she would like to have some say over the governance of that people's institutions, she has a good moral claim to certain political rights relative to those people events. These rights are not the whole basket of citizens' rights, but they are rights of political participation. For example, the Vietnam War is a people event of the American people. Consider then the case of a Viet Cong soldier whose husband, brothers, and father—also Viet Cong—are killed in battle with American forces. Her life and interests have now been intensely affected by an American people event. She therefore partakes of the American people. If in addition she would like to have some say over the course of the American people's actions, then on this theory she partakes of the American people and is entitled to some rights and obligations derived from this partaking. (This helps explain why the American government felt obligated to admit many Vietnamese immigrants in the 1970s and 1980s.) Take another case: an Indian living in servitude in colonial Peru. Obviously, this servant was intensely affected by the practices of the governing institutions of the Spanish empire. But to the extent that events in his life contributed to changing institutions in the Peruvian colony, one could say that he partici-pated in these practices, and thus partook of the people of Spain.[51] Had

50. Unless the choice of broiling rather than grilling can importantly affect the institu-tions of highest authority in your state, as would happen if, say, grilling had acquired sym-bolic value and you grilled as part of an organized public demonstration. Most grilled chicken parts are not so important, though.

51. See Forment, *Democracy in Latin America,* 39–66.

the viceroyalty of Peru or the Spanish empire been democratic republics, the servant, as part of the people, could have demanded some political rights. Moreover, he had a good moral claim to those rights. Or consider an illegal immigrant working in the United States, who took to the streets on May 1, 2006, to demonstrate in favor of immigration reform. To the extent that she participated in changing the highest political institutions in the United States, she partook of American people events. Moreover, living and working in the Unites States, she is intensely affected by institutions that are the highest authority for her. Hence, on my theory, if she would like to have some say over American politics, then she is so entitled in a degree proportional to her participation in the American people. (Again, notice that partaking of the American people does not entitle you to citizenship. It may, however, entitle you to certain rights against the American state, like visas or circumscribed political rights while residing in the country. It may also impose certain obligations on you.)

But how does this people conception differ from considering a people as an aggregation of citizens or affected individuals? Is it not the same for all practical purposes? The main constituents of the people are not persons, but rather other processes and events. Many of the events making up the people directly involve only citizens, but many do not. For example, the people includes events involving individuals who are not full citizens (like aliens, children, the mentally ill, and convicted felons), as well as events constituting collective persons, like corporations, civic associations, churches, and governmental organizations. On my conception, all of these can partake of the people. Moreover, the relevant events may also involve animals, plants, and other parts of the physical environment. Again, on my theory, all of these can partake of the people. For example, think of the people events described above. "Paul Revere's Ride" cannot be part of the people without the horse and the Charles River. So these, too, partake of the American people. In the same way, Lazaro Cárdenas's nationalization of Mexican oil does not make much sense if we do not consider the oil. So the oil also partook of the Mexican people. These nonhuman elements also feature prominently in the event and are important in determining the course of the complete series of people events.

You might think that this view of the people is odd and incompatible with some basic metaphysical truths, such as the idea that there are stable things. Yet, as I argued in the previous part of this chapter, a philosophy of process does not do away with things. It merely holds that events are more basic than things, and that all things presuppose processes and their constitutive events. Seeing the people as an unfolding series of events (a process) is compatible with seeing the people as a stable, identifiable thing. Yet when the people is conceived only as a thing (say, a definite collection of individuals), the conception is poorer and less descriptive. A series of events can include an aggregation of individuals (e.g., the counting of votes in an election, or the signing of a new constitution), but it also incorporates the changes that occur among and within individuals when they do not aggregate. Moreover, not all the people events that go into the people as process must occur within the procedures that aggregate individual wills. The people includes such events as when a group of individuals gives the law to themselves, as well as the events that obtain when a group raises up in arms against the institutions legitimated by the constitution. It encompasses discussions of politics in coffeehouses, public demonstrations, the counting of votes, and the rallies preceding Election Day.

The idea of the people as process is compatible with more traditional conceptions of the people, such as those of a historical social contract, of a hypothetical account of those individuals who would agree to constitute the state, and of the descriptions of the people as a process in the theories of dynamic constitutionalism and dualist democracy. But the people as process is more expansive than these conceptions. It can incorporate aspects of other related processes, like the market, the environment, and international pressures, and it can exclude the private aspects of individual lives. As I discuss in the following chapter, being more expansive in respect to other public processes, and more restrictive in regard to other private processes, is what allows the people as process to avoid the logical problems that arise in other conceptions of the people.

Individuation of a People as Process

A people is constituted by events, but how can you distinguish one people from another? The normative justification for popular self-determination, the right to physically exclude and include individuals in a state, and the rights of citizenship all hinge on our capacity to determine which specific events and relations belong to one people rather than another. To resolve this issue, I claim that one people may be individuated from another according to three criteria (none of which is independently sufficient for individuation): the time and place in which the process occurs; the character of the practices that constitute, govern, or change a particular set of supremely authoritative institutions; and whether the individuals who are under the authority of the process's authoritative institutions conceive of themselves as part of different peoples.

To begin, if you conceive of the people as a process, you can partly tell an individual people from others because it occupies a concrete spatiotemporal expanse—that is, it is a particular instantiation of a generic process of peoplehood. In general, you can distinguish an individual process from others because it is a particular instantiation (a token) of a process type. For example, how can you tell a yawn from another? Presumably, you can tell your yawns apart, even if they are both the same type of process and they are yours, because one yawn happened in a particular time and place (by your computer, after lunch), different from the other (by the fire, late at night). Similarly, we know that there is a type of process that we call a people and that there have been many different, concrete instantiations of this type.[52] For example, the Japanese people occupies a particular spatio-temporal expanse that no other people completely occupies.

The second criterion that helps individuate peoples is differences in the characteristic practices of constituting, governing, and changing a set of institutions. These practices are varied and obtain in different places and at different historical periods, even if there are similarities among abstract practices.[53] For example, the practice of enthroning a monarch existed in twentieth-century Britain as well as in ninth-century Japan. But the *sokui-rei*, the ancient Japanese "ceremony of ascending the throne and announcing the succession to the gods of heaven and earth, to the spirits of the imperial ancestors" is easy to tell apart from the practice whereby the English monarch is anointed by the archbishop of Canterbury and vested in garb of alb, dalmatic, and stole.[54] Each practice, a discernible pattern of events, occurs habitually in different places and different times, and allows us to tell one people from another.

At first it may seem that this approach is not so different from traditional views that distinguish different peoples according to their ancestral culture or other essential traits. Yet it is quite different because the political practices that help distinguish one people from another are not *essential* to the people in question. The character of these practices does not determine who these people essentially *are*. Rather, a people's character is an abstraction that gives you an account of a set of characteristic activities: the

52. Again, the types themselves are not Platonic forms but rather conceptual processes. They can be seen as both statistical regularities framed retroactively, or as part of conceptual processes interacting with ontological processes. This is Whitehead's position. See *Adventures of Ideas*, especially "Objects and Subjects" (175–90). Rescher holds a similar view. See Rescher, "Replies," 318, and Siebt, "Process and Particulars."

53. I use the term "practice" in the sense of "habitual doing." I use the term "pattern" interchangeably because a practice is made up of a pattern, a regular sequence of events.

54. Oakley, *Kingship*, 20, 134.

abstract form of what the people regularly *does*. These repeated events give a character to the series they constitute, but there is nothing essential about this character, for the changes in the activities can transform that character. For this reason, we can only discern a people's character in retrospect, as recurrent activities that establish patterns of recognizable events over time.

Specifically, we can conceive of this character as constituted by the particular practices through which coordinated events constitute, govern, or change a set of institutions. The practices that give a people its particular character may be habitual. For example, they may refer to informal institutional mechanisms that describe how organizations work (a custom of dressing in a certain way in Parliament, for example), or how organizations enforce formal rules for governing (for instance, elections are held every four, six, or eight years). But the patterns that define a character may also apply to exceptional events, such as to the periodic bursts of political energy that challenge and change a constitution, expand the franchise, or revolutionize organizations. These events, though unforeseen, are part of the practices of constituting, governing, and changing authoritative institutions, and are thus characteristic of the complete series.

But why do peoples manifest different characteristic practices? The repetition of characteristic practices that differentiate one people from another is partially determined by past events and is partially self-creative. A people's governing practices have a causal history, which partially determines what that people will do in the future. Like any other process, the series of events that constitutes a people does not exist as an abstraction or as an ideal, but rather must exist in real time. Past events condition the way a people will change, just as the passing of time makes a thing decay, adds rings to the tree trunk, or adds wrinkles to a person's face.

Yet the history of past events does not completely determine the process. In any series of events, there is some space for causal indeterminacy, which allows for self-creation. Self-creation is the second element that determines the practices that coordinate a people and allows us to distinguish it from others. It is this creativity that leads the process in one direction rather than others and allows a people to determine its own character.

At this point you might ask why this is not like saying that the people has a will. If a people as process can be distinguished from other such people processes because it has a particular character and capacity for self-determination, how is this different from saying "the people has spoken" or "this is the people's will"? Unlike the traditional conceptions of the people, the people as process does not have a capacity to decide in the same way a person does. The self-creative drive is not like the personal decision of the autonomous individual as traditionally conceived; it does not have one single voice. Every people event incorporates creativity in the indeterminacy of the future. Yet the changes that determine the process are not completely random. They also arise from a past that causally determines future events, as well as the interactions of conscious (and unconscious) memories, personal ideals, and collective expectations. The interaction of these events eventually sets the process on an individual course, but they do not close it to the future.

Finally, regarding the last criterion for individuation, when those individuals who partake in people events believe they are part of a particular people, they may preserve or alter the characteristic practices that constitute the said people to the point that they preserve or alter the people itself. For example, if enough individuals who partake of a given people at a given time believe they do not partake in it, they may bring about the end of the people in question, or create a new one. In this manner different peoples can fuse into one if individuals partaking of different peoples believe they have merged and choose to harmonize their practices of constituting, governing, and changing authoritative institutions. The converse occurs in cases of independence, secession, and partition.

Spatial and Temporal Boundaries of the People as Process

A problem that is closely related to that of how to individuate peoples is how to discern the exact location of the spatial and temporal boundaries between peoples. As I argued above, processes do not have well-defined edges, hence their boundaries are not clear-cut either in space or in time. Yet this may be an advantage if you want to understand the processes by which peoples emerge, interact, diverge, or merge, while avoiding the difficulties that follow from conceiving the people as a collection of individuals.

As I argued in the previous section, different people processes can be distinguished from one another when characteristic practices repeat themselves with a certain frequency. It would not be hard to distinguish two peoples with very different characters in different places and times. For example, you wouldn't have any difficulty telling apart the Chilean people in the twentieth century from the Japanese people in the fifteenth century. Yet these discriminations become very difficult when the interactions between peoples are very frequent and intense, or when in a given territory there are overlapping jurisdictional claims of different authorities that have some institutional clout.[55] Such distinctions become almost impossible when these interactions are governed by two different sets of institutions, both claiming to be the highest authority in a given geographical area, and where the individuals participating in these interactions have mixed allegiances.[56]

For example, perhaps it was easy to distinguish the American from the Mexican people when there were almost no relevant political events occurring in the plains and desert stretches from Chihuahua to Kansas. What political events there were up to the nineteenth century pertained to local peoples, rather than to the peoples of the neighboring national states. But things became different as soon as individuals, whose political practices linked them to either Mexico City or Washington, D.C., moved to the desert. The relative frequency of interaction among settlers who had exclusive and mixed political allegiances made people events belonging to either people hard to discern. These interactions have increased up to a point that today even the most inhospitable parts of the Arizona desert have become rife with political events coordinated by the legal institutions of the two countries. In the U.S.-Mexico border region, the political processes that a physical barrier formerly kept separated are now hardly distinguishable because of creative pressures coming from many quarters. But this does not mean that the Mexican and American peoples have merged. That is obvious as you cross the border between, say, Laredo, Texas, and Nuevo Laredo, Tamaulipas. The differences in the way roads are built, differences in the way business is conducted, and differences in the interaction between denizens and authorities on either side of the river remind you that many people events are in fact divided by the political and geographical border. Yet many events that pertain to the governing and changing of relevant border institutions do substantially overlap. There is a distinct Mexican American border culture that includes institutions governing border interactions.[57] In sum, peoples as

55. This occurs whenever borders are disputed, or when there are claims to secession, partition, or independence. For discussion of these issues that considers the people as a collection of individuals (including the difficulties this view poses for democratic theory), see Buchanan, *Secession;* Buchanan, "Making and Unmaking of Boundaries"; and Beran, "Border Disputes and the Right of National Self-Determination."

56. To address disputed borders we need a theory of territory, which is a relatively unexplored area of political philosophy. Recently, however, there has appeared an interesting treatment of the relation of people to territory according to their perception of land and land use; see Kolers, *Land, Conflict, and Justice.* Other political theorists have dealt with the role of space in political theory, particularly in regard to identity. On this, see Keith and Pile, *Place and the Politics of Identity,* and Bauböck and Rundell, *Blurred Boundaries.*

57. For an example of these interactions, see Andreas, *Border Games.* For a theoretical discussion of border institutions, see Gavrilis, *Dynamics of Interstate Boundaries.*

processes can be independent and follow distinguishable patterns, but they can also merge[58] or diverge.[59] We can illustrate these dynamics of people processes using the historical creation of nation-states.

This view of peoples and their dynamics differs from most conceptions of the people now current in the study of international relations. It particularly differs from those views that see peoples as legally bound groups of individuals in a given territory, with common sympathies and a legal personality. According to such a view, states are morally equivalent to persons, and the world community must be conceived as an aggregation of political peoples or states. Peoples as processes do not fit well with this view because according to the theory, peoples can only exist if they are legally recognizable by a third party and have fixed borders. Yet peoples as processes can exist without such external legal recognition and without fixed borders. Their existence depends only on internal institutions and interactions, and they may be nested in one another, flow into one another, or separate from one another if the rate and intensity of interactions ceases.

As discussed above, the spatial boundaries of peoples are hard to determine if the jurisdictional claims of institutions overlap. A similar indeterminacy obtains when we think about the people's temporal boundaries. The people as process does not have a clearly marked beginning in time. There are no precise moments when peoples are born. All political foundings are events difficult to distinguish from their predecessor events. A political founding is always part of a series of political events unfolding in time, and thus there can be no political creation ex nihilo.

It is true that many peoples seem to have a precise founding moment, especially in cases of the independence of former colonies and the drafting of new constitutions. Given that the character of a people depends on institutional practices, one can identify the first time something was done in a given manner and think of this event as a founding moment. But this is a "first time" only in retrospect. Even if the practice is novel, when it first came into being it was partially determined by past events. Take, for instance, the enthronement of kings. You could say that the events that

---

58. The process of merging independent regional peoples into a nation correlated with a given state is often called "nation building." For an illustration of this process with specific reference to the concept of a democratic people, see Rosanvallon's trilogy: *La démocratie inachevée, Le peuple introuvable,* and *Le sacre du citoyen.*

59. Peter Sahlins shows how the enforcement of the Spanish-French border for more than two hundred years created a French Cerdagne and a Spanish Cerdaña, where once there was just a Cerdagna, a territory of the Catalonian people. See *Boundaries.*

solemnized the accession of Queen Elizabeth to the throne in 1953 occurred for the first time in the tenth century, as described by the Anglo-Saxon's manual of coronation, the "Edgar *ordo.*"[60] But you could only say this in retrospect (after the practice was established). Moreover, when the alleged first instantiation of the practice took place, it built on already existing practices. Hence it would be difficult to determine that any one occasion was the first because any given concrete instantiation of the practice is never exactly the same as the next. You might object that this is a bad example, and note that some very important practices, like those codified in a written constitution, do have clearly defined beginnings. Yet even those exceptional moments are preceded by recognizably similar patterns of constituting, governing, and changing institutions. The precise moments of initiation and termination of practices are difficult to determine precisely, even though peoples do have beginnings and ends.

It is true that the temporal boundaries of some processes are very precise. For example, we can see (and measure) the precise moment when some chemical reaction begins to take place, as well as when it has ended. Yet other processes have only vague temporal boundaries. Organic and social processes are the best examples. Organic processes, including the lives of individuals, have a beginning and an end, but these beginnings and ends are vague, as the debates over abortion and end-of-life issues illustrate. Obviously, the temporal boundaries of the processes that define a people are even more vague than the temporal boundaries of an individual person. The Roman and Aztec peoples are long gone, but the precise dates of their respective demises are the subject of much discussion.

In sum, a people as process differs from other conceptions of the people with respect to the type of constituents that make up the people, its criteria of individuation, its views on the people's spatial boundaries, and its theory of the people's vague temporal boundaries. Given that one can individuate peoples and establish their continuity in time, this conception may help us to determine what is a democratic people and to solve the problem of indeterminacy of popular unification in democratic theory.

Conclusion

According to the processual theory that I developed in these pages, a people is an unfolding series of events coordinated by the practices of constituting, governing, and changing a set of institutions. These institutions

60. Oakley, *Kingship*, 20.

are the highest authority for all those individuals intensely affected by these events and these institutions. This definition incorporates creativity and novelty. The creativity in question comes from the freedom of those individuals who partake in the process of peoplehood, but also from the partial indeterminacy of nature and unforeseen events. Moreover, this theory of the people provides a tool to individuate peoples and answer questions regarding their origin, their termination, and their territorial borders. Finally, and most important, this account shows how a people can be self-creative.

This processual theory of peoplehood is quite different from common views of the people. So why adopt it? The theory still needs an argument to show that it is preferable to the standard conceptions. That is my task in the following chapter. There I will argue for the theory of the people as process by considering the nature of democratic peoples. I defend the theory on the ground that it does not fall prey to the logical difficulties I found in other views. Moreover, this theory can legitimize the democratic state because it shows that there can be a kind of unified people without the unification of will and reason of a collection of individuals in a popular sovereign.

7

A Democratic People as Process

A democratic people rules itself. This assertion contains the problem in democratic theory that has been this book's main concern. The problem arises because it is mysterious how an aggregation of individuals could rule if it is not unified at some point. But how can the people be unified at any given time? As I have shown, the problem of indeterminacy of popular unification plagues all democratic theories that rely on the aggregation of individual wills. Moreover, even if a collection of individuals could be unified at a given time, how can this moment of unification guarantee a continuous identity over time? Unless we can establish such continuity, it makes no sense to say that a unified people gave itself law or that it coerced itself into obedience.

Many political theorists have appealed to time and process to solve these problems. Yet few have tried to show exactly how a theory of process can be a foundation for a theory of democratic legitimacy.[1] This is what I seek to do in this chapter. In what follows, I use the processualist theory of peoplehood developed in chapter 6 to tackle the indeterminacy problem. I claim that when you conceive of the people as a process, the people can then genuinely support and buttress the arguments that legitimize the state in traditional democratic theory. I make my point by showing that the people as process does not fall victim to the logical problems I described in the previous chapters. The reason the theory is spared these difficulties is

---

1. Past philosophers who have tried to connect theories of time and process to theories of democracy include Bergson and Dewey. Contemporary theorists who have tackled this task include Connolly (*Pluralism*) and Rubenfeld (*Freedom and Time*).

that self-reference within a process does not produce a vicious circle or an infinite regress. Moreover, process provides sufficient stability over time to say that the people is a single entity that rules itself. Given these traits, we can say that the people as process is better able to sustain democratic legitimacy than are other conceptions because it can make sense of core ideas of the theory of democracy that did not make full sense in other theories of the people.

I develop the argument in two parts. In the first part, I define the democratic people as process. I argue that this conception can solve the indeterminacy problem because it can explain how a people has a stable identity that persists over time, even if we cannot show that all individual wills in the state do (or could) unify through reason. In the subsequent sections, I show how the people as process stops the infinite regress and breaks the vicious circle of self-constitution of the people, and how the people as process can solve the problem of continuity over time, or "the problem of generations." With these arguments in hand, I show in the second part that a justificatory democratic theory that rests on process philosophy can coherently claim that a democratic people creates itself and rules itself, and for this reason can claim that the people is sovereign. In the last two sections I respond to two possible objections: First, if process philosophy does away with the ideal of unifying reason and will in a popular sovereign, what is the normative standing of the idea of popular sovereignty and popular self-rule according to a democratic theory of the people as process? Second, this processualist solution to the paradoxes of democracy requires an unusual ontology. Is adopting an ontology too high a price to pay in order to legitimize the state democratically?

The Democratic People as Process and the Indeterminacy of Popular Unification

The problem of the indeterminacy of popular unification, which I described in chapter 2, is that democratic theories require that the people, as a collection of individuals, unify in their consent (actually or hypothetically) in order to create and justify the state. This unification allows you to say that the people rules itself, and thus that democratic institutions do not impinge on any individual's autonomy, that government respects equality, and that these ruling institutions are as a result justified. But the theories that conceive of the people as a collection of individuals cannot show that these individuals do or could unify, since a collection of free individuals is necessarily indeterminate. (Individuals cannot unify their wills through reason to constitute a people because any such unification presupposes an already existing people, which leads to a vicious circle or an infinite regress.) As a result, these theories cannot justify the state on that basis.

I argue here that the democratic people as process can solve the indeterminacy problem because such a people is individuatable and persists over time without the need to unify the wills of a collection of individuals through reason. Thus this theory allows you to say that the people makes and rules itself while remaining undetermined and open to the future. Hence the theory of the democratic people does not fall into either the problem of self-constitution or the problem of the people in time (described in chap. 2). I will argue for this claim in the following sections, but in order to substantiate this solution to the indeterminacy, I must first define a *democratic* people as process.

A Democratic People as Process

A democratic people as process is a people whose practices of constituting, governing, or changing a set of supremely authoritative institutions formalize the freedom and equality of all individuals who partake in it. A people, in turn, is an unfolding series of events coordinated by the practices of constituting, governing, and changing a set of institutions. These institutions are the highest authority for all those individuals intensely affected by these events and these institutions (described in chap. 6). By "formalize their freedom and equality," I mean that this type of people explicitly incorporates the freedom and equality of individuals as the coordinating aim of the institutions in question, and the practices that constitute these institutions effectively further this aim. This view of the people makes it possible that all those persons ruled be publicly treated as equals, which as I argued in chapter 2 is the justificatory aim of democracy.[2] This means that the practices that coordinate ruling institutions allow all individuals to have a say in setting the most fundamental laws and mechanisms of rule in their polity.[3] Given that all individuals who partake of the

2. Christiano, "Authority of Democracy"; Waldron, *Law and Disagreement,* chap. 13.

3. This condition could also be formulated by consent—for example, "that all individuals ruled consent to be ruled by democratic mechanisms." But as Simmons has pointed out in *Moral Principles and Political Obligations,* consent theories are particularly vulnerable to criticism. I follow Christiano (*Rule of the Many*) in conceiving democracy as reconciling differential political power with equality. It does this by ensuring that individuals have "an equal say" in determining who will wield political power and what are the polity's fundamental laws.

people have an equal say in the making of institutions, it becomes possible for the people to create itself and rule itself. But in order for the people to actually create and rule itself, it must be individuatable; further, it must persist over time, regardless of the wills of individuals who partake of the people at any given time. Self-creation and self-rule require these two conditions because without them, the problem of indeterminacy arises anew.

A people can be individuated without any need to assume that there was or will be a moment of unification. A people, like all processes, does not have very precise spatiotemporal edges, but it can be individuated by the particular way events are coordinated within the process, as I argued in chapter 6. The coordination of a people, or its practices of governing, has a particular character that distinguishes it from other instantiations of the process of peoplehood. That is, even if the character of all democratic peoples is built on the same principles, democratic peoples are not all alike. For example, we can individuate among democratic peoples because each democratic people process has a characteristic set of practices of government. For instance, the declarations of rights incorporated in most democratic constitutions differ from one another in their precise formulations and the context of their enunciations. For example, given the precise circumstances in which the 1689 English Bill of Rights became the highest law of the land, and the circumstances in which the first ten amendments to the U.S. Constitution came into existence, each of these events gave rise to different practices of rule. In turn, these practices settled into distinct institutional structures, which continue to change along different paths of development. (But note that there *could* be a worldwide people if the same institutional practices developed toward convergence and the same authoritative institutions extended throughout the world.) Individuation, then, does not require that a group of people unify in their consent because the practices of government exist regardless of the precise set of individuals who partake in them. In sum, we can individuate democratic peoples by appeal to differences in their characteristic practices of governing.

The second condition, persistence over time, is also satisfied if you conceive of the democratic people as a process, and this without any need to assume popular unification. As I argued in chapter 5, persistence over time is difficult to explain if you conceive of a collective agent as an aggregation of individual wills. Once the generation who designed the fundamental practices of rule in a state dies out, there is no good reason why the older generation's mutual promises should bind younger generations. But in a democratic people as process, continuity does not depend on the strength of individual promises or on the bequeathal of this commitment to younger members of family lines. Instead, the continuity of the people comes from the actual repetition of a given kind of institutional practice, considered by its practitioners to be the highest authority. So democratic institutions persist, even when different individuals participate in the democratic process. At different times, different sets of individuals partake in events, but these events reproduce particular institutional practices. Democratic peoples, in particular, can be said to persist over time if their governing practices have the following traits. First, the people's practices are relatively stable; second, those individuals affected by the highest political institutions must actually have a say in creating and modifying these institutional practices; and third, the practices must in fact further freedom and equality of these individuals. These conditions do not require popular unification because the practices can exist independently of the particular individuals who take part in the events constituting the series.

In sum, a democratic people as process is individuatable and can persist over time without the need for unification. Now, the people as process that I have just described is democratic by definition. In that sense, it is an abstract ideal, similar to Rousseau's democratic people, which actualizes collective and individual freedom by acting according to the general will. Unlike Rousseau's ideal people, the people as process is not an impossible object, like a round square. Unlike the people of classical democratic theory, the democratic people as process can rule itself without falling into the two problems of self-reference I described in chapter 2 and elsewhere. The first is the vicious circle of self-constitution, or the synchronic problem of unification. The second is the problem of the people in time, or the diachronic problem of unification. Let us see how the democratic people as process can avoid them.

The People as Process and the Vicious Circle of Self-Constitution

When you conceive of the people as an aggregation of individuals, a democratic people seems impossible. Such a people cannot come into being because there is a circularity between institutions and citizens: you need democratic citizens to create legitimate democratic institutions, but you need democratic institutions to determine who are the citizens who would create those very institutions.[4] At first blush, all solutions to this circularity

---

4. Bonnie Honig holds that this paradox "cannot be resolved, transcended, managed, or even affirmed as an irreducible binary conflict." "Between Decision and Deliberation," 1. See also her treatment of this topic in *Emergency Politics*.

problem seem futile. For example, if you appeal to geography or ethnicity to define a citizen, then you compromise legitimacy. If you instead appeal to the principle of "all affected interests" as a democratic criterion for constituting the demos and dissolving the vicious circle, then you fall into a philosophical regress: a democratic decision can alter whose interests are affected, and thus you cannot know in advance whom to include in the demos.[5] Hence, if the democratic people is not already there, then democratic theory faces a seemingly insurmountable "chicken-and-egg" problem; but if the people is defined by criteria external to a democratic decision, then you may exclude individuals who ought to be included in the demos, thus endangering democratic legitimacy.

At first, it might seem that this problem also bedevils a view of the people as process. You might think that if a people is a series of people events coordinated by authoritative institutions, then people events require the prior existence of authoritative institutions—while, at the same time, these institutions must be created by people events. So the vicious circle seems to arise here as well. Not so. A people as process does not yield a vicious circle because some of the authoritative institutions in question can be created by events other than people events. For example, the right to trial by jury is now an institution of the highest authority for the British people. But it did not become so because of a people event. Rather, the institution gradually became more and more widespread and authoritative, in the way that social conventions like handshakes do. As it became more authoritative, the right to trial by jury gradually became a full member of the set of institutions coordinating people events. But there is no precise moment we could select that marks when it became an authoritative institution.

My full-blooded processual solution to the vicious circle of self-constitution thus is similar to that proposed by theorists of dynamic constitutionalism: the chicken-and-egg problem does not arise if you dissolve it in the past (see chap. 4). The past can save the theory because the people as process effectively eliminates the illusion that there is a state of nature or a founding moment that legitimized the state once and for all. According to a processual theory of the people, a democratic people is a process that feeds on a previous culture and consciously changes itself over time. A people as process can be creative and generate novelty, but novelty does not arise out of nothing.[6] Wherever there is an individual, there will be

5. For a recent treatment of this problem, see Goodin, "Enfranchising All Affected Interests." See also chapter 2.
6. See the discussion of novelty and creativity in chapter 6.

social processes, including political institutions and a highest source of authority for this individual. An individual participates in a people that may become democratic as it gives law to itself, and a people may found a new order of free and equal individuals by transforming existing institutions into the practices of a liberal democracy. A people may thus become democratic, even if its boundaries are partially determined by history and chance.

You might object that this solution breaks the problem of self-reference but at the price of eschewing the democratic goal of relying on the people to legitimize the state. Now a people as process legitimizes the state by appeal to a people that was not itself created along democratic lines. But a people created by such means will have characteristic practices that a liberal democracy cannot consider legitimate. For example, such practices might make the boundaries of the people depend on morally irrelevant traits, like geography or ethnicity. If a people depends on its nondemocratic history, it may perpetuate such nondemocratic practices. After all, this was my own criticism of the other, semi-processual theories of the people, such as those of Habermas and Ackerman. So how can my own theory clear this hurdle?

This brings me to the second way my thoroughly processual theory of democracy can solve the problem of self-constitution. A democratic people can itself be created democratically by the self-same people, but only if the people is a process in my sense, a series of events unfolding in coordination. If you conceive of the people as an aggregation of individuals, circularity inevitably sets in because in that case the people cannot exist without set boundaries for the demos. Thus the criteria of exclusion must be logically prior to the people, and for this reason it cannot be determined democratically. If the democratic people is a process in my sense, however, the criteria of exclusion can be modified over time and alter the people's boundaries *retroactively*. This means that, within a process as I conceive it, the boundaries of the people can be legitimized from the standpoint of the future. As I argued in chapter 6, this retroactive modification can occur because every event within a process is still unfinished. If you alter the process as a whole, then you alter each of its parts, including the events that have already occurred, because these are not completely determined as far as the process continues. This means that while the ground of legitimacy in the state may be partially undemocratic at some point, it can be affected by subsequent events, such that the process effectively alters what has already occurred. In sum, subsequent events in the series can change the authoritative institutions in question, and retroactively define or change their character by changing the process as a whole.[7] This temporal trait, together with the fact that democratic institutions (including citizenship) are not a requisite for participation in the events that constitute the people, allows you to say that there is no circularity between the people and democratic institutions. It also means that democratic peoples need not perpetuate undemocratic practices, even if they rely on an appeal to nondemocratic peoples.

Even if my people as process does not fall into the vicious circle, you might still wonder how it deals with the further logical problems that arise from the principle of all affected interests. On my theory, individuals who partake in the people as process are those whose interests are intensely affected by the people events and the institutions that constitute the people. So the people as process, as I conceive it, depends on the principle of all affected interests. Hence, the objector might say, in order to make a democratic decision, a people should give an equal say to all those individuals whose interests are affected by these events. But, the objector would argue, this creates a problem. You cannot know who will be affected by the decision unless the people makes the decision first because who will be affected depends on the precise decision made and on who participates in making it.[8] So it would be impossible to democratically decide whether to expand or restrict the electorate on the basis of an election because the very decision to expand or restrict intensely affects those who are excluded from the vote. It seems that the only way out of this is to make everyone possibly affected by a decision a member of the electorate. This means that in order to be faithful to the principle of affected interests, you would have to enfranchise all parties with any possible interest in the decision about to be made, but this implies that in principle you must include every person in every democratic decision *ever* to be made! So, for example, imagine that we apply the principle of all affected interests to determine the question of whether to give the right to vote to all children above sixteen years of age in a given demos. This decision obviously affects all sixteen- and seventeen-year-olds. So, according to a theory of democratic participation that conceives of the demos as a collection of individuals, all sixteen- and seventeen-year-olds ought to participate in making this decision. That is, they ought to be allowed to participate in the election that would settle the question by aggregation of individual wills. But it will soon become clear

7. Lawmakers can in fact claim to represent something that doesn't exist *yet*. The future can effectively change the past, since it affects the whole people as process. See chapter 6.

8. Goodin, "Enfranchising All Affected Interests"; Miller, "Democracy's Domain."

that you cannot settle the question this way; in order to have these children participate in the election, it would be necessary to include them prior to the decision about whether to include them. This leads us to the following dilemma: either you include all those who could possibly be affected in each decision by making the people universal,[9] or you give up on the principle of affected interests. Robert Goodin prefers the first horn. He concludes that this logical difficulty compels us to accept the universalization of the demos.[10] But this has the disadvantage that we cannot govern democratically, for we lack worldwide electoral institutions. Others, then, grasp the dilemma's second horn. In this vein, David Miller argues that since universalization leads to countless difficulties, we must give up on the principle of affected interests in order to preserve independent peoples.[11] But this is not a good solution either, because relying on a people that is solely defined by chance jeopardizes democratic legitimacy. Can the people as process deal with this dilemma?

My theory of the people as process does not have to clear this hurdle, for the problem of circularity with respect to all affected interests does not even enter its path. As I argued in chapter 6, my processualist view of a democratic people does not claim that a person has a right to vote in all the decisions that could affect her. It says merely that a person has a right to participate in the process of governing and of making fundamental laws once her interests are intensely affected by a particular people event and a set of institutions. According to my theory, this is all that the principle of affected interests requires. If you conceive of the people as a process, the problem of circularity does not arise, for participation in the process of government does not require prior enfranchisement. You can see this in the specific case of lowering the voting age. Any decision on children's rights to participate in elections would affect all children and immediately make sixteen- and seventeen-year-olds partake in people events, so in a democratic state the decision would give all these children, as partakers in the people, a right to participate in the process of peoplehood. But the principle of affected interests, as interpreted by my processual theory, would not invalidate the decision to restrict the franchise to adults. For

9. This horn of the dilemma is more dangerous than it may appear at first sight. The universalization of the demos does not solve the indeterminacy problem. As I argue in chapter 2, this could avoid the circularity only if the set of all humans was found naturally and uncontroversially. But it is not. In order to establish who belongs to the universal demos, a prior demos would still be required to decide who or what counts as a human person.

10. Goodin, "Enfranchising All Affected Interests."

11. Miller, "Democracy's Domain."

even if the sixteen- and seventeen-year-olds did not vote in this particular decision, they could still participate in the process of making and governing institutions, either now or in the future, by voting or by other means, such as participating in public protests or extra-electoral political organizations. So long as a person's right to participate in the ongoing process as a whole is respected, then the principle has been satisfied in her case. Taking my processualist view of the process of making fundamental laws, and of the right to participate in that process, allows us to evade the objection. For it arose by fixating on whether a person had a right to vote—that is, a right to participate in aggregating wills in a particular decision—rather than a right to participate in the ongoing process of governing a set of institutions.

So, in conclusion, the people as process can avoid the problem of self-constitution. How about the problem of continuity?

The Problem of the People in Time

The problem of the people in time, or the diachronic problem of popular indeterminacy, is usually equated with the "problem of generations,"[12] or the "problem of precommitment."[13] How can the law that a unified people enacts in a given moment bind future generations? If it is the original commitment of a group of individuals in a founding moment that binds future generations to the basic laws, this seems to rob the present people of their right to make their own fundamental institutions. Thus, if you conceive a people as a collection of individuals, a people can always disown, on democratic grounds, the law established in the past by prior members of the people.

This problem has traditionally been addressed by claiming that the people is a collective agent with a continuous identity.[14] As a collective perduring agent, the people has obligations to itself, and these generate obligations for the individual members of the people over time. But it is difficult to give a coherent argument for the continuity of such collective agents because if you conceive of the people as a collection of individuals, then the people's continuity depends on the continuous harmony of individual wills. Yet the harmonization of individual wills cannot be sustained by actual or hypothetical consent (as I argued in chaps. 2 and 3). So the

---

12. Michelman, "Constitutional Authorship," 78.
13. Waldron, *Law and Disagreement*, 257.
14. See, for example, Rubenfeld, *Freedom and Time*.

continuity of the people in time remains a problem in democratic constitutional theory.

In this book I have looked at this problem from a different angle than do constitutional theorists (see chap. 5). On my view, the diachronic problem, or what I call the temporal problem of the indeterminacy of popular unification, arises when you require individual consent to legitimize the state, something that you cannot do at *any given moment*. That is to say, the problem arises because the people constantly changes in composition. As a result, you cannot establish that there has been popular unification at any moment in time. But because you cannot establish that individuals self-constituted as a democratic people, you cannot presume that individuals would be autonomous, either individually or collectively, at any subsequent moment or hypothetical occasion.

If you accept my theory of the people as process, however, then neither problem arises. For if you take the people as a series of people events, then the state's legitimacy does not come from the popular will, from a mutual promise to obey the constitution, or from an original moment of allegiance. Rather, democratic legitimacy comes from the possibility that each individual affected by people events participates in creating, governing, and changing the democracy's institutions. An individual participates in the democratic process if and only if she has a say in governing and changing the institutions that rule her, and she partakes in the people-events that constitute institutional practices. (Recall that these practices are made up of events, which, in their turn, constitute the people itself.) In that way, the state and the constitution can still be legitimate for those who did not themselves found them; legitimacy does not require explicit consent or a promise from individuals.

It might be objected that a theory of legitimacy that allows institutions to operate without the explicit consent of individuals is bound to inherit and perpetuate unjust practices that have become habitual. But this need not be the case if the people as process formally recognizes an equal right to participate and acknowledges creativity, or the possibility of modifying a particular pattern of government. Creativity can be formally incorporated in institutions as an explicit recognition that governing processes (such as the crafting of laws) are not settled and complete. As I argued in chapter 6, creative freedom, both individual and collective, is not something that a people or a constitution declares; rather, it is something that individuals do by participating in ongoing practices. Free, individual actions grant a liberal democratic character to a series of events, and this character becomes recognizable in settled practices. The democratic people as process is constituted through these practices rather than in a constitutive moment that legitimizes the state once and for all. It is true that a mutual promise to grant one another respect can jump-start a habit of cooperation. But what grounds liberal institutions and constitutes a liberal democratic people are not such promises, but rather the repeated instances of not cheating and not bailing out.

In sum, the people as process can legitimize the state as the people constantly changes in composition because legitimacy does not require a moment of unification or a temporal link to that moment, either as an image of the past or a vision of the future. All it requires is the present instantiation of an ongoing practice of democratic governance.[15] The changing people could eventually legitimize the state if the people is conceived of as a self-creative process, if state institutions aim at attaining the freedom and equality of individuals that partake of this very process, and if these institutions effectively further this aim. In conclusion, the people as process can tell you how the people can legitimize the state even if its composition is constantly changing. Thus it solves the diachronic problem of the indeterminacy of popular unification.

It is worth noting, however, that this solution does not guarantee that a people as process will continue to be democratic in the future, or that it will progress toward a liberal democratic ideal. All this conception can do is to open the possibility of a self-constituting and self-governing people, one that can govern itself according to the principles of freedom and equality if individuals consciously choose this aim, and if the conditions for achieving it are adequate. My theory of a democratic people as process cannot guarantee that a state will be legitimate in the future. All it does is restore the *possibility* of legitimizing the state on the basis of practices that further freedom and equality. It allows us to reasonably hope that as participants in the events that create the people, we can also alter it. For if we conceive of the people as a changing assemblage of many nested processes and crisscrossing relations, then we can alter the process as we work on ourselves and change for the better.

Popular Sovereignty and the Normative Status of the People as Process

I have argued that our individual actions and decisions can change the practices and institutions that create the people, and that they can also change the course of the people as process. But how do they do this? Can

---

15. There is no need to establish a link to the past if the past subsists in the present. As Deleuze puts it, "A scar is the sign not of a past wound but of 'the present fact of having been wounded.'" *Difference and Repetition*, 77.

a process decide and govern? Can a people be sovereign? In this part I
show how a democratic theory based on process philosophy could claim
that the people decides and rules—in short, I show that the people is sovereign. But even if it were possible for a people to make decisions, does this
give popular decisions a special normative weight? If process philosophy
does away with the ideal of unifying reason and will in a popular sovereign,
then what implications does this have for the normative standing of the
idea of popular sovereignty and popular self-rule? What is left of the people
if it lacks the power of the Leviathan, the dignity of "We the People," or
the inspiring strength of Marianne in her Phrygian cap? After addressing
these issues, I deal with a final concern regarding my full-blooded theory
of the people as process: is adopting this unusual ontology too high a price
to pay in order to legitimize the state?

Process, Self-Rule, and Popular Sovereignty

The people as process does not fall into the logical problems that beset
traditional conceptions of the people as a collection of individuals. A processualist theory of peoplehood can coherently hold that the people is an
individual entity persisting over time. But can this allow the theory to claim
that the people is, or ought to be, sovereign? The people as process is an
entity that creates and rules itself, but in order to do so the individuals
who partake in the process do not have to unify their wills through reason.
Thus a people as process does not require the unification of will and reason that, according to the traditional theories of popular sovereignty, constitutes the highest authority in the polity. This means that a people can
be sovereign without claiming to have a normatively indefeasible sovereign
will. This, I will argue, is a gain for democratic theory.

Most formulations of liberal democratic theory require the idea of popular sovereignty. As I argued in chapter 2, democratic theories rely on popular sovereignty to justify the state because they legitimize rule according to
a set of principles on which everybody ought to agree. According to most
of these theories, a popular sovereign is just the outcome of harmonizing
all individual wills around these principles. It follows from these assumptions that the popular sovereign is necessarily right, for the will of the
people only unifies around true principles (hypothetically). A democratic
state, according to these theories, then establishes its authority by claiming
to represent all individuals in one single will unified by reason. Thus this
unification invests the state with a single authoritative will; further, this
unification itself *explains* why this single will is authoritative and deserving

of each individual's obedience and respect. As I argued in chapters 2 and 3, however, this unification of will and reason cannot obtain in practice because the people never unify. Further, it cannot obtain hypothetically because hypothetical unification leads to intractable logical problems. Thus traditional liberal democratic theories seek to legitimize the state on the basis of popular sovereignty, but they all ultimately fail.

Once you identify this problem and recognize that the people cannot unify its will and reason at any given time, it is tempting to give up on the people as the legitimizing ground of democratic rule. According to many political theorists nowadays, a paradox itself is a better ground for democratic politics because the indeterminacy reminds you that legitimacy is never settled.[16] Relying on paradox, these theorists claim, allows you to sustain democracy in the long run. Yet if you get too smitten by the depths of logical paradox you risk sacrificing the very possibility of democratic legitimacy—even as a standard or ideal reference. Instead, I hold, we can avoid the logical problem and use process thought to rescue the people as the ground of democratic theory. Let us see how the people as process can do this.

First of all, if you rely on the people as process you can claim that a democratic people creates itself and rules itself without contradiction. You can claim this in two different senses. First, as I argued in chapter 6, all processes are partly self-creative: they produce internal syntheses that use prior events to create new subsequent events in the series. Given that a new people event requires a prior people event to go on, we can say that all peoples create their own institutions. In this sense, we can claim that all peoples are self-creative and self-ruling. But self-rule in a second sense is more important for democratic legitimacy. The term "self-rule" is most commonly used in the political sense, which is roughly equivalent to "collective autonomy." In this regard, a people rules itself if it can govern and legislate without external interference from other peoples or individuals, and if, simultaneously, those individuals governed by the people have a say in making and changing fundamental institutions that constitute the people, so that they can all be individually autonomous as well. A people as process can create itself and rule itself in this second sense when those individuals who partake in the people have the opportunity to influence actively and consciously the construction of institutional practices of rule.

16. "The paradox of politics highlights the chicken and egg circle in which we are law's authors and law's subjects, always both creatures and authors of law. Thus, the paradox teaches us the limits of law and calls us to responsibility for it. And it teaches that the stories of politics have no ending, they are never ending." Honig, *Emergency Politics*, 3.

This occurs when institutions allow all individuals intensely affected by people events and institutional practices to have an equal say in the shaping of these practices (by voting, deliberation, or other noninstitutionalized forms of collective action), and also when the conditions for the actualization of this aim are favorable (e.g., when there exist relatively good economic circumstances and the individuals who partake in these events live in a relatively stable and secure society). In these conditions, institutions and individuals can mutually reinforce the democratic character of practices of rule that coordinate the events making up the people in question. Thus a people as process is self-creating and self-governing in the second sense of the term as well. A people as process can have a democratic government because a process can rule.

That a process can rule may seem strange at first, for ruling—that is, guiding, judging, administering, and legislating—is often associated with individual leaders and single wills. It is true that a single person can perform the actions required for rule. But a process—a coordinated series of events—can also guide, administer, and legislate by constraining individual decisions, by keeping other causal constraints in check, and by minimizing (or channeling) contingencies. It is not difficult to grasp how social processes can guide individual decisions and formulate conscious goals if you make an analogy with simpler social processes. Take, for example, the practices that coordinate the process of training a sports team (using sporting facilities, determining meeting times, designing workouts, and doing the workouts). These practices can effectively rule the actions of the individuals involved in the process, even if the team does not have a coach making these decisions. Other social processes, like creating a family or participating in a market, can also guide, control, and administer the actions of the individuals involved. For example, the existing structure of family relations reproduces and guides further events in the life of the family and each of its members. It constrains individual decisions and it may minimize contingencies. For another example, an existing market effectively rules individuals' actions by constraining individual decisions, and minimizing or exacerbating the role of unforeseen events. Similarly, a people as process can effectively guide the actions of individuals involved because what coordinates events in the process is also a set of practices: those of constituting, governing, or changing a set of institutions. In this way, the process itself guides, judges, administers, and legislates.

Take a real example. In July 2000, Mexico underwent a momentous people event. The party that had ruled in semi-dictatorial fashion for more

seventy years lost a presidential election for the first time. This event sig-
naled an important political change in the country. Can we say that *the
people* decided to uphold electoral practices and abide by their outcomes?
Yes, I claim. But notice that this change was not the result of a single
event, but rather of a long political process started many years before. The
process involved electoral decisions and institutional practices of rule, but
it also involved noninstitutionalized events seeking to challenge and
change these practices. Many events of different kinds configured this
series over those seventy years: countless individuals conforming to existing practices of rule (accepting favors from the regime, joining its organizations) and many others resisting them (voting for the opposition without
much hope of winning); innumerable individual decisions proposing and
resisting changes (joining protest movements or advocating institutional
stability); and organized and informal undercurrents of social and economic interests informing, influencing, and constraining political decisions (the messages of official media, the support of economic actors, the
activities of urban guerrillas, the organization of an independent electoral
institute). All these prior events partially configured the important event
that occurred in July 2000, in which a people decided to choose their new
president according to fair electoral procedures. In that process culminating in that moment, the Mexican people judged, decided, and ruled. In
general, therefore, we can say that a democratic people as process per-
forms activities associated with rule without having a single will, and thus
we can say that a people can rule itself democratically without unifying
reason and will.

A democratic people as process is thus self-governing and embraces
creative freedom for those individuals partaking in it. Nonetheless, like
any process, a democratic people is partially constituted by circumstances
beyond individuals' control. Thus, even when the process incorporates
institutional elements for making it self-governing (like elections and protection of individual political rights), these may not completely coordinate
the process. External circumstances of many types often constrain processes such that they are never purely democratic and never completely
self-determining. Examples of such circumstances are the influence and
overlap of other peoples, the unconscious drives and habits of those who
participate in governing, changes in the environment, the unexpected consequences of conscious decisions, and sheer luck. All these are forces that
temper the influence of the creative freedom of conscious individuals. All
these forces also steer the people in unforeseen directions and shape the
character of the practices in the process. The more that self-government

becomes an entrenched and characteristic pattern of political action, however, the more likely are democratic practices to survive. All of this shows how a democratic people can create itself and rule itself without logical contradiction.

A corollary of this view is that a people can be sovereign. To the extent that the people rules itself, it can be the highest source of power and authority in the state. Notice, however, that from what has been said so far, popular sovereignty has no normative weight. A popular decision may be good or bad. For example, it seems like the Mexican people made a good decision when it turned to democracy in 2000. But the very same people exerted their sovereignty to turn away from democratic practices in the 1930s and 1940s. The twentieth century alone offers more examples than we could print of self-governing peoples making stupid or evil decisions. This means that my people as process is sovereign only in the descriptive sense of the term. That is, the people is sovereign in the sense associated with legal realism and Carl Schmitt's well-known definition: "Sovereign is he who decides on the exception."[17] It is not sovereignty in the normative sense of the term, according to which the people's will is right by definition. In the descriptive sense, a people can make political decisions when mechanisms of rule or explicit laws of decision making are suspended or not already in place. This might strike some as odd because democratic theorists usually associate popular decisions with democratic institutions, and theorists of sovereignty often think of sovereign decisions in terms of unified individual wills. How could there be a democratic sovereign decision if there are no established practices of decision making? A people as process can decide without such established practices, just as an individual would. Strictly speaking, any decision (personal or collective) in such a situation is not just an unconstrained personal choice, but rather the result of the many causal constraints placed on individuals embedded in a political and historical process. As William Connolly says, sovereignty is not "he who decides that there is an exception" but "*that* which decides an exception exists."[18] In this case, *that* which decides the political course of action in exceptional circumstances is the people as process: a crisscrossing set of individual and collective processes partially composed by

17. Schmitt, *Political Theology*, 5.
18. "The sovereign is not simply (as Agamben and Schmitt tend to say) he (or she) who first decides that there is an exception and then decides how to resolve it. Sovereign is *that* which decides an exception exists and how to decide it, with the *that* composed of a plurality of forces circulating through and under the positional sovereignty of the official arbitrating body." Connolly, *Pluralism*, 145.

personal decisions, which in their turn are influenced and constrained by external circumstances.

So you can say that the people is self-creating and self-ruling, and thus that the people can be sovereign. This means that in my processual theory of peoplehood there is also popular sovereignty. But popular sovereignty was the pitfall of traditional theories of the people because it led to the indeterminacy problem. Does this mean that a democratic theory based on process philosophy would also get caught in the logical traps of popular sovereignty and popular indeterminacy?

The Sovereign People as Process as a Normative Ideal

Popular sovereignty has a very special normative status in traditional democratic theory. In the classic Rousseauian formulation, for example, the people as a whole could only agree on that which is true and right. Therefore, the outcome of popular unification (actual or hypothetical) is necessarily right. By contrast, the sovereign people as process does not have an equivalent normative standing. In my processual theory, the people can be sovereign and still make terrible choices. In this view, the popular sovereign is not necessarily right, the people as a whole do not embody rationality, and the theory does not entail any intrinsic obligation on individuals to obey the sovereign's decisions.[19] My processualist theory of popular sovereignty does not depend on individual consent, so you cannot say that a people has an obligation to obey the law of the state just because everybody agreed and promised to do so (or because everybody could agree, or everybody could promise). If the decisions of the sovereign people as process do not have special normative standing, then why is popular sovereignty relevant to my theory of democracy?

So far I have argued that the justificatory aim of democracy is the freedom and equality of individuals.[20] A sovereign democratic people as process is required to achieve this aim because it is only when such a people obtains that those individuals who partake in the people, and who are affected by its decisions, have an equal say in the process of making, governing, and changing the institutions that rule them. As I argued in chapters 2, 3, and 5, other accounts of the people do not allow you to make this claim because they fall into the vicious circle of self-constitution or the

---

19. It may be that democratic decisions are the best decisions from an epistemic point of view, but one would require an independent argument to sustain such a claim. For one such argument, see Estlund, *Democratic Authority*.

20. See the introduction and chapter 2.

problem of the people in time. But if you treat the people as a full-blooded process, you *can* say that the people rules itself, and also that democratic theory maintains internal coherence. Under this conception, we can say that, ideally, democratic institutions do not impinge on any individual's autonomy and that government respects equality. In short, a people as process allows you to make sense of the normative core of any theory of democracy: the ideas of freedom and equality under collective rule. Thus the people as process has a special normative standing because it allows you to make sense of the normative principles that did not work fully in a democratic theory grounded on a collection of individuals or on semi-processual views of the people, like those of Habermas and Ackerman.

A democratic theory based on a full-blooded process is different from other traditional liberal democratic theories in at least one other important aspect. It is true that all democrats share the principles of freedom and equality, but democrats disagree on how the people relates to these principles. A common point of disagreement is over whether, as most liberals claim, the justification of democracy (the normative standing of freedom and equality) cannot be itself democratic. According to most liberals, you cannot democratically justify the principles that ground democracy for the same reason that a people cannot create itself: any such attempt would be circular. Faced with this, traditional liberal theories justify democracy by appeal to extra-democratic principles that are not necessarily considered true by any actual people.[21] Hence most liberals hold that the proper normative standard for evaluating democracy is external to democracy. But this is not the case for a democratic theory based on process philosophy.

According to my processual theory of peoplehood, the principles of freedom and equality are not completely independent of the individuals who hold them. In a democratic people as process there are no independent normative standards. These standards, such as freedom and equality, are not timeless guiding goals; rather, they are a result of the actual experiences of those individuals who participate in the making of the people. The principles are themselves dynamic conceptual processes that may change as individuals live and the people transforms itself. For example,

---

21. Thomas Christiano formulates this insight clearly. In his view, a conception of democracy founded on the principle of equal consideration of interests can break the vicious circle because it "is grounded on an appeal to the truth, or correctness, of the principles of equal consideration and democratic equality." *Rule of the Many*, 78. This appeal to the truth breaks the vicious circle, but it also makes democracy likely to fall into the constitutional paternalism I discussed in chapter 2. In such situations a group institutionalizes its views of truth or correctness and imposes them on the rest, thus wrecking the very normative goal of the theory.

freedom and equality cannot have the exact same meaning in the metropole and in the colonies. Equal participation changes its meaning once the makers of institutions include former colonial subjects. The same occurs when equality extends to former slaves, women, or immigrants. Equality cannot mean the same thing for individuals who think of one another as equal members of a homogenous ethnic nation as it does for those who accept the principle of all affected interests.

These variations associated with the development of each specific people are the second reason why the people must form part of a theory of democracy, and why popular sovereignty has a certain normative weight. The people must be a part of democratic theory because it is popular sovereignty that sustains the people's creative freedom. Publicly acknowledging these capacities and fostering the people's collective autonomy is itself important. It is this very recognition that would have to be the ground of a democratic theory built on process philosophy.

So the normative standing of the popular sovereign, and the relation between the people and its normative aims are two important traits that distinguish my processual democratic theory. These traits have implications for any attempt to build a full-blown theory of democracy. In what follows, I describe some of these implications, noting that in this book I have not offered a theory of democracy, but only one of democratic legitimacy. For that reason, there are many other aspects of process thought, not addressed here, that a full-blown processual theory of democracy would have to take into account.

The first implication of my view of the people and popular sovereignty is that the people and its normative aims are always changing. That is, they are not complete at any given time. Holding this view of the people commits you to accepting novelty, change, and transience in the people's constitution, in its ruling institutions, and in the very principles that justify the state. The people changes as new events take place, and with these changes it may include new partakers, such as young people or immigrants, as well as the partakers' relations with animal, vegetables, and inanimate things and processes. Moreover, the changing people may bring new habits and practices of rule to institutions, but these changes may also come from new technologies, from changes in the environment, and from other unforeseen events. Further, this view commits you to incorporating into the people not just new citizens, but new *kinds* of citizens; not just new practices and institutions, but new *kinds* of practices and institutions. Lastly, accepting novelty and change also commits you to accepting transience: in this view, things that were very important can become irrelevant with the passing of time.[22]

A second implication is that a processual democratic theory would have to make relatedness a central trait. That is, this view has to acknowledge that the people and its normative goals are not isolated and self-sufficient. Peoples as process are composed of subprocesses, and they are themselves part of other, bigger processes. Some of these are conceptual processes, and others are processes of formation of beliefs, including the process that defines what democracy is and when the state is justified. This means that you cannot justify democratic rule, either philosophically or sociologically, in isolation from the processes that make the people, and you cannot construct an abstract standard of democratic rule appealing only to timeless ideals. This implication has a corollary: you cannot justify the state solely on the basis of hypothetical consent. As I have argued, a successful justification of the state requires abstract reasons, but it also requires the actual process and subprocess that together generate these reasons. For example, a justification based on the principle of affected interests has to consider actual practices that made it true that those affected ought to have a say. These include historical practices of rule, political processes that generated the expansion of rights, and the accompanying social processes, such as those that structure markets, religion, the family, and so forth. In this view, one cannot justify a state only with hypothetical reasons that individuals would accept; you also need to think of a dynamic process of development, which includes the lived experience of those participating in it.

A third implication follows from the second. Even if freedom and equality are universal principles (in the sense that every individual does or ought to accept them), and even though they are the ground of a democratic people, we cannot conclude from this that there should be a global democracy. Even if they could be shown to be universal, the principles are still

22. Accepting transience can be very difficult in politics, and it often leads to errors in judgment. For example, in his *Who Are We?* Samuel Huntington argues that Latin American (particularly Mexican) immigration to the United States is dangerous because it challenges American cultural identity. According to him, this cultural identity is rooted in Anglo-Protestantism, a religious culture that grounded characteristic American institutions in the early days of the United States. Huntington's argument assumes that because this cultural form was important in the past, that cultural change is dangerous today. But this assumption is false. Just because this cultural form was important in creating the original practices does not mean that the culture must be important in retaining the practices or institutions. The fallacious argument rests on the *temporal* gap between the premises. Process thought helps us to focus on change and transience, and thus it helps us to assess and address similar arguments in a way that fosters democratic governance in the face of (inevitably) changing circumstances.

part of independent people events and processes. In order to ground global democracy, a global people would be required in addition to global principles. (But notice that the connection between the people and its driving goals is not itself an obstacle to developing a universal democratic people. Such a people *could* exist if there were universal institutions coordinated by a goal that all living persons considered their own.)[23]

The last implication that I can treat here is more important to the internal politics of the state. This is that popular mandates alone do not generate legitimacy. A popular mandate is often associated with an overwhelming majority in an election, or the approval of a supermajority of the electorate as discovered by polling. In politics, pundits and politicians often assume that an electoral mandate can bestow legitimacy on a decision. Yet, as I argued above, the decisions of a popular sovereignty are not necessarily correct, they are not always authoritative, and they do not generate obligations. All that a popular mandate can tell you is that right now a majority of the electorate publicly approves of a decision. That may give politicians real power to act, but it is not equivalent to having *the people's* permission to act in a particular way. Taking the democratic people as process as the legitimizing ground of state institutions does not allow you to say that the people have a unified will; thus you cannot say after a referendum or an election that "the people has spoken." My theory of the democratic people as process does not allow you to disguise a politician's decision under the cloak of the general will. The people rules and decides by constraining options over time, but it does not formulate closed or final rulings at any given time. To assess a closed or final ruling, we require reasons that can stand on their own, and a popular mandate does not provide these reasons. Popularity alone cannot tell you whether a decision is right. As the sad experiences of the early twentieth century illustrate, the masses congregated in the public square are often wrong. So taking a decision on the basis of a thumbs-up or thumbs-down from the public square does not absolve rulers from having responsibility for their choices. In sum, popular mandate and popular sovereignty are not, on their own, a justifying ground for political decisions. Saying that the people is sovereign is analogous to saying that the people is free. Both claims testify that peoples as processes can make choices, but they do not say anything about the wisdom or rightness of the chosen path.

These are four of the most important implications for democracy that stem from popular sovereignty as conceived in my processual theory of

---

23. This position does not hold that global solidarity is incoherent. For a similar view, see Abizadeh, "Does Collective Identity Presuppose an Other?"

peoplehood. But I reiterate that, so far, I have developed a theory of the people rather than a full theory of democracy. A fully developed processual theory of democracy would require much more elaboration. I have only cleared the ground and solved a preliminary problem standing in the way of a coherent democratic theory: adopting a processual theory of peoplehood makes it *possible* to say that the people rule.

Why the People as Process?

We have seen that my democratic people as process can solve some difficult problems in political philosophy. But is that enough of a reason to prefer a new definition of the people to a familiar conception that most people already hold? Moreover, the new definition commits you to an unusual ontology. Is this too high a price to pay, just in order to clear democratic theory of its logical problems?

There are at least two reasons why my full-blooded conception of the people as process is better suited to both political philosophy (and perhaps also to everyday language) than are the rival conceptions examined in this book. The first is that my processual definition can deal with the problem of the indeterminacy of popular unification. This issue was my main source of concern throughout the previous chapters, where I showed that all the leading theorists of the people succumb to this same pitfall. That the people as process can solve the indeterminacy problem is important because it allows you to hold two valuable tenets that would be incompatible with any of the other definitions of the people I have discussed. Only if both tenets are true can democracy legitimize the state. One of these tenets holds that in a democracy the people rule. The other holds that in a democracy there can be both individual and collective autonomy. The people as process makes these elements possible by adding time and incorporating indeterminacy in democratic theory.

You may object that changing metaphysical commitments for the sake of making these tenets compatible is not worth the effort. With the anarchist, you might perhaps wonder why anyone would pay such a high price for the state's legitimacy. Many believe that the state cannot be legitimate, and that the difficulties and tensions in democratic theory are proof of this. They believe that trying to solve the logical problems of democracy is a form of servility to a master who does not deserve their allegiance. I agree with the philosophical anarchist critics that all currently existing states are illegitimate, and also that you must tolerate the state as a necessary evil.[24]

24. For a recent formulation of the philosophical anarchist position, see Simmons, "Philosophical Anarchism."

But I also hold that if you don't have at least the logical possibility of legitimate government, then there is no good reason to try to improve it. This means that without a coherent theory of democratic legitimacy, there is no direction to follow in our efforts to make the state less bad. And while it may be true that we do not have any experience of a perfectly legitimate political order, we do know that trying to achieve a "less bad" state is a realistic goal. If we want to retain the possibility of political improvement in democratic terms, then we must change our conception of the people. Nonetheless, critics might reply that while changing the conception of the people may be necessary, we do not need a vocabulary of processes, events, and relations to accomplish that. Why can you not do this in common-sense terms? This takes me to the second reason why I stand by my full-blooded conception of the people.

My conception better fits the phenomenon that we are trying to describe than do alternative conceptions. All other theories talk about the people—either the aggregation of individuals or a semi-process—as an idea, or an ideal. As such it is never available: in their accounts we can never see the people, hear the people, or access the people empirically. None of them can account for the experience of collective action, or for the feeling of political freedom that often arises from political participation. Yet by relying on creativity and the feeling of novelty, my conception of the people as process incorporates the experience of politics into the concept. But the phenomenology of process is not the only reason why my definition is a better fit. From the perspective of a detached observer, the people is better conceived as a process extended in time than as a bounded thing that obtains at a given moment. A collective extends beyond the presence of those individuals it comprises at a given time. It changes, but it is real and can be individuated. The people is a process, and it can be better described as such.

To this you might object, with Sheldon Wolin, that we must resist the temptation to define the experience of concerted action. In his view, the feeling of democracy is evanescent, and every effort to bind it conceptually—to make it effable—harms the experience somehow. I believe that democracy and concerted action seem ineffable only because we have thus far lacked an appropriate vocabulary. Our words tend to describe stable things and to speak of being. They are clumsy when it comes to talking about processes. Of course, you might think that my processual definition is rather clumsy itself. It is certainly not as graceful as everyday words could be, but it allows you to affirm self-creation and to describe reality more accurately. The language of process may seem cumbersome at first, but it renders more understandable entire areas of reality that otherwise are difficult to grasp. It allows you to talk of all sorts of phenomena, such as waves, pulses, noises, and intensities. Many of these are simple, everyday, commonsense entities, the kind you could even discuss with children, such as clouds, streams, tantrums, emotions, and relations. Others are the very stuff that politics is made of: political movements, social and market forces, power relations, and the like.

Conclusion

A democratic people as process, as I have described it here, is a people whose practices of constituting, governing, or changing a set of institutions formalize the freedom and equality of all individuals who partake in it, where these institutions are the highest authority for all those individuals intensely affected by these events and institutions. This conception of the people as process can solve the problem of the indeterminacy of popular unification, which I have discussed throughout this book. This conception dispels the three logical puzzles at the core of the problem: the problem of constituting the demos, the vicious circle of self-constitution, and the problem of the people in time.

The processual theory of the people that I have presented here allows you to avoid the logical impasses that arise when you conceive of the people as a collection of individuals, or as a semi-process (as do Habermas and Ackerman). These problems do not arise for my theory because the people cannot be unified—it is not complete and it is not completable. As a series of events, the people is flexible and open to change, yet it is stable enough to offer a moral ground for the people's political organization, and to provide an ideal toward which you can direct your hopes and political energy. The theory also gives reasons for holding that a people is the moral ground of governing institutions. Given that the people is not completable, however, the framework does not commit you to drawing a rigid legal boundary that excludes immigrants, ethnicities, classes, or future generations. Moreover, my thoroughly processual theory of peoplehood allows you to legitimize the democratic state because it grounds the democratic principles of freedom and equality.

Defining the people as process requires that you accept process metaphysics. Accepting a new metaphysical theory may seem too onerous if the aim is just to solve a problem within democratic theory. But process philosophy does much more than solve the indeterminacy problem. It gives you the tools to describe a whole new range of phenomena that could be objects of study for political philosophy and political science. But more important, process philosophy frees you from the choice that has hitherto bedeviled liberal democratic theory. The alternatives were that either you accept a theory riddled with problems for the sake of stability, or you reject democracy for the sake of theoretical consistency. Instead, my conception of the people as process restores the possibility of legitimizing rule on the basis of individual and collective freedom, and of developing a theory of democracy in terms of the experience of creative freedom. This alone may be worth the price of accepting process thought.

Conclusion:
Radical Realism

A people is a process, an unfolding series of events coordinated by the practices of constituting, governing, or changing a set of institutions. This conception helps democratic theory to deal with the logical problems that arise when it tries to legitimize the state. Specifically, it makes internally coherent and compatible the claims that a people can constitute an electorate democratically, that a people creates and rules itself, and that the people can have continuity in time. As it deals with these problems, my theory of the people as process also answers the question of how to legitimize the state democratically as the people changes composition. Moreover, by defining a democratic people as a process, the theory tells you how the people can be the normative ground of the democratic state. We can say, then, that my theory of the people as process is better able to sustain democracy than other conceptions of the people because it can make sense of core ideas of the theory of democracy while the other conceptions cannot.

Now, it is worth repeating that this book has offered only a theory of the people, not a theory of democracy; as such, it is fairly limited in scope. My theory is just a fragment of a full processual theory of democracy. Such a theory would have to deal with many other problems that stand in the way of a full democratic legitimization of the state. For example, a complete democratic theory would have to explain how a people that fosters freedom and equality can actualize these aims. It would thus have to deal with contemporary problems related to citizenship, such as how to make available equal rights of political participation through electoral mechanisms and deliberation. It would have to examine the obstacles to achieving this aim, beginning with the problems that arise from the reliance of contemporary states on an administrative bureaucracy and the rule of experts, and how this bureaucracy blocks or enables the way government responds to collective concerns. A processual democratic theory would also have to deal with how individuals and citizens create individual and collective interests, and how they negotiate them within subprocesses that overlap with the people, such as markets, wider cultural and social processes, families, and individual lives. The theory would have to specify the terms of political representation, including how to represent events and relations rather than persons, as well as how to hold public leaders accountable and determine to whom they should be accountable. Moreover, the theory would have to include reflections on how to govern peoples that overlap and intersect, and how to manage problems that affect interrelated peoples at a global level. In sum, while the problem of popular indeterminacy is just the most obvious difficulty in legitimizing the state democratically, it is not the only one, or the most important. For this reason, a processual theory of peoplehood cannot answer the question of how should democracy work, or when are democracies fully legitimate; all it can do is clear a hurdle in order to make that goal possible.

Even though this processual theory of the people is limited in scope, it has some theoretical implications that may be interesting and useful in other branches of democratic theory and political theory in general. An important implication of this new theory of peoplehood is that it challenges the entrenched belief among political theorists that the people is a collection of individuals. Instead, according to this theory, the constituents of the people are political events and relations. This claim may sound implausible at first, but when you consider that all those individuals who participate in the events that shape institutions are part of the people, as are those who are intensely affected by the events in question, it becomes clear that the claim is not counterintuitive. All these individuals participate in the process of peoplehood as they participate in relevant political events, such as elections, public discussions, and popular mobilizations. Yet this view challenges and enriches traditional individual-based views by positing that other entities besides individuals partake in these events as well. Examples of such entities that constitute the people include parts of the environment in which these individuals live, as well the creatures that populate it. The events that make up the people also include products that individuals make and the objects they value. In this view, a people includes a group's institutional relation to the environment, its affective and symbolic ties to the land and other objects, as well as production forces, financial institutions, and market trends. This conception of the people, then, could be useful in the development of new theories of environmental politics, as well as in research dealing with territorial claims and the relationships among territory, population, and economic processes.

A second theoretical implication stems from the criterion this theory uses to tell peoples apart from one another. In the traditional conceptions of the people, you can distinguish one people from another because each aggregation of individuals has a particular identity. This identity is essential to the group; in fact, it is what binds it together. Some theorists call this the people's essence, the "national character," or the "spirit of the people." It is made of "common sympathies" or memories, and it constitutes the cultural substrate of institutions. In contrast, a people as process does not have a fixed identity or any essential traits. It is bounded by causal constraints, like physical barriers and path dependence. But these constraints are subject to change, transformed by the will of individuals who partake in the people or by sheer luck as events occur and time passes. You can tell processes apart not by what they essentially *are,* but by what they habitually *do.* For example, a democratic people can be distinguished from nondemocratic peoples because it governs itself, it determines its own path of development, and it formalizes and seeks to further the freedom and equality of those individuals who partake in it. But the way it does these things can change substantially over time, to the extent that the change may blur the people's edges. This view, then, presents an alternative approach to problems concerning political and personal identity in politics. It could help political theorists to unblock the discussions regarding the politics of group identity, an area of debate that has reached a stalemate in recent years.

A third implication comes from the criterion that a processual political theory uses to deal with boundaries. Given that a people changes constantly, it can be difficult to see its precise territorial and temporal edges. Traditionally, a people conceived as an aggregation of individuals has a clearly marked beginning in time. In the traditional view, a member of the democratic people can turn to the calendar and find a date on which the people began, corresponding to the proclamation of independence or a constitutional enactment. In contrast, a person who partakes in a people as process may not know the precise date when the people came about, since the practices that characterize a people are hard to date. But she may be able to trace the process by which certain practices become more frequent and more intense. Eventually, the frequency and intensity of characteristic practices may allow her to claim that a part of the people has diverged sufficiently to constitute a different people, or that peoples that were formerly alien to each other have now merged into one. By conceiving of borders in terms of frequency and intensity of relations, this view compounds time and space. Hence it can deal with problems regarding flows and trends that extend beyond territorial jurisdictions and rigid time frames. For example, this conception of borders may help us better understand the political aspects of commerce, flows of immigration, and traffic in illegal products. It may also help us better understand political movements that result in shifting political borders, such as decolonization, partition, and secession, as well as overlapping jurisdictions and other processes associated with globalization.

Finally, my processual approach to the people has a wider theoretical implication. Just as process thought helped us see the stubborn paradoxes of democracy in a new light, it can also help us think differently about difficult problems in other areas of political philosophy. A processual approach can offer new ways of dealing with some stubbornly difficult problems within political theory, and it may even help to solve them. For example, one of the attractive aspects of process philosophy is its capacity to avoid dualistic thinking. So process thought can help us deal with the many political challenges that arise from dualism's tendency to oppose part to the whole, or of the individual's tendency to oppose the collective. Unlike most dualism-inspired approaches, process philosophy does not reduce one of the two poles to the other (e.g., part to whole, or whole to part). Rather, by introducing time it allows for pluralism. At every moment, the relations among individuals form contingent arrangements that shape events, without reducing these arrangements to either the individuals or to the whole. Thus the part and the whole can coexist harmonically in contingent arrangements of relations that occur over time, and we can schematize this coexistence as relations and events.

In sum, process allows us to see political problems in a new theoretical light. I like to refer to this light as a "radical realism." This position is *realist* because it is based on concrete facts and because it recognizes the power of causal and final constraints in every social and political process. But unlike those "realist" theories that focus on power politics and hold that moral beliefs do not matter, this realism is *radical* because it goes to the root of reality as it is felt and perceived by individuals, and it holds that reality so experienced includes individuals' moral beliefs and value relations. This root is what José Ortega y Gasset called "radical reality": my life, each one's own life.[1] This theory gets to the root because the real world is not constituted of objective material things, but rather of the interplay among external circumstances and events and each individual's awareness of the passing of time. Reality, that is, consists of processes, events, changes, and relations, and these include beliefs, expectations, and unconscious drives and desires, as well as unexpected turns of events in the natural world. Radical realism holds that these are the building blocks of social life. It also holds that they change because time passes. Further, it affirms that there is novelty and creativity in the world.

Radical realism, then, has a distinctive character and a distinct attitude toward logical difficulties, paradoxes, and theoretical impasses. According to this view, these aporias should not be interpreted as signs that political reality is stubbornly irreducible to theories and interpretations, or as signs warning philosophical thought to stay away. Instead, the logical difficulties suggest that currently dominant theories are blocking a more adequate view of reality. In response, radical realism faces reality directly and seeks to think again. Hence, when looking at the concept of the people under the light afforded by radical realism, it becomes apparent that the people is not a concept that has to be framed in scare quotes. The people is not a trace, an image, an illusion, a signifier without a signified, a fictitious symbolic reference, or an empty space. The people is real, and there cannot be democracy without a people. Recognizing this fact alone should vaccinate us against the mysticism of popular sovereignty and any romanticizing of the people's power. But although the people is real, it is not a concrete thing but rather a process. In the passing of time intrinsic to process, the people retains something of that ethereal quality that people often associate with hope.

Let us return to the black-and-white photograph with which this book began. What I had in mind as I described it was a mixture of Sebastião Salgado's photo of peasants occupying the Cuiabá plantation in Sergipe, Brazil, in 1996, and the newspaper pictures of scenes I had just witnessed in Mexico City, where in July 2006 hundreds of thousands took to the streets to protest against the official decision of an exceptionally close election.[2] These images bring with them memories of the social and political struggles of the twentieth century throughout the world: social revolution, independence from colonial rule, and the progressive expansion of political and social rights. At their core, however, these images provide static

---

1. See Ortega y Gasset's *Obras completas*, 404–7, and *Revolt of the Masses*, 79.
2. Salgado, *Terra*, 132–33.

pictures of unity, and hence they remain an unreachable ideal. Appealing to the people to justify change at a given time requires both a frame and the static qualities of the painting and the snapshot: a fixed composition, a clear origin and end. Yet the real people is a process composed of relations and events that transcend any visual frame. It cannot be captured in a single image. Unlike the people depicted in those static images, the real people is still going on.

BIBLIOGRAPHY

Abizadeh, Arash. "Does Collective Identity Presuppose an Other? On the Alleged Incoherence of Global Solidarity." *American Political Science Review* 99, no. 1 (2005): 45–60.

Ackerman, Bruce. *Foundations*. Vol. 1 of *We the People*. Cambridge, Mass.: Harvard University Press, 1991.

———. "The Living Constitution." *Harvard Law Review* 120, no. 7 (2007): 1738–1810.

———. *Transformations*. Vol. 2 of *We the People*. Cambridge, Mass.: Harvard University Press, 1998.

Agamben, Giorgio. *Homo Sacer: Sovereign Power and Bare Life*. Stanford: Stanford University Press, 1998.

———. "What Is a People?" In *Means Without End: Notes on Politics*, translated by Vincenzo Binetti and Cesare Casarino, 29–36. Minneapolis: University of Minnesota Press, 2000.

Aguilar Rivera, José Antonio. "Dos conceptos de república." In *El republicanismo en hispanoamérica: Ensayos de historia intelectual y política*, edited by José Antonio Aguilar Rivera and Rafael Rojas, 57–85. Mexico City: Fondo de Cultura Económica, 2002.

———. *En pos de la quimera: Reflexiones sobre el experimento constitucional atlántico*. Mexico City: Fondo de Cultura Económica, 2000.

Alexander, Larry, ed. *Constitutionalism: Philosophical Foundations*. Cambridge: Cambridge University Press, 1998.

Aljovín de Losada, Cristóbal. "Ciudadano y vecino en Iberoamérica, 1750–1850: Monarquía o república." In *Diccionario político y social del mundo iberoamericano: La era de las revoluciones, 1750–1850*, edited by Javier Fernández Sebastián, 179–98. Madrid: Fundación Carolina, Centro de Estudios Políticos y Constitucionales, 2009.

Anderson, Benedict. *Imagined Communities*. London: Verso, 1991.

Andreas, Peter. *Border Games: Policing the U.S.-Mexico Divide*. Ithaca: Cornell University Press, 2000.

Angle, Paul, ed. *The Complete Lincoln-Douglas Debates of 1858*. Chicago: University of Chicago Press, 1958.

Annino, Antonio. "Pueblos, liberalismo, y nación en México." In *Inventando la nación: Iberoamérica, siglo XIX*, edited by Antonio Annino and François-Xavier Guerra, 399–431. Mexico City: Fondo de Cultura Económica, 2003.

———. "Soberanías en lucha." In *Inventando la nación: Iberoamérica, siglo XIX*, edited by Annino Antonio and François-Xavier Guerra, 117–51. Mexico: Fondo de Cultura Económica, 2003.

Arendt, Hannah. *Between Past and Future: Eight Exercises in Political Thought*. New York: Penguin, 1977.

———. *On Revolution*. New York: Penguin, 1990.

Arrhenius, Gustaf. "The Boundary Problem in Democratic Theory." Draft paper, Department of Philosophy, Stockholm University, 2007.

Arrow, Kenneth. *Social Choice and Individual Values*. New Haven: Yale University Press, 1951.

Balibar, Etienne. *We the People of Europe? Reflections of Transnational Citizenship*. Princeton: Princeton University Press, 2004.

Barry, Brian. *Justice as Impartiality*. Oxford: Clarendon Press, 1995.

Bartelson, Jens. *A Genealogy of Sovereignty*. Cambridge: Cambridge University Press, 1995.

Bauböck, Rainer, and John Rundell, eds. *Blurred Boundaries: Migration, Ethnicity, Citizenship*. Aldershot, U.K.: Ashgate, 1998.

Beitz, Charles R. *Political Equality: An Essay in Democratic Theory*. Princeton: Princeton University Press, 1989.

Benhabib, Seyla. *Another Cosmopolitanism: Hospitality, Sovereignty, and Democratic Iterations*. Oxford: Oxford University Press, 2006.

———. "Borders, Boundaries, and Citizenship." *PS: Political Science and Politics* 38, no. 4 (2005): 673–77.

———. "Deliberative Rationality and Models of Democratic Legitimacy." *Constellations* 1, no. 1 (1994): 26–52.

Benn, Stanley I. "The Uses of Sovereignty." In *Political Philosophy*, edited by Anthony Quinton, 67–82. Oxford: Oxford University Press, 1967.

Bennett, Jane. *Vibrant Matter: A Political Ecology of Things*. Durham: Duke University Press, 2010.

Beran, Harry. "Border Disputes and the Right of National Self-Determination." *History of European Ideas* 4 (January 1993): 470–86.

———. *The Consent Theory of Political Obligation*. New York: Croom Helm, 1987.

Bergson, Henri. *Creative Evolution*. Translated by Arthur Mitchell. Mineola, N.Y.: Dover, 1998.

———. *The Creative Mind*. Translated by Mabelle L. Andison. New York: Philosophical Library, 1946.

———. *Matter and Memory*. Translated by N. M. Paul and W. S. Palmer. New York: Zone Books, 1988.

———. *Time and Free Will: An Essay on the Immediate Data of Consciousness*. Translated by F. L. Pogson. New York: Macmillan, 1921.

———. *The Two Sources of Morality and Religion*. Translated by R. Ashley Audra and Cloudesley Brereton, with the assistance of W. Orsfall Carter. New York: Henry Holt, 1935.

Bernal, Angelica. "The Concept of Founding." Ph.D. diss., Yale University, 2008.

Bohman, James. *Democracy Across Borders: From Demos to Demoi*. Cambridge, Mass.: MIT Press, 2007.

Brading, David A. *Mexican Phoenix: Our Lady of Guadalupe: Image and Tradition Across Five Centuries*. Cambridge: Cambridge University Press, 2001.

———. *Mito y profecía en la historia de México*. Mexico City: Vuelta, 1988.

Breña, Roberto. "Mexico." In *Diccionario político y social del mundo iberoamericano: La era de las revoluciones, 1750–1850*, edited by Javier Fernández Sebastián, 259–70. Madrid: Fundación Carolina, Centro de Estudios Políticos y Constitucionales, 2009.

Brettschneider, Corey. *Democratic Rights: The Substance of Self-Government.* Princeton: Princeton University Press, 2007.

Buchanan, Allen. "The Making and Unmaking of Boundaries: What Liberalism Has to Say." In *States, Nations, and Borders: The Ethics of Making Boundaries,* edited by Allen Buchanan and Margaret Moore, 231–61. Cambridge: Cambridge University Press, 2003.

———. "Political Legitimacy and Democracy." *Ethics* 112, no. 4 (2002): 689–719.

———. *Secession: The Morality of Political Divorce.* Boulder, Colo.: Westview Press, 1991.

Canovan, Margaret. "Patriotism Is Not Enough." *British Journal of Political Science* 30, no. 3 (2000): 413–32.

———. *The People.* Cambridge: Polity Press, 2005.

———. *Populism.* London: Junction Books, 1981.

Carens, Joseph. "Aliens and Citizens: The Case for Open Borders." *Review of Politics* 49, no. 2 (1987): 251–73.

Casati, Roberto, and Achille Varzi. *Events.* Brookfield, Vt.: Dartmouth, 1996.

Castro Leiva, Luis, and Anthony Pagden. "Civil Society and the Fate of the Modern Republics in Latin America." In *Civil Society: History and Possibilities,* edited by Sudipta Kaviraj and Sunil Khilnani, 179–203. Cambridge: Cambridge University Press, 2001.

Chiaromonte, Nicola. *La paradoja de la historia.* Translated by Antonio Saborit. Mexico City: Instituto Nacional de Antropología e Historia, 1999.

Christiano, Thomas. "The Authority of Democracy." *Journal of Political Philosophy* 12, no. 3 (2004): 266–90.

———. *The Rule of the Many.* Boulder, Colo.: Westview Press, 1996.

Chust, Manuel. "Legitimidad, representación, y soberanía: Del doceañismo monárquico al republicanismo federal mexicano." In *Poder y legitimidad en México en el siglo XIX,* edited by Brian F. Connaughton, 209–48. Mexico City: Universidad Autónoma Metropolitana, 2003.

Cicero, Marcus Tullius. *On the Commonwealth.* Translated by George Holland Sabine and Stanley Barney Smith. New York: Macmillan, 1976.

Cleary, Matthew, and Susan Stokes. *Democracy and the Culture of Skepticism: Political Trust in Argentina and Mexico.* New York: Russell Sage Foundation, 2006.

Colomer, Josep. "Taming the Tiger: Voting Rights and Political Instability in Latin America." *Latin American Politics and Society* 46, no. 2 (2004): 29–58.

Connolly, William E. *The Ethos of Pluralization.* Minneapolis: University of Minnesota Press, 1995.

———. *Pluralism.* Durham: Duke University Press, 2005.

Cortázar, Julio. *Historias de cronopios y de famas.* Buenos Aires: Alfaguara.

Cristi, Renato. "The Metaphysics of Constituent Power: Carl Schmitt and the Genesis of Chile's 1980 Constitution." *Cardozo Law Review* 21, no. 5 (2000): 1749–75.

D'Agostino, Fred. "Public Justification." In *Stanford Encyclopedia of Philosophy.* Stanford University, 1996. Article revised January 19, 2007. http://plato.stanford.edu/entries/justification-public/.

D'Agostino, Fred, and Gerald Gaus, eds. *Public Reason.* Aldershot, U.K.: Ashgate, 1998.

Dahbour, Omar. "Borders, Consent, and Democracy." *Journal of Social Philosophy* 36, no. 2 (2005): 255–72.

Dahl, Robert A. *Democracy and Its Critics.* New Haven: Yale University Press, 1989.

Decock, Lieven. "The Taming of Change." In *After Whitehead: Rescher on Process Metaphysics,* edited by Michel Weber, 95–112. Frankfurt: Ontos Verlag, 2004.

Deleuze, Gilles. *Difference and Repetition.* Translated by Paul Patton. New York: Columbia University Press, 1994.

Derrida, Jacques. "Declarations of Independence." Translated by Tom Keenan and Tom Pepper. *New Political Science* 15, no. 1 (1986): 7–15.

Dryzek, John S. "Critical Theory as Research Program." In *The Cambridge Companion to Habermas,* edited by Stephen K. White, 97–119. Cambridge: Cambridge University Press, 1995.

Dworkin, Gerald. "Paternalism." *The Monist* 56, no. 1 (1972): 64–84.

Eisenstadt, Todd, and Alejandro Poiré. 2006. "Explaining the Credibility Gap in Mexico's 2006 Presidential Election, Despite Strong (Albeit Perfectable) Electoral Institutions." Working Paper 4, School of International Service, American University, Washington, D.C., 2006.

Elster, Jon. *Nuts and Bolts for the Social Sciences.* Cambridge: Cambridge University Press, 1989.

———. *Ulysses and the Sirens.* Cambridge: Cambridge University Press, 1984.

———. *Ulysses Unbound.* Cambridge: Cambridge University Press, 2000.

Elster, Jon, and Aanund Hylland, eds. *Foundations of Social Choice Theory.* Cambridge: Cambridge University Press, 1986.

Elster, Jon, and Rune Slagstad, eds. *Constitutionalism and Democracy.* Cambridge: Cambridge University Press, 1988.

Engster, Daniel. *Divine Sovereignty: The Origins of Modern State Power.* DeKalb: Northern Illinois University Press, 2001.

Escalante Gonzalbo, Fernando. *Ciudadanos imaginarios: Memorial de los afanes y desventuras de la virtud y apología del vicio triunfante en la república mexicana: Tratado de moral pública.* Mexico City: El Colegio de México, 1992.

———. "La imposibilidad del liberalismo en México." In *Recepción y transformación del liberalismo en Mexico: Homenaje al profesor Charles A. Hale,* edited by Josefina Zoraida Vázquez, 13–18. Mexico City: El Colegio de México, 1999.

Estlund, David. *Democratic Authority: A Philosophical Framework.* Princeton: Princeton University Press, 2008.

———. "Jeremy Waldron on Law and Disagreement." *Philosophical Studies* 99, no. 1 (2000): 111–28.

Ferrara, Alessandro. "Of Boats and Principles: Reflections on Habermas's 'Constitutional Democracy.'" *Political Theory* 29, no. 6 (2001): 782–91.

Fishkin, James S. *The Voice of the People: Public Opinion and Democracy.* New Haven: Yale University Press, 1995.

Forment, Carlos. *Democracy in Latin America, 1760–1900: Civic Selfhood and Public Life in Mexico and Peru.* Chicago: University of Chicago Press, 2003.

Gavrilis, George. *The Dynamics of Interstate Boundaries.* Cambridge: Cambridge University Press, 2008.

Geuss, Raymond. *History and Illusion in Politics.* Cambridge: Cambridge University Press, 2001.

Goodin, Robert. "Enfranchising All Affected Interests, and Its Alternatives." *Philosophy and Public Affairs* 35, no. 1 (2007): 40–68.

Guerra, François-Xavier. *México: Del antiguo régimen a la revolución.* Translated by Sergio Fernández Bravo. 2 vols. Mexico City: Fondo de Cultura Económica, 1988.

———. *Modernidad e independencias*. Madrid: Editorial MAPFRE, 1992.

Gutmann, Amy, and Dennis Thompson. *Democracy and Disagreement*. Cambridge, Mass.: Harvard University Press, 1996.

Habermas, Jürgen. "Apologetic Tendencies." In *The New Conservatism and the Historian's Debate*, edited by Shierry Weber Nicholsen, 212–29. Cambridge, Mass.: MIT Press, 1990.

———. *Between Facts and Norms: Contributions to a Discourse Theory of Law and Democracy*. Translated by William Rehg. Cambridge, Mass.: MIT Press, 1996.

———. "Citizenship and National Identity." In *Between Facts and Norms: Contributions to a Discourse Theory of Law and Democracy*, translated by William Rehg, 491–515. Cambridge, Mass.: MIT Press, 1996.

———. *Communication and the Evolution of Society*. Translated by Thomas McCarthy. Boston: Beacon Press, 1979.

———. "Constitutional Democracy: A Paradoxical Union of Contradictory Principles?" *Political Theory* 29, no. 6 (2001): 766–81.

———. "The Limits of Neo-historicism." In *Autonomy and Solidarity: Interviews with Jürgen Habermas*, edited by Peter Dewes, 237–44. Revised and enlarged ed. London: Verso, 1996.

———. *Moral Consciousness and Communicative Action*. Translated by Christian Lenhardt and Shierry Weber Nicholsen. Cambridge, Mass.: MIT Press, 1990.

———. "On Law and Disagreement: Some Comments on 'Interpretative Pluralism.'" *Ratio Juris* 16, no. 2 (2003): 187–94.

———. "Popular Sovereignty as Procedure." In *Between Facts and Norms: Contributions to a Discourse Theory of Law and Democracy*, 463–90. Translated by William Rehg. Cambridge, Mass.: MIT Press, 1998.

———. *The Structural Transformation of the Public Sphere: An Inquiry into a Category of Bourgeois Society*. Translated by Thomas Burger. Cambridge, Mass.: MIT Press, 1989.

———. *The Theory of Communicative Action*. Translated by Thomas McCarthy. 2 vols. Boston: Beacon Press, 1984–87.

———. "What Is a People? The Frankfurt 'Germanists' Assembly' of 1846 and the Self-Understanding of the Humanities in the Vormärz." In *The Postnational Constellation: Political Essays*, edited by Max Pensky, 1–25. Cambridge, Mass.: MIT Press, 2001.

Hale, Charles A. *The Transformation of Liberalism in Late Nineteenth-Century Mexico*. Princeton: Princeton University Press, 1989.

———. "The War with the United States and the Crisis in Mexican Thought." *The Americas* 14, no. 2 (1957): 153–73.

Hardt, Michael, and Antonio Negri. *Empire*. Cambridge, Mass.: Harvard University Press, 2001.

———. *Multitude: War and Democracy in the Age of Empire*. New York: Penguin, 2004.

Haslanger, Sally, and Roxanne Marie Kurtz, eds. *Persistence: Contemporary Readings*. Cambridge, Mass.: MIT Press, 2006.

Hausman, Carl R. *Charles S. Peirce's Evolutionary Philosophy*. Cambridge: Cambridge University Press, 1993.

Hazlitt, William. "What Is the People?" In *Selected Writings*, edited by Jon Cook, 3–28. Oxford: Oxford University Press, 1991.

Held, David. *Democracy and the Global Order: From the Modern State to Cosmopolitan Governance*. Cambridge: Polity Press, 1995.

Herzog, Tamar. "Communities Becoming a Nation: Spain and Spanish America in the Wake of Modernity." *Citizenship Studies* 11, no. 2 (2007): 151–72.

Hinsley, F. H. *Sovereignty*. Cambridge: Cambridge University Press, 1986.

Hollis, Martin. *The Philosophy of Social Science*. Cambridge: Cambridge University Press, 1994.

Holmes, Stephen. *Passions and Constraint: On the Theory of Liberal Democracy*. Chicago: University of Chicago Press, 1995.

Honig, Bonnie. "Between Decision and Deliberation: Political Paradox in Democratic Theory." *American Political Science Review* 101, no. 1 (2007): 1–18.

———. "Dead Rights, Live Futures." *Political Theory* 29, no. 6 (2001): 792–805.

———. "Declarations of Independence: Arendt and Derrida on the Problem of Founding a Republic." *American Political Science Review* 85, no. 1 (1991): 97–113.

———. *Democracy and the Foreigner*. Princeton: Princeton University Press, 2001.

———. *Emergency Politics*. Princeton: Princeton University Press, 2009.

Hont, Istvan. "The Permanent Crisis of a Divided Mankind: 'Contemporary Crisis of the Nation State' in Historical Perspective." Special issue, *Political Studies* 42 (1994): 166–231.

Huntington, Samuel. *Who Are We? The Challenges to America's National Identity*. New York: Simon and Schuster, 2004.

Illades, Carlos. "La representación del pueblo en el segundo romanticismo mexicano." *Signos Históricos* 5, no. 10 (2003): 16–36.

Jaffa, Harry. *Crisis of the House Divided: An Interpretation of the Issues in the Lincoln-Douglas Debates*. Garden City, N.Y.: Doubleday, 1959.

Kalyvas, Andreas. *Democracy and the Politics of the Extraordinary: Max Weber, Carl Schmitt, and Hannah Arendt*. Cambridge: Cambridge University Press, 2008.

———. "Popular Sovereignty, Democracy, and Constituent Power." *Constellations* 12, no. 2 (2005): 223–44.

Kammen, Michael. *A Machine That Would Go of Itself: The Constitution in American Culture*. New York: Knopf, 1986.

Kant, Immanuel. *Critique of Pure Reason*. Translated by J. M. D. Meiklejohn. Amherst, N.Y.: Prometheus Books, 1990.

———. "On the Common Saying: That May Be Correct in Theory, but It Is of No Use in Practice." In *Practical Philosophy*, edited by Mary J. Gregor, 273–310. Cambridge: Cambridge University Press, 1996.

Kantorowicz, Ernst. *The King's Two Bodies: A Study in Mediaeval Political Theology*. Princeton: Princeton University Press, 1997.

Keenan, Alan. *Democracy in Question: Democratic Openness in a Time of Political Closure*. Stanford: Stanford University Press, 2003.

Keith, Michael, and Steve Pile, eds. *Place and the Politics of Identity*. London: Routledge, 1993.

Kelly, Paul. *Liberalism*. Cambridge: Polity Press, 2005.

Kim, Jaegwon. "Causation, Nomic Subsumption, and the Concept of Event." *Journal of Philosophy* 70, no. 8 (1973): 217–36.

———. "Emergence: Core Ideas and Issues." *Synthese* 151, no. 3 (2006): 457–559.

Klesner, Joseph L. "The 2006 Mexican Election and Its Aftermath: Editor's Introduction." *PS: Political Science and Politics* 40, no. 1 (2007): 11–14.

Kohlberg, Lawrence. *The Philosophy of Moral Development*. Vol. 1 of *Essays on Moral Development*. San Francisco: Harper and Row, 1984.

———. *The Psychology of Moral Development*. Vol. 2 of *Essays on Moral Development*. San Francisco: Harper and Row, 1985.

Kolers, Avery. *Land, Conflict, and Justice: A Political Theory of Territory*. Cambridge: Cambridge University Press, 2009.

Laclau, Ernesto. *On Populist Reason*. London: Verso, 2005.

Lintott, Andrew W. *The Constitution of the Roman Republic*. Oxford: Oxford University Press, 1999.

Lipset, Seymour M. "Some Social Requisites of Democracy: Economic Development and Political Legitimacy." *American Political Science Review* 53, no. 1 (1959): 69–105.

Locke, John. *Two Treatises of Government*. Edited by Peter Laslett. Cambridge: Cambridge University Press, 1988.

López-Guerra, Claudio. "Should Expatriates Vote?" *Journal of Political Philosophy* 13, no. 2 (2005): 216–34.

Loveman, Brian. *The Constitution of Tyranny: Regimes of Exception in Spanish America*. Pittsburgh: University of Pittsburgh Press, 1993.

Lutz, Donald. *Principles of Constitutional Design*. Cambridge: Cambridge University Press, 2006.

Machamer, Peter, Lindley Darden, and Carl Craver. "Thinking About Mechanisms." *Philosophy of Science* 67, no. 1 (2000): 1–25.

Manin, Bernard. *The Principles of Representative Government*. Cambridge: Cambridge University Press, 1997.

Markell, Patchen. "Making Affect Safe for Democracy: On 'Constitutional Patriotism.'" *Political Theory* 28, no. 1 (2000): 38–63.

———. "The Rule of the People: Arendt, Archê, and Democracy." *American Political Science Review* 100, no. 1 (2006): 1–14.

Marrati, Paola. "Time, Life, Concepts: The Newness of Bergson." *MLN* 120, no. 5 (2005): 1099–1111.

Michelman, Frank I. *Brennan and Democracy*. Princeton: Princeton University Press, 1999.

———. "Constitutional Authorship." In *Constitutionalism: Philosophical Foundations*, edited by L. Alexander, 64–98. Cambridge: Cambridge University Press, 1998.

———. "Human Rights and the Limits of Constitutional Theory." *Ratio Juris* 13, no. 1 (2000): 63–76.

———. "Law's Republic." *Yale Law Journal* 97, no. 8 (1988): 1493–1537.

Mill, John Stuart. *Considerations on Representative Government*. Edited by Currin Shields. Indianapolis: Bobbs-Merrill, 1958.

Miller, David. *Citizenship and National Identity*. Cambridge: Polity Press, 2000.

———. "Democracy's Domain." *Philosophy and Public Affairs* 37, no. 3 (2009): 201–28.

———. "Immigrants, Nations, and Citizenship." *Journal of Political Philosophy* 16, no. 4 (2008): 371–90.

———. *On Nationality*. Oxford: Oxford University Press, 1995.

Modgil, Sohan, and Celia Modgil, eds. *Lawrence Kohlberg: Consensus and Controversy*. London: Falmer Press, 1986.

Monsiváis, Carlos. "Prólogo a *El Zarco*." In *El Zarco*, edited by Carlos Monsiváis. Mexico City: Ediciones Océano, 1999.

Morgan, Edmund. *Inventing the People: The Rise of Popular Sovereignty in England and America*. New York: W. W. Norton, 1988.

Morris, Randall C. *Process Philosophy and Political Ideology: The Social and Political Thought of Alfred North Whitehead and Charles Hartshorne*. Albany: SUNY Press, 1991.

Morse, Richard. "The Heritage of Latin America." In *The Founding of New Societies: Studies in the History of the United States, Latin America, South Africa, Canada, and Australia*, edited by Louis Hartz, 159–65. New York: Harcourt, Brace and World, 1964.

Mueller, Dennis C. *Public Choice III*. Cambridge: Cambridge University Press, 2003.

Müller, Jan-Werner. *Constitutional Patriotism*. Princeton: Princeton University Press, 2007.

Nagel, Ernest. *The Structure of Science: Problems in the Logic of Scientific Explanation*. London: Routledge and Kegan Paul, 1961.

Näsström, Sofia. "The Legitimacy of the People." *Political Theory* 35, no. 5 (2007): 624–58.

Negretto, Gabriel, and José Antonio Aguilar Rivera. "Rethinking the Legacy of the Liberal State in Latin America: The Cases of Argentina (1853–1916) and Mexico (1857–1910)." *Journal of Latin American Studies* 32, no. 2 (2000): 361–97.

Nozick, Robert. *Anarchy, State, and Utopia*. New York: Basic Books, 1974.

Oakley, Francis. *Kingship: The Politics of Enchantment*. London: Blackwell, 2006.

Ochoa Espejo, Paulina. "Does Political Theology Entail Decisionism?" *Philosophy and Social Criticism*. Forthcoming.

———. "On Political Theology and the Possibility of Superseding It." *Critical Review of International Social and Political Philosophy*. Forthcoming.

———. "Paradoxes of the People in Spanish American Political Thought." Unpublished manuscript. Yale University, 2010.

O'Connor, Timothy, and Hong Yu Wong. "The Metaphysics of Emergence." *Noûs* 39, no. 4 (2005): 658–78.

Olson, Kevin. "Paradoxes of Constitutional Democracy." *American Journal of Political Science* 51, no. 2 (2007): 330–43.

———. *Reflexive Democracy*. Cambridge, Mass.: MIT Press, 2006.

Olson, Mancur. "Dictatorship, Democracy, and Development." *American Political Science Review* 87, no. 3 (1993): 567–76.

Ortega y Gasset, José. *Obras completas*. Vol. 7. Madrid: Revista de Occidente/Alianza Editorial, 1983.

———. *The Revolt of the Masses*. Translated by anon. New York: W. W. Norton, 1932.

Palti, Elías José. "Introducción." In *Política del disenso: La "polémica en torno al monarquismo" (México, 1848–1850) . . . y las aporías del liberalismo*, edited by Elías José Palti, 7–58. Mexico City: Fondo de Cultura Económica, 1998.

———. *La invención de una legitimidad: Razón y retórica en el pensamiento mexicano del siglo XIX*. Mexico City: Fondo de Cultura Económica, 2005.

————, ed. *Política del disenso: La "polémica en torno al monarquismo" (México, 1848–1850) . . . y las aporías del liberalismo.* Mexico City: Fondo de Cultura Económica, 1998.

Panizza, Francisco, ed. *Populism and the Mirror of Democracy.* London: Verso, 2005.

Pettit, Philip. "Rawls's Political Ontology." *Politics, Philosophy, and Economics* 4, no. 2 (2005): 157–74.

————. *Republicanism: A Theory of Freedom and Government.* Oxford: Oxford University Press, 1997.

Philpott, Daniel. "Sovereignty: An Introduction and Brief History." *Journal of International Affairs* 48, no. 2 (1995): 353–68.

Plato. *Cratylus.* In *The Dialogues of Plato,* 3rd ed., translated by Benjamin Jowett, 1:323–89. London: Oxford University Press, 1892.

————. *Theaetetus.* In *The Dialogues of Plato,* 3rd ed., translated by Benjamin Jowett, 1:193–280. London: Oxford University Press, 1892.

Pols, Edward. *Whitehead's Metaphysics: A Critical Examination of Process and Reality.* London: Feffer and Simons, 1967.

Post, Robert. *Constitutional Domains: Democracy, Community, Management.* Cambridge, Mass.: Harvard University Press, 1995.

Przeworski, Adam. "Minimalist Conception of Democracy: A Defense." In *Democracy's Value,* edited by Ian Shapiro and Casiano Hacker-Cordón, 23–55. Cambridge: Cambridge University Press, 1999.

Rabasa, Emilio. *"La bola" y "La gran ciencia."* Mexico City: Porrúa, 1999.

————. *La constitución y la dictadura.* Mexico City: Porrúa, 1912.

Rancière, Jacques. *Dis-agreement: Politics and Philosophy.* Translated by Julie Rose. Minneapolis: University of Minnesota Press, 1998.

Rawls, John. "Justice as Fairness: Political Not Metaphysical." In *John Rawls: Collected Papers,* edited by Samuel Freeman, 388–414. Cambridge, Mass.: Harvard University Press, 1999.

————. *Political Liberalism.* New York: Columbia University Press, 1996.

————. *A Theory of Justice.* Cambridge, Mass.: Harvard University Press, 1999.

Raz, Joseph. *The Morality of Freedom.* Oxford: Clarendon Press, 1986.

Rescher, Nicholas. *Process Metaphysics: An Introduction to Process Philosophy.* Albany: SUNY Press, 1996.

————. *Process Philosophy: A Survey of Basic Issues.* Pittsburgh: University of Pittsburgh Press, 2000.

————. "Replies." In *After Whitehead: Rescher on Process Metaphysics,* edited by Michel Weber. Frankfurt: Ontos Verlag, 2004.

Richardson, Henry S. *Democratic Autonomy: Public Reasoning About the Ends of Policy.* Oxford: Oxford University Press, 2001.

Ricoeur, Paul. "The Political Paradox." In *Legitimacy and the State,* edited by William E. Connolly, 289–321. New York: New York University Press, 1984.

Riker, William H. *Liberalism Against Populism: A Confrontation Between the Theory of Democracy and the Theory of Social Choice.* Long Grove, Ill.: Waveland, 1988.

Riley, Patrick. *The General Will Before Rousseau: The Transformation of the Divine into the Civic.* Princeton: Princeton University Press, 1986.

————. *Will and Political Legitimacy: A Critical Exposition of Social Contract Theory in Hobbes, Locke, Rousseau, Kant, and Hegel.* Cambridge, Mass.: Harvard University Press, 1982.

Rocafuerte, Vicente. *Bosquejo ligerísimo de la revolución de México, desde el grito de Iguala hasta la proclamación imperial de Iturbide*. Philadelphia: Imprenta de Teracrouef y Naroajeg (Rocafuerte y Bejarano), 1822.

———. *Ideas necesarias a todo pueblo americano independiente que quiera ser libre*. Philadelphia: D. Huntington, 1821.

Roldán Vera, Eugenia. "'Pueblo' y 'pueblos' en México, 1750–1850: Un ensayo de historia conceptual." *Araucaria* 9, no. 17 (2007): 1–12.

Rosanvallon, Pierre. *La contre-démocratie: La politique à l'âge de la defiance*. Paris: Seuil, 2006.

———. *La démocratie inachevée: Histoire de la souveraineté du peuple en France*. Paris: Gallimard, 2000.

———. *Le peuple introuvable: Histoire de la représentation démocratique en France*. Paris: Gallimard, 1998.

———. *Le sacre du citoyen: Histoire du suffrage universel en France*. Paris: Gallimard, 1992.

Rousseau, Jean-Jacques. *On the Social Contract*. Translated by Judith Masters. Edited by Roger D. Masters. New York: St. Martin's Press, 1978.

Rubenfeld, Jed. *Freedom and Time: A Theory of Constitutional Self-Government*. New Haven: Yale University Press, 2001.

———. *Revolution by Judiciary: The Structure of American Constitutional Law*. Cambridge, Mass.: Harvard University Press, 2005.

Runciman, Walter G., and Amartya K. Sen. "Games, Justice, and the General Will." *Mind* 74, no. 296 (1965): 554–62.

Sábato, Hilda. "On Political Citizenship in Nineteenth-Century Latin America." *American Historical Review* 106, no. 4 (2001): 1290–1315.

Sahlins, Peter. *Boundaries: The Making of France and Spain in the Pyrenees*. Berkeley and Los Angeles: University of California Press, 1989.

Salgado, Sebastião. *Terra: Struggle of the Landless*. Translated by Clifford Landers. London: Phaidon Press, 1998.

Schiller, Friedrich. *Wilhelm Tell*. Frankfurt: Suhrkamp, 2002.

Schilpp, Paul Arthur, ed. *The Philosophy of Alfred North Whitehead*. Evanston: Northwestern University Press, 1941.

Schmid, Michael. "Habermas's Theory of Social Evolution." In *Habermas: Critical Debates*, edited by John B. Thompson and David Held, 162–80. Cambridge, Mass.: MIT Press, 1982.

Schmitt, Carl. *Constitutional Theory*. Edited and translated by Jeffrey Seitzer. Durham: Duke University Press, 2008.

———. *The Crisis of Parliamentary Democracy*. Translated by Ellen Kennedy. Cambridge, Mass.: MIT Press, 1985.

———. *Political Theology: Four Chapters on the Concept of Sovereignty*. Translated by George Schwab. Cambridge, Mass.: MIT Press, 1985.

Schumpeter, Joseph. *Capitalism, Socialism, and Democracy*. New York: Harper and Brothers, 1942.

Schwartzberg, Melissa. *Democracy and Legal Change*. Cambridge: Cambridge University Press, 2007.

Shapiro, Ian. *Democratic Justice*. Princeton: Princeton University Press, 1999.

Shapiro, Ian, and Casiano Hacker-Cordón, eds. *Democracy's Edges*. Cambridge: Cambridge University Press, 1999.

Siebt, Johanna. "Process and Particulars." In *After Whitehead: Rescher on Process Metaphysics,* edited by Michel Weber, 113–34. Frankfurt: Ontos Verlag, 2004.

Simmons, A. John. *Moral Principles and Political Obligations.* Princeton: Princeton University Press, 1979.

——. "Philosophical Anarchism." Chap. 6 in *Justification and Legitimacy: Essays on Rights and Obligation.* Cambridge: Cambridge University Press, 2001.

Singer, Peter. *Democracy and Disobedience.* Oxford: Oxford University Press, 1974.

Smith, Rogers. *Stories of Peoplehood: The Politics and Morals of Political Membership.* Cambridge: Cambridge University Press, 2004.

Stark, Cynthia. "Hypothetical Consent and Justification." *Journal of Philosophy* 97, no. 6 (2000): 313–34.

Taylor, Charles. *The Explanation of Behaviour.* New York: Humanities Press, 1964.

——. *Modern Social Imaginaries.* Durham: Duke University Press, 2004.

Thomassen, Lasse. *Deconstructing Habermas.* New York: Routledge, 2008.

Vallenilla Lanz, Laureano. *Cesarismo democrático: Estudio sobre las bases sociológicas de la constitución efectiva de Venezuela.* Caracas: Empresa El Cojo, 1919.

Van Young, Eric. *The Other Rebellion: Popular Violence, Ideology, and the Mexican Struggle for Independence.* Stanford: Stanford University Press, 2001.

Véliz, Claudio. *The Centralist Tradition of Latin America.* Princeton: Princeton University Press, 1980.

Waldron, Jeremy. *Law and Disagreement.* New York: Oxford University Press, 1999.

——. "Theoretical Foundations of Liberalism." *Philosophical Quarterly* 37, no. 145 (1987): 127–50.

Weber, Michel, ed. *After Whitehead: Rescher on Process Metaphysics.* Frankfurt: Ontos Verlag, 2004.

——. *Whitehead's Pancreativism: The Basics.* Frankfurt: Ontos Verlag, 2006.

Whelan, Frederick G. "Democratic Theory and the Boundary Problem." In *Liberal Democracy,* edited by J. R. Pennock and J. W. Chapman, 13–47. New York: New York University Press, 1983.

Whitehead, Alfred North. *Adventures of Ideas.* New York: Free Press, 1967.

——. *Modes of Thought.* New York: Free Press, 1966.

——. *Process and Reality: An Essay in Cosmology.* New York: Free Press, 1978.

——. *Science and the Modern World.* New York: Free Press, 1967.

Whitton, Brian J. "Universal Pragmatics and the Formation of Western Civilization: A Critique of Habermas's Theory of Human Moral Evolution." *History and Theory* 31, no. 3 (1992): 299–313.

Widder, Nathan. *Reflections on Time and Politics.* University Park: Pennsylvania State University Press, 2008.

Wolff, Robert Paul. *In Defense of Anarchism.* New York: Harper and Row, 1970.

Wolin, Sheldon. "Contract and Birthright." In *The Presence of the Past: Essays on the State and the Constitution,* 137–50. Baltimore: Johns Hopkins University Press, 1989.

——. "Fugitive Democracy." *Constellations* 1, no. 1 (1994): 11–25.

——. *The Presence of the Past: Essays on the State and the Constitution.* Baltimore: Johns Hopkins University Press, 1989.

Woodfield, Andrew. *Teleology.* Cambridge: Cambridge University Press, 1976.

Yack, Bernard. "Popular Sovereignty and Nationalism." *Political Theory* 29, no. 4 (2001): 517–36.

Ypi, Lea L. "Statist Cosmopolitanism." *Journal of Political Philosophy* 16, no. 1 (2008): 48–71.